Editor
Dorinda Mas

Editorial Project Manager
Evan D. Forbes, M.S. Ed.

Editor in Chief
Sharon Coan, M.S. Ed.

Illustrator
Howard Chaney

Cover Artist:
Karen Fong

Art Coordinator
Cheri Macoubrie Wilson

Creative Director
Elayne Roberts

Imaging
Alfred Lau
James Edward Grace

Product Manager
Phil Garcia

Acknowledgments:
Apple, the Apple Logo, and Macintosh are trademarks of Apple Computers, Inc., registered in the United States and other countries.

Trademarks:
Trademarked names and graphics appear throughout this book. Instead of listing every firm and entity which owns the trademarks or inserting a trademark symbol with each mention of a trademarked name, the publisher avers that it is using the names and graphics only for editorial purposes and to the benefit of the trademarked owner with no intention of infringing upon that trademark.

Publishers:
Rachelle Cracchiolo, M.S. Ed.
Mary Dupuy Smith, M.S. Ed.

MANAGING TECHNOLOGY IN THE MIDDLE SCHOOL CLASSROOM

Author:
Paul Gardner

Teacher Created Materials, Inc.
6421 Industry Way
Westminster, CA 92683
www.teachercreated.com

ISBN-1-55734-667-4

©*1996 Teacher Created Materials, Inc.*

Reprinted, 1999

Made in U.S.A.

The classroom teacher may reproduce copies of materials in this book for classroom use only. The reproduction of any part for an entire school or school system is strictly prohibited. No part of this publication may be transmitted, stored, or recorded in any form without written permission from the publisher.

W9-CHG-725

TABLE OF CONTENTS

INTRODUCTION

A NEW ERA IN EDUCATION

Welcome to a new era of education. In this era, the traditional walls of the classroom have been removed. Students are leaving the classroom aboard educational tools like CD-ROM, laserdiscs, multimedia, and telecommunications. They are creating projects in partnership with not only their peers in the classroom, but with people all over the world. Teachers have access to tools that allow them to reach and challenge students in ways they could only dream of before.

Like most change, the use of educational technology does not happen overnight. It requires a commitment to continuing education and, for some, a total shift in the way they think about delivering instruction. Although this sounds like a monumental task, the good news is that it can be very exciting and satisfying.

There is no way to duplicate all the different hardware and software configurations used in education. It does not make a difference whether your school has chosen IBM or Apple, Windows or Mac. What we are concerned with is how to match the tool to the job. In short, how can technology help us do our jobs better?

Consider how teaching can be enhanced with technology and how these tools can help you make your students better readers, writers, problem solvers, and thinkers.

INTRODUCTION *(cont.)*

WHAT IS TECHNOLOGY?

The definition of technology, like the examples we use to illustrate it, is ever-changing. Simply put, technology is a tool human beings use to complete a job more efficiently and/or creatively. Since the beginning of time we have striven to create tools that make our lives easier or allow us to push the window of creativity. In most cases, the effects of these inventions on our every day lives have been less than earth shaking. However, at certain times in our history, technology has been developed that changes how we think, feel, work, and live. Consider the effects of the following technologies on human beings:

- The Plow
- The Printing Press
- The Internal Combustion Engine
- The Electric Light
- The Radio
- The Television
- The Computer

Furthermore, consider the evolution of education in comparison to the invention of these technologies. The plow turned a world of mostly subsistence farmers into one that could produce excess food and feed many people. The result was the growth of cities, and from this, the need and time for wide spread public education. The rest of the list's contributions to the education system are more obvious, but no less profound. The computer is the latest invention to change the way we think about education. This technology has already changed our lives and will make profound changes in the way we educate ourselves and our children.

Computer technology has come a long way since IBM's first computer. The IBM Mark I had 760,000 parts, 500 miles of wire and required four seconds to perform a simple multiplication equation. The personal computers of today handle thousands of calculations per second and fit on a teacher's desk top, with plenty of room for books and coffee.

Modern personal computers can display color pictures or video and digital audio can be played. Voice recognition by the computer is no longer a dream of the future; it is shipped as standard equipment on many models. Interactively, the ability to choose one's own path through an educational experience has aided people in finding the information they must have to make informed decisions.

INTRODUCTION *(cont.)*

THE HISTORY OF EDUCATIONAL TECHNOLOGY

In order to evaluate attitudes about the educational technology of today, it is important to see the attitudes of people involved with new technologies in the past. Here are a few quotes from people involved in education during the time when new technologies were being introduced.

"Students today can't prepare bark to calculate their problems. They depend on their slates which are more expensive. What will they do when the slate is dropped and it breaks? They will be unable to write!" (Teacher's Conference, 1703)

"Students today depend on paper too much. They don't know how to write on a slate without getting chalk dust all over themselves. They can't clean a slate properly. What will they do when they run out of paper?" (Principal's Association, 1815)

"Students today depend too much upon ink. They don't know how to use a pen knife to sharpen a pencil. Pen and ink will never replace the pencil." (National Association of Teachers, 1907)

"Students today depend upon store bought ink. They don't know how to make their own. When they run out of ink they will be unable to write words or ciphers until their next trip to the settlement. This is a sad commentary on modern education." (The Rural American Teacher, 1928)

"Students today depend on these expensive fountain pens. They can no longer write with a straight pen and nib. We parents must not allow them to wallow in such luxury to the detriment of learning how to cope in the real business world which is not so extravagant." (PTA Gazette, 1941)

"Ballpoint pens will be the ruin of education in our country. Students use these devices and then throw them away. The American values of thrift and frugality are being discarded. Business and banks will never allow such expensive luxuries." (Federal Teachers, 1950)

"Students today depend too much on handheld calculators . . ."

Detractors from today's vision of education will no doubt have the same view of the use of computers. What we must realize is that like bark, slate, pencils, pens, and calculators, computers are nothing but the vehicles we use to deliver instruction. It is not the paint or brush or canvas that makes a great painting, it is the artist's product.

INTRODUCTION *(cont.)*

THE FIRST EDUCATIONAL COMPUTER REVOLUTION

In the early 1980s, the mind set for computer using educators was that of an individual, basic skill building model. This was due partially to the limited ability of the technology and partially because educational trends, drill and practice programs were the mainstay of computer use in schools.

Computer labs full of computers began to spring up throughout the educational system. Scheduling students into the lab for regular "computer time" has been the practice. While there, the students would be taught to use the computer in isolation from the regular curriculum, sometimes working on skills that were unrelated to the activities taking place in the classroom. Where students were working on subject-related computer activities, they were limited to simple word processing due to the limited capability of early machines.

THE NEW PHILOSOPHY OF TECHNOLOGY IN EDUCATION

In the new vision of education, technology is an integral component. Technology is used to provide basic skills support. However, this is a supplement to the overall usefulness of technology tools. More importantly, technology helps interface with information sources outside of the school, provides support for individual creativity, manages information about student performance and achievement, assists teachers in their dual roles as instructors and clerks, and provides students with greater control over their own learning.

This new model puts technology into the role it serves in the "real world"; as a tool. This tool aids the teacher and the student in gathering and communicating information. We don't teach computers, we teach curriculum. Using the technology tool is just a very good way of teaching curriculum.

THE FUTURE OF EDUCATIONAL TECHNOLOGY

The rapid advancements and increased affordability of technology as well as the overall support for the use of it in preparing our students for the modern workplace, leads one to believe that technology will become as integral a part of the classroom as the chalkboard. In fact, technology will help the teacher make education a realistic experience.

Here are a few technologies that will surely make their way to our classrooms:

Video Conferencing: Imagine your students working jointly with students in other countries, talking with them face to face through the computer screen.

Virtual Reality: Imagine your students experiencing an important event or simulation, historical or current, through VR.

Teacher Assessment Tools: Imagine tools that would automatically, immediately, and constantly give you information you need to assess your student needs.

INTRODUCTION *(cont.)*

WHY USE TECHNOLOGY?

Reason Number 1: Society Is Changing

The fact that computer technology touches our lives on a daily basis is a good enough reason in itself to teach using technology. From the time we wake, drive our automobiles, do our jobs, purchase our groceries, cook our food, until we tuck our children in at night, we are in contact with computerized technology. The more we are able to understand and interact with it, the better we will get along in the world we have created using these technologies.

Reason Number 2: Preparing the Twenty-First Century Work Force

Fortune 500 executives were recently polled to find out what skills they would want in the twenty-first century work force. The following is a list of the most wanted traits:

- a generalist
- a problem solver
- a good communicator
- computer literate

The list was very general except for a single item, "computer literate". Not so coincidentally, the computer literate individual is often a generalist who is a good problem solver and communicator and vice versa. Each of these skills is aided by the other. If one is able to problem solve enough to access information, it follows that one would learn to generalize and communicate that information.

New technology is creating a demand for workers who have increased computation, communication, and science skills. According to the United States Department of Labor, the fastest growing segment of the job market in the 1990s has been and will continue be low to mid-level occupations, with three out of four of those jobs requiring some education or technical training beyond the high school level.

Reason Number 3: Meeting the Needs of Students

Technology also helps meet the needs of our students who have differing needs and talents. Students who are academic, in nature, have very little trouble coping in the classroom. However, the visual or performing arts and our more hands-on, kinesthetic learners sometimes slip through the cracks. Computers offer these students the tools they need to succeed. Students with special needs can be aided to overcome handicaps by using computers.

INTRODUCTION *(cont.)*

Reason Number 4: Efficiency and Professionalism

With all the hats teachers are being asked to wear, time is at a premium. The everyday classroom administrative tasks, although necessary, are extremely time consuming. Teachers must be given, and then utilize the tools that help complete these tasks more efficiently. Technology can aid the teacher in this endeavor.

At the same time, teachers must be able to access the information they need to make decisions regarding their students. This information must then be communicated to the student, parents, and colleges in a professional manner. Technology can support the teacher in the gathering and communicating of this information.

Reason Number 5: Our Role as a Teacher Has Changed

The role of the teacher has changed from the "sage on the stage" to the "guide on the side." We have found, partly because of societal changes and partly because of research on how we learn best, that a thinking curriculum leads to more active learning. In the past teachers needed paper, pencils, and books to ensure that their students got the knowledge they needed to succeed. To succeed in the twenty-first century, our students have to move beyond memorization to synthesizing and analyzing information. With the total human knowledge base doubling every 18 months, computers are they only way to sort through this vast amount of information in order to glean what is needed.

Classrooms are the wagon trains of the future. Teachers need to be the trail guides, pointing out obstacles and suggesting routes. The destination and the decisions on what route to take will be up to the students.

INTRODUCTION *(cont.)*

HOW TO USE THIS BOOK

Hardware Section

In this section begins a description of the hardware components most commonly found in the classroom. What do these devices look like, what do they do, and how can they be utilized to deliver instruction?

Software Section

This section is designed to look at the five families of technology tools (Electronic Learning and Research, Data Analysis, Writing and Publishing, Presentation and Creativity, Telecommunications) that teachers use to deliver curriculum. Within each section is included a detailed description of the tool, a justification for using it, strategies for teaching the software, recommendations for hardware and software, and tips.

Management

The Management section includes teacher technology tools that can help you with the everyday administrative tasks in the classroom, as well as some tips for helping the technology-using classroom to run smoothly.

Lesson Plans

This section includes several lesson plans that utilize technology tools to deliver them. You simply plug in the content, software, and hardware configurations that you currently have available.

Appendix

Finally the Appendix includes a glossary of terms, bibliography, grant writing resources, and suggested software.

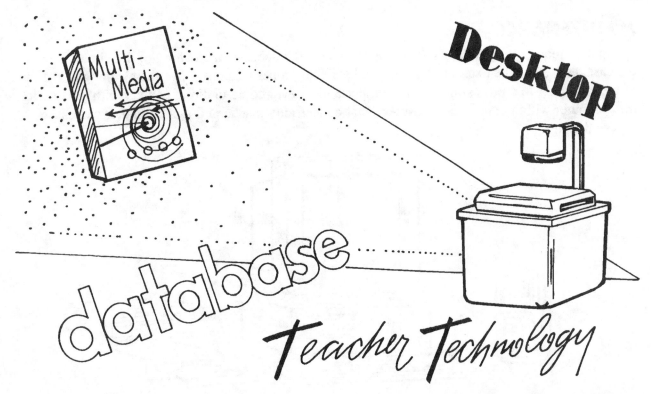

WHAT IS HARDWARE?

Hardware, simply put, is any computer technology that one can touch. The computer, printer, monitor, keyboard, and mouse are all hardware components. These are the tools that carry out the instructions that the software gives them. Your brain, for instance, is the greatest piece of computer hardware known to man. It is a maze of interconnected circuits which carries out instructions that have been loaded through a lifetime of experience. What makes the brain such a perfect piece of hardware is that it is continually being upgraded to process faster and remember things better. Computer hardware, on the other hand, needs to be physically upgraded or even replaced periodically in order to run new or more powerful software.

Educators are faced with having to know what the capabilities of their hardware are in order to use it to its potential. This section will provide the background you need to determine the capabilities of different pieces of hardware. Each piece of hardware and its function are described, as well as tips on care and maintenance.

OPERATING SYSTEMS

An attractive member of the opposite sex is nice to look at, but when you are looking for a long term relationship, personality has to be a major concern. The same holds true for a computer; fast processors and lots of memory are nice, but if you can't interact with it, they are useless. There are several computer manufacturers on the market today, but each has its roots with one of two companies. International Business Machines, or IBM, and Apple Computer have dictated the way personal computers have been made since their inception. However, the differences between the computers are mostly in the software that is used to control it, called the operating system. Much like our nervous systems, computers must have a set of instructions that help them run. These operating systems tell the computer where and how to save things and help the user to interact with it. Although mostly dedicated to hardware, this section will also discuss software integral to the use of the machines.

MAINTENANCE

Computers require very little maintenance other than the occasional cleaning of the circuit boards inside the case, as well as the exterior. Unless you have had proper training, leave the cleaning of the interior of the computer to a professional. Most importantly, never come in direct contact with the interior of the computer without antistatic measures. Static electricity discharged in a computer can cause **severe** damage.

COMPUTERS

CHOOSING A COMPUTER

Much like choosing an automobile, choosing a computer can be a daunting task. There are several manufacturers that package computers in hundreds of ways. They use model numbers and slick names to steer us away from "what's under the hood."

PLATFORM

Platform refers to the type of computer/operating system that you require. There are two major choices: Windows or Macintosh (DOS ships standard on all IBM and compatibles). In the past this was a major decision when considering a purchase, in that IBM and compatible machines could not run Macintosh programs and vice versa. With the development of software translators and dual platform (they can run both) machines, the problem has become less significant. However, this is still a consideration. Here are a few questions that will help you or your school make the platform decision.

1. What platform is shared by the people with whom you most often share documents (office staff, fellow teachers, school sites)? If only one is used, choose that platform. If both are utilized, choose a platform that can easily operate in both environments.

2. What platform offers the software which you use or are interested in using? Most companies produce software versions for both platforms, however, because of the abundance of IBM compatibles, you will usually find them more accessible through retailers. Macintosh software, although available, tends to be easier to get through mail order sources such as Mac Mall, Mac Warehouse, and educational suppliers.

PROCESSOR

The brain of any computer is its processor. The ability to handle large computing jobs with speed and accuracy depends largely on the processor. Computer manufacturers have evolved through several microprocessors, each generation more fleeting and powerful than the last. Don't focus on the name or model number of the microprocessor. Compare the speed of the processor with other models in your price range. The computing speed of a processor is listed in megahertz or MHz.

RAM

RAM or Random Access Memory is the computer's short term memory, which it needs to carry out a program's instructions. As software becomes more and more memory intensive, it is important to buy a computer with enough RAM to handle it. RAM's unit of measure is the Megabyte or MB. Here are a few questions to ask when considering a purchase:

1. How much RAM does the operating system software use? Windows and MacOS require a large amount of RAM just to run the computer.

2. What types of programs am I going to run? Many graphic intensive programs like educational CD-ROM's, require several megabytes RAM to run. Look at the backs of software packages that you are interested in and check the minimum RAM requirements, then add at least 25% more as a safety net.

COMPUTERS *(cont.)*

RAM *(cont.)*

3. Will you run more than one program at a time? If you are a first time computer user, you may not think that you will; however, the time savings of being able to move information from one program to another is extremely useful. If so, add the minimum memory requirements for both programs together and add 25% for safety.

4. Is the RAM easily upgradable, and what is the maximum RAM upgradability? As computer programs are developed that require more memory, it is important that you are able to "keep up".

STORAGE

Storage is the amount of long term memory that a computer can file or store. There are several storage devices on the market. Like RAM, storage is also measured in megabytes (MB) or gigabytes (GB). There are 1,000 megabytes in a gigabyte. Almost all computers now come with an internal hard disk drive and at least one removable disk drive. Both of these would be considered storage.

MONITOR

A monitor is the screen for the computer. They are available in many sizes and configurations. If you are to take advantage of the multimedia (text, sound, animation, video, photographs, drawings, etc.) available in programs, you will need a good quality monitor that supports at least 256 colors. Monitors that support thousands and millions of colors are also available. Be aware that high end large screen monitors will require the addition of special parts called "video cards" installed into your computer.

PERIPHERALS

Peripherals are things that you add to your computer, such as printers, scanners, modems, video input cards, digital cameras, etc., that enhance what it can do. When shopping for peripherals, study the job that you want to do and the software you need to do it. Ask the following questions:

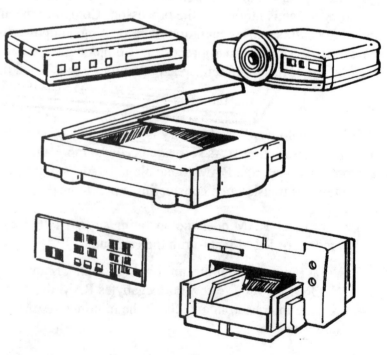

1. What quality are you expecting?

2. Will you need to add anything to the computer in order for the peripheral to work?

3. Does the peripheral require any software?

COMPUTERS *(cont.)*

DIAGRAM OF COMPUTER PARTS

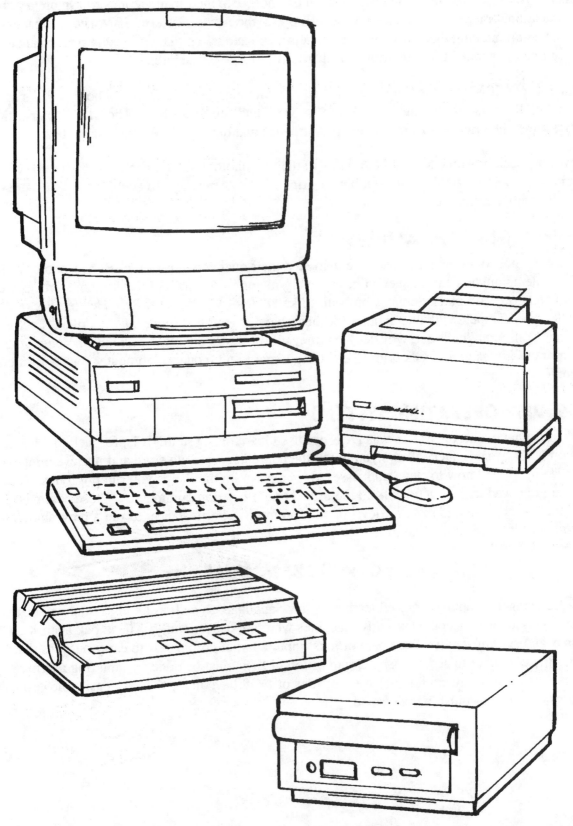

COMPUTERS *(cont.)*

IBM AND COMPATIBLES

In recent years, International Business Machines, Inc. (IBM) has made strides to capture a portion of the educational market. Although schools still prefer the Apple platform, IBM and compatible computers are making their way into the schools more and more. The price and performance of IBM and compatibles make them an attractive alternative to Apple Macintosh.

Unlike Apple, IBM sold the right to manufacture computers that use their technology years ago. This opened up the personal computer market to "clones" and "compatibles". The added competition has driven down the price and increased the performance and quality of personal computers.

However, recently Apple has sold the rights to their technology to companies that want to clone the Macintosh. Begin watching for even bigger price wars as Apple trys to acquire a larger share of the personal computer market.

CLONES AND COMPATIBLES

There are a host of companies that have marketed their own versions of the IBM technology. IBM compatible computers can be seen in nearly every major electronic and department store, as well as "mom and pop" computer stores. Companies like Dell, AT&T, Packard Bell, Hewlett Packard, NEC and Compaq compete with one another for their share of your computer buying dollar. Each machine may have different "bells and whistles," but they all run using the same basic technology. It is important to assess your needs prior to choosing a make and model of computer for your school or home.

DOS (DISK OPERATING SYSTEM)

IBM's original operating system was DOS or Disk Operating System. It is, for lack of a better analogy, the computer's maid. DOS allows you to tell the computer where to store and retrieve things, how to organize itself, and how to clean up messes. It is a program that helps you run programs. This piece of software received its instructions from the user through typed in commands. These commands were the code that users needed to save, retrieve, or start programs. For instance, to run a program in DOS the user might type something like this:

C:/PROGRAMNAME.EXE

Because using a computer required learning a new language, as well as an understanding of the operating systems concept, these early machines were not user friendly. The knock against DOS is that it has been user unfriendly. The operator must input a list of commands to carry out jobs that he/she wishes the computer to accomplish. Organization of files must be done by inputting a string of information on a command line. Newer versions of DOS have made this task easier, however DOS still remains difficult for most to understand.

COMPUTERS *(cont.)*

MICROSOFT WINDOWS

Probably the most significant change in personal computer technology this decade was the production of *Windows* from the Microsoft Corporation. *Windows* provides the IBM and compatible user with an environment similar to the Macintosh operating system. The system is menu driven, with choices made by pointing and clicking a mouse, rather than inputting strings of commands. This operating system also allows the user to work on different programs simultaneously, easily exchanging text, graphics, and numbers from one application program to another. (See Operating Systems page 10.)

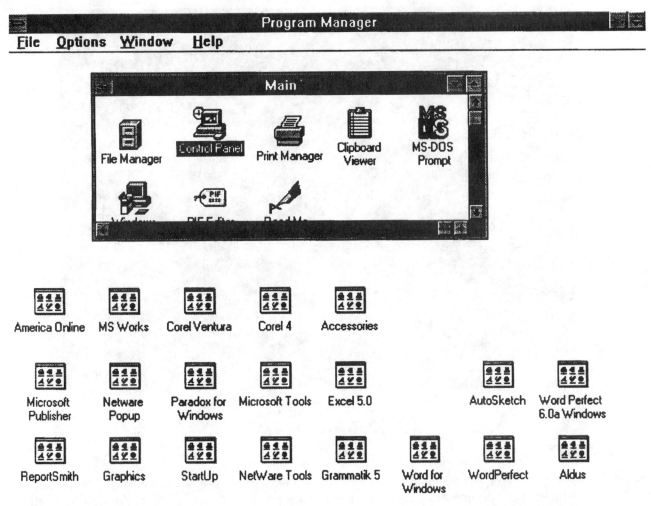

Microsoft Windows 3.1 © (Screen shot reprinted with permission from Microsoft Corporation)

MICROPROCESSORS

The brain of any computer is its microprocessor. The ability to handle large computing jobs with speed and accuracy depends largely on the microprocessor. IBM and Compatibles have evolved through several microprocessors, with each generation increasing in speed and power. (See Choosing a Computer page 11.) Microprocessors are not the only consideration when looking for speed and power in an IBM or compatible; they are, however, a good rule of thumb.

COMPUTERS *(cont.)*

APPLE MACINTOSH: MACOS

With the advancements in personal computers came the graphic interface. In the 1980s, Apple computer developed a computer and operating system that changed the way people thought of the tool. The Macintosh Operating System or MacOS uses graphics called icons to represent the files stored on the computer. Using an innovative piece of hardware called a mouse, the user was easily able to start, move, and organize files by simply manipulating the icon. Apple continues to improve on the operating system even today.

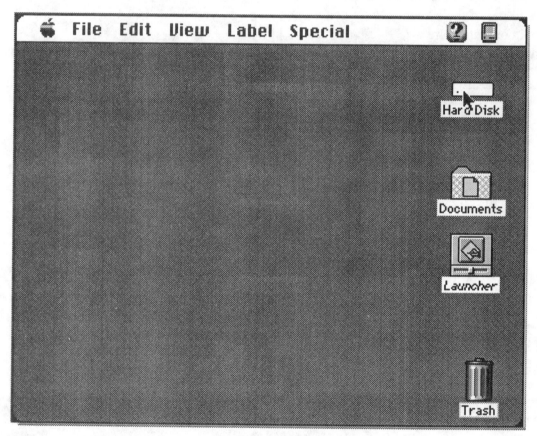

MacOS Desktop

MAC COMPATIBLES

As of 1995, several computer companies have begun to make Mac compatibles and clones. Like the IBM compatibles, these computers perform as well, if not better in some cases, as Apple's Macintosh. Some of the companies include Power Computing, UMAX, Daystar, and Radius.

MICROPROCESSORS

The brain of the Mac is much like that of the IBM and compatibles. It is continually changing. More speed and power come with each generation. When buying a Mac, concentrate on the speed of the processor, not the model number or name. These speeds are expressed in megahertz or MHz. The higher the number, the faster the machine. Remember that this is not the only benchmark of performance. (See Choosing a Computer page 11.)

COMPUTERS *(cont.)*

MONITORS

The monitor is the screen that the user looks at when interacting with the computer.

Size

Monitors, like TV's, come in several different sizes. The measurement of a monitor is a straight diagonal line from corner to corner of the screen. Most home and school computers are a 13"–15" (32.5 cm–38 cm) diagonal picture. Prices of monitors over 15" (38 cm) increase rapidly and are usually overkill for student use unless used for school newspaper or yearbook layout.

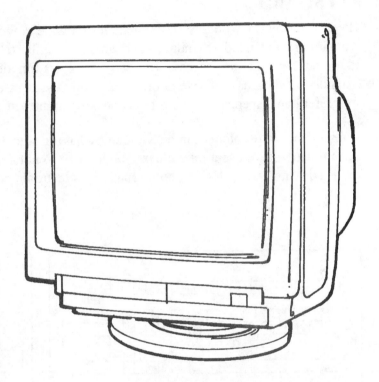

Resolution

The resolution of the picture refers to the amount of tiny pixels (or lights) there are on a monitor screen. This is usually expressed in a number sentence that shows the dimensions of the screen in pixels (e.g., 640 x 480). The more pixels, the more true the picture is on the screen.

High Resolution Video Cards

In order to display high resolution computer images on larger monitors you must have a high resolution video card. The circuit board that is installed inside your computer contains VRAM or Video Random Access Memory. This memory is there solely for the purpose of allowing you to draw an image on the screen without tying up
your work.

Projecting on a TV

Displaying an image on a TV is a very good way to use the computer as a presentation tool. Whether teaching the class how to use a program or as a visual aid for a science lesson, it is advantageous to connect a computer to a television. Because computers are based on high resolution video signal, you cannot simply plug one into a TV. You must first use what is known as a "print to video" or "video conversion box" to convert the high resolution signal to regular TV RF signal. Some examples are listed in the Large Screen Projection Section on page 23.

INPUT DEVICES

Input devices are those items that allow the user to interact or input information into the computer. Input devices include the keyboard, mouse, touch pad, trackball, graphics tablet, touch screen, and microphone.

KEYBOARD

There are several keyboards on the market in a wide range of prices. Most fall into two categories: standard and extended. Standard keyboards are similar to most typewriter keyboards except for a few additional keys that are necessary to carry out extra functions that are assigned by the software. Extended keyboards add several other function keys, as well as a ten key calculator type keypad. These are preferable, especially if math concepts are taught with the computer.

Many keyboard problems can be avoided by having students wash their hands prior to using them. To clean the keyboard use a mild cleaner on a rag. Do not spray the cleaner directly on the keyboard. If a key is sticking, use a cleaning spray made for electronic components to remove the obstructing grime.

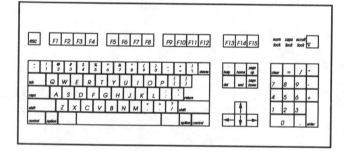 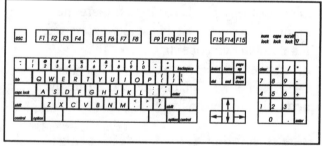

PORTABLE KEYBOARDS

Several manufacturers have developed portable keyboards that allow the student to enter and edit text, then transfer it to a computer for formatting and printing. These relatively inexpensive machines are perfect for classrooms which do not have enough computers to allow the students enough keyboard time. For example, the student can write a story or report on the keyboard, do the preliminary editing, then "dump" the text into the computer's word processor. From there the student can spell check, format, add pictures, and print the document. Since the initial keyboarding is the most time consuming of these tasks, the portable keyboard saves precious computer time at a fraction of the cost of a computer. Other models even allow the user to connect directly to a printer, allowing a student to print out the text for editing prior to publishing with a computer.

INPUT DEVICES *(cont.)*

PORTABLE KEYBOARDS (cont.)

These keyboards require little user maintenance aside from cleaning. To avoid damaging connectors on cables that interface with the computer, pull gently at a right angle to the computer. Make these connections easily assessable, as they will need to be used quite often during a project.

MOUSE

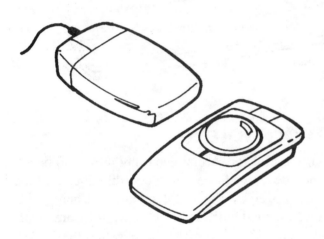

Named because of its resemblance to the rodent, the mouse is an input device that controls the cursor on the screen. The ball on the underside rolls against smooth gears which, in turn, send a signal to the computer and control the cursor. Mice come in several configurations containing from one to three buttons. Once the user has the cursor where he/she wants it, the button or buttons on the top of the mouse can be clicked to move the cursor or select an item or items. The mouse works best on a mouse pad. Better mouse pads are made of dense foam rubber with a non slide surface on the table side and a tightly woven cloth material on the side that comes in contact with the mouse.

Many times the gears in the mouse can become dirty or entangled with hair or fibers. To clean the mouse, turn it over and remove the ring that covers the rubber ball. Wash the rubber ball thoroughly with a mild soap. Remove any dirt or fiber from the gears with a cotton swab and a small amount of alcohol. Make sure that the ball is completely dry before replacing it in the mouse.

TOUCH PAD

A touch pad is a device that is an alternative to a mouse. Instead of rolling a mouse around, the user moves the tip of his/her finger on the surface of the pad. The cursor reacts much as it does with a mouse. A touch pad needs to be cleaned periodically with a mild soapy solution. Again, this should be applied conservatively to a soft cloth and never sprayed directly on the pad.

INPUT DEVICES *(cont.)*

GRAPHICS TABLET

A graphics tablet is a device that allows the user to draw free hand on it while it duplicates the drawing on the computer screen. Aside from the use in a graphics environment, this type of device comes in handy when teachers are presenting using the computer. For instance, if a picture is shown on the computer or large screen projection device, the teacher can use the tablet to circle or make notes right on the screen. (See page 23.) Sports commentators use these same devices to call attention to details on a replay by drawing directly on the screen.

Care of a graphics tablet is much the same as a touch pad. Keeping the tablet clean will enhance its performance and extend its life.

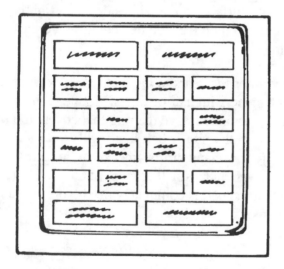

TOUCH SCREEN

Very useful for special needs children who have underdeveloped fine motor coordination, the touch screen is an overlay to the monitor. When accompanied with the appropriate software, users touch the screen to make the selection they require in a program. These are used in informational kiosks. (e.g., Wedding registers at major department stores.)

Once again, keeping the touch screen clean by dusting and wiping with a slightly damp cloth will help to avoid problems.

MICROPHONES

With the proliferation of multimedia computers and the use of recorded sound has evolved the ability to record oneself on the computer. In addition, many new computers have a voice recognition capability. Many computers have microphones built in to do this, although the quality and flexibility of these is not usually very good. Several electronics stores sell microphones starting at as little as five dollars. Any of these will work as long as the plug is the right size. Most computers accept the 1/8 inch diameter mini plug.

Take care not to bump the plug while in the socket of the computer, as it can cause the socket to be damaged or shear off the plug. Again, occasionally cleaning the microphone will assure that it lasts a long time.

OUTPUT DEVICES

AV INPUT/OUTPUT CARDS

Some computers are equipped or can be installed with AV cards. These circuit boards allow the connection of audio and video equipment such as VCRs, video cameras, laserdisc players, audio CD players, and tape recorders. When connected to appropriate equipment and running appropriate software, these AV cards can record audio and video clips for use in multimedia presentations by students or teachers. If the card has an output capability, the computer can be linked directly to a TV, VCR, or tape recorder. Computer sounds and images can then be viewed or recorded. This eliminates the need for a separate print to video box.

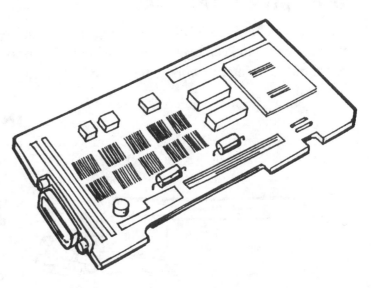

Since these are inside the computer, the only maintenance required would be the occasional (one to three times a year depending on the amount of dust in the environment) cleaning of the computer's circuit boards.

OUTPUT DEVICES

Output devices are mechanisms that allow you to receive some type of product from a computer. Some output devices are printers, large screen projectors, and speakers.

PRINTERS

There are several brands of printers on the market. However, there are only three types of printers most commonly found in schools: dot matrix, ink jet, and laser.

DOT MATRIX PRINTERS

Dot matrix printers are characterized by very fast printing at a lower visual quality than other printers. A dense grid of metal pins impact against an ink ribbon to form the shapes of letters and symbols. It takes several pins to make the shape of a letter. Most of these printers are equipped with tractor and friction feed. Tractor feed requires a continuous roll of special paper with holes on either side that engage in the gears of the printer for advancement. "Friction feed" means that the paper can be fed through the printer by friction, much like a typewriter.

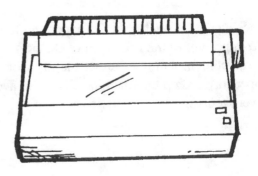

OUTPUT DEVICES *(cont.)*

DOT MATRIX PRINTERS (cont.)

Most care and upkeep involves changing ribbons and keeping the platen (rubber cylinder) clean. It is very important to keep continuous feed paper free of obstruction so that tangling does not occur. Do not allow the printer to work without paper. Printing directly on the platen can cause damage to the dot matrix pins.

INK JET PRINTERS

Ink jet printers are very popular because of their flexibility. Although slower than dot matrix, ink jet printers can print type and pictures in shades of gray, and with some models, even in color. These printers work by spraying ink through very small jets in order to form the shape and shade required. Color ink jets combine layers of red, green, and blue to achieve different hues and shades.

Maintenance includes the changing of the ink cartridge and the occasional cleaning of metal contacts and the jets themselves. Many models are self-cleaning, eliminating the bother of a cleaning ritual. Avoiding low quality paper will result in a better quality print job and a longer time period between cleaning.

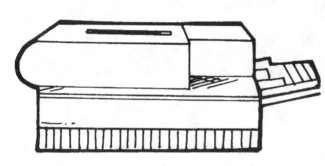

LASER PRINTERS

Laser printers work much like photocopiers. A thin layer of toner powder is distributed over the surface of the paper. A laser draws the shapes, and increases or decreases the intensity of the light in order to achieve shading. The toner which is hit by the laser, adheres to the paper, and the rest is removed.

Once again the quality of the paper and toner are important to the operation of the printer. Avoid contamination of either the toner or the paper tray. Keep the machine clean and avoid severe temperature fluctuations.

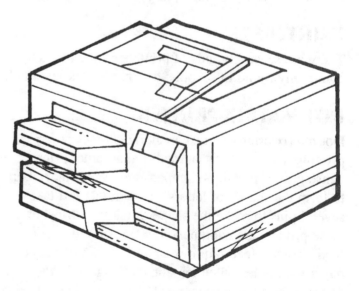

OUTPUT DEVICES *(cont.)*

LARGE SCREEN PROJECTION DEVICES

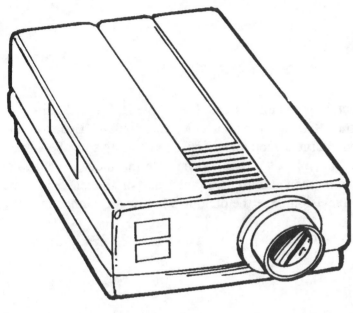

High End Multimedia Projectors

These large screen projectors are incredible and incredibly priced. It is not likely that you will see this all-in-one projector at your school unless you have found an extra $3,000 to $10,000 dollars in the student body account. These pieces of equipment are used to project computer, video, and laserdisc images onto a large movie screen. They are portable and usually include a sound system built in. Some examples include the LitePro 580 (InFocus), nFinity P115 (nView) and the Sharp XGE65OU (Sharp).

Advantages: Durability; extremely clear picture even at large sizes

Disadvantages: $$$$

LCD Panels

Liquid crystal display, or LCD panels, work using the same technology as the digital watches many of us own. The difference being that the liquid crystals float between two sheets of glass that are embedded with electrodes. This panel is then placed on an overhead projector, connected to a computer or video source, and projected on to a large screen. These devices are still very pricey for use in a single classroom, with the average price ranging from just under $1,000 for a black-and-white model to several thousand for the top of the line active matrix color model. In addition, most of these panels will require a special, extra bright overhead projector, which is an additional cost. The most cost effective use of an LCD panel is to share it between a number of classes. The price of these devices has dropped dramatically in the past few years and industry experts believe the cost will continue to decrease. Many suppliers will loan panels on a trial basis to schools who are in the market to buy.

OUTPUT DEVICES *(cont.)*

Advantages: Large screen projection

Disadvantages: $$$$, many models don't support the amount of colors found in many newer CD-ROM software.

PROJECTING ON THE TELEVISION

Older Computers?

A more affordable option for large screen projection is the television. The Apple II, Laser, Radio Shack, and Commodore computers popular in the 1980s used regular video line signals. Because of this, these computers are very easy to display on a large screen television. You simply split the video line coming out of the back of the computer by attaching a "Y" cable (available for under $7.00 at any Radio Shack Store). This allows the computer to be seen at both its monitor and on the television. You can also videotape anything that is seen on the television. See the diagrams below for connecting.

If your television has a video line input use this diagram.

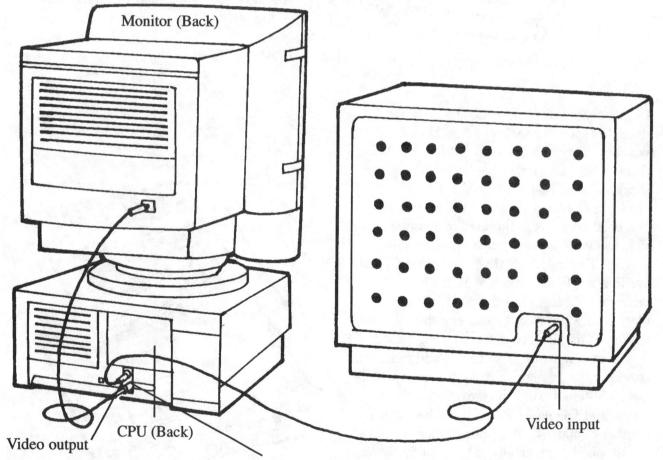

Monitor (Back)

Video output

CPU (Back)

"Y" Cord (1 male RCA connector to 2 females

Video input

If your television does not have a video line input or you wish to videotape what is on the computer, use the diagram on page 25. If you do not have a VCR or a TV that has video line input or S video input, you will need to purchase an RF converter from a consumer electronics store like Radio Shack.

OUTPUT DEVICES *(cont.)*

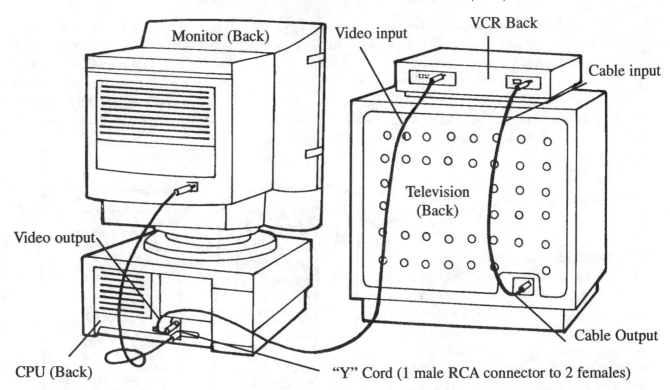

Monitor (Back) · Video input · VCR Back · Cable input · Video output · Television (Back) · Cable Output · CPU (Back) · "Y" Cord (1 male RCA connector to 2 females)

Tech Tip: Use VCR Companion, a program written for the Apple II series of computers, to make opening or closing credits on video tape projects. This inexpensive program will let you script several special effects like rolling credits and dissolving transitions for use in video reports.

Newer Computers

In order to accomplish the higher resolution graphics we are used to on today's computers, computer companies such as IBM and Apple had to move away from line video used for television signals. Because of this, special hardware called "video conversion" or print to video boxes are needed to convert these high resolution video signals to that which can be handled by televisions. These boxes are much more affordable than other large screen projection devices. If televisions and VCRs are available, they give the user the added dimension of being able to video tape student presentations and projects for replay at school or home. Some of the video conversion devices available on the market include the following:

LTV Pro and Portable Pro (Focus Enhancements): Available as internal cards that are added to the interior of the computer and external boxes that are connected to the computer.

The Presenter Plus (Consumer Technology): Available as external connections only, these devices are available for both IBM and Macintosh.

TelevEyes (Digital Vision): Available in both external and internal options for IBM and Macintosh.

If your computer is an all-in-one design (CPU and monitor are built into the same case) and does not have an external video connector, you will need to purchase an adapter. These internally installed cards are usually around $75.00.

OUTPUT DEVICES *(cont.)*

If you do not have a VCR and your computer does not have a video line input or S video input, you will need an RF modulator available through Radio Shack and other consumer electronic stores. Use the diagram on page 25 as a reference only. Read the instructions that come with the unit carefully. Once you have the converter hooked up, tune the TV to the station that the VCR transmits on (usually 3 or 4), and switch the VCR to receive the "Video In" signal. This is usually accomplished by pushing the channel button on the VCR until AV or "Video In" is displayed. Sometimes there is a button on the VCR or its remote that switches the signal to "Video In."

SPEAKERS

Most computers purchased in the last five years are equipped with or have the capability of producing sound. In order to produce sound, computers must have a sound card installed. You can usually find out if your computer has a sound card installed by looking for a speaker jack at the back panel of the computer. This is usually labeled with the word "speaker" or an icon that represents it. Computer speakers must be amplified in order to be heard. Make sure that amplified speakers are specified when purchasing.

Amplified speakers require very little maintenance other than occasional cleaning. Make sure that volume levels during use stay below the level at which distortion is heard. If they do not, it can cause irreparable harm to the speaker mechanism.

CAPTURING PICTURES AND TEXT

One of the strengths of microcomputers is their ability to capture pictures and text so that they can be used in other applications. The following pieces of hardware are used to capture pictures and or text.

SCANNERS

Scanners are peripheral devices that can take an image from the printed medium and digitize it for use in your computer. For instance, if your class is writing reports about ancient Greece and your text book has an excellent picture of the Parthenon, you could use a scanner to save the image for use in reports. If the scanner has OCR (optical character recognition) software, scanned text can be used in a word processor and may be edited just as if you had typed it yourself.

OUTPUT DEVICES *(cont.)*

SCANNERS (cont.)

Scanners come in a variety of configurations, only two of which schools need or can afford: hand held and flatbed scanners. Handheld scanners are less costly, but provide a lower-quality image reproduction. These scanners are held in the hand and pulled across the document. Flatbed scanners are more like photocopy machines. The document is placed on the scanner, and an image is taken. Flatbed scanners are available in several different price ranges, depending much on the speed and resolution in which they scan a document. In most cases, schools require a color scanner that

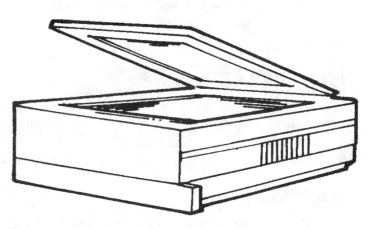

will accept up to a legal size document at a minimum resolution of 1200 dpi (dots per inch). OCR software can be expensive if purchased separately; however many scanners come with lesser versions. All scanners come with the software they require to function.

Maintenance for scanners usually consists of cleaning the glass or plastic scanning surface with a mild window cleaner. Avoid spraying the cleaner directly on the surface and use a soft cloth. Scratches in the glass will cause the transfer of lines onto scanned images.

DIGITAL CAMERAS

There are several digital cameras on the market that allow students and teachers to take pictures and bring them directly from the devices into the computer. Since the cameras save the image in a digital format, they require no film. The pictures are stored as numbers in the memory of the camera. The memory can be transferred from the camera to the computer through a cable. The computer software can then assemble the digital information into an image that can be used in a variety of writing and presentation programs. These cameras come in both black and white and color. Some models are portable, with the ability to be taken anywhere; whereas, others require the connection of a computer in order to be utilized.

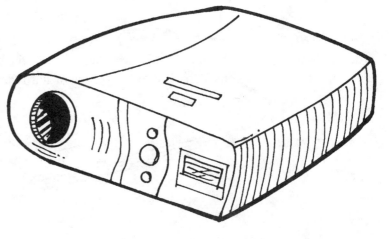

These cameras take very little maintenance other than the cleaning of lenses with a soft cloth. Portable cameras require batteries, therefore the batteries will have to be recharged or replaced occasionally.

OUTPUT DEVICES *(cont.)*

COMMUNICATION DEVICES

In order to communicate with other computers, for example, when using the Internet, a computer requires either a modem or network card. The use of a modem or network card depends on your connectivity (the way in which computers are connected).

NETWORK CARDS

If your school's computer is networked, your computer will require a network card similar to those used throughout the school. These devices allow your computer to share files, share devices (like printers), and communicate with one another. If your network is directly connected to the Internet, your network card will allow you to access information on other computers and networks around the world.

MODEMS

Most schools, however, do not have the resources for such costly connections to the Internet. In this case, modems are used to make this connection. These devices can be inside the computer in the form of a circuit board or external in the form of a box that is connected to the rear of the computer by a cable. The devices translate the digital information that your computer understands to analog or sound information that can be sent over a normal phone line. Because this translation takes time, modems are typically slower than directly connecting to a network. Modems are, however, much less expensive than the infrastructure required for a network and can offer the ability to fax documents from your computer. In order to access the Internet, one would only need a modem, dedicated phone line, and an Internet service provider (ISP). When shopping for a modem, one should look at the rate at which it can send and receive information. This is known as the baud rate and is expressed in bytes per second (bps). The industry standard is 28,000 bps, or 28.8K bps as of the date that this book was published.

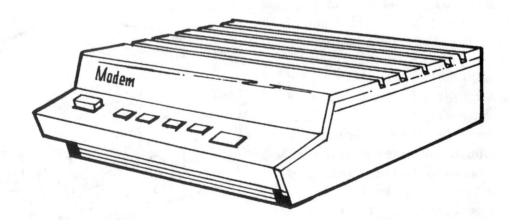

Modems take little to no maintenance. Keeping all electronic equipment clean prevents the build up of heat which can cause damage.

OUTPUT DEVICES *(cont.)*

Hardware Checkout Sheet

Type of Hardware	Equipt. Number	Reserved From:	Reserved To:	Signature	Room Number	Additonal Information

WHAT IS SOFTWARE?

In the past, teachers interested in using technology quickly discovered that software resources were limited. Applications software such as word processors and spreadsheets could be adapted for classroom use. And, of course, there was a growing collection of drill and practice, tutorial, and simulation software designed for classroom use. Many teachers who used this software in their classes could keep all their program disks in a small plastic box.

Now there are thousands of educational software packages, and new types of applications software have appeared, such as desktop publishing programs and presentation software. Many new forms of educational software have also emerged. Computer supported laserdisc packages, hypermedia software, and multimedia packages are popular. Today the computer-using educator is faced with a problem of overabundance rather than scarcity. With all the software on the market, it is a daunting task to decide which one to use. Among all the glitz we sometimes forget curriculum comes first and the technology is nothing but a tool to deliver it. The problem with the abundance of technology tools available is that teachers are led to believe, consciously or unconsciously, that they must use them all. This isn't true. The fact is, many software tools duplicate each other. This section will describe the five software tool groups that should be available in the classroom, as well as their possible uses. The perfect tool kit would include the following software:

Software	Tool Description	Amount of programs needed
Electronic Learning Tools	Software that teaches the skills, concepts, and content in the curriculum.	Amount and type depend on curriculum.
Word Processing	Software that enables user to write on the computer.	One: can be purchased as an integrated package with data analysis tools.
Creativity and Presentation	Software that enables the user to draw, paint and present information.	One.
Data Analysis	Software that enables the user to compare, sort, and break down information in order to analyze it.	One database and one spreadsheet. These can be purchased as an integrated package with word processors.
Telecommunication	Software that allows the use of the Internet.	Amount depends on the type of connection.

ELECTRONIC LEARNING TOOLS

Electronic learning is the gathering of information and/or skills by way of some type of technology, such as a computer, CD-ROM, or laserdisc. It is, for the most part, the easiest use of the computer. The technology is used as a vehicle to deliver instruction.

Most electronic learning is delivered in five forms:

- Reference
- Simulations
- Literature
- Drill and Practice
- Thinking Games

Many of the more modern electronic learning environments are multimedia CD-ROMs and Laserdiscs.

WHAT IS MULTIMEDIA?

The integration of text, sound, photographs, and motion pictures has turned the mostly number-crunching computers of the 80s into the multimedia computers of the 90s. These computers can not only present text about certain subjects, but display pictures or movies and play recorded sounds. Most software packages are very interactive allowing the user to pick his/her path while learning about a subject. These machines can be powerful learning tools if used correctly.

WHAT IS HYPERMEDIA?

If the user can choose his/her own path through the program, it is said to be interactive multimedia. The term "hypermedia" is sometimes used as an alternative to "interactive multimedia". Hypermedia learning stations allow the user to browse through a learning experience rich with text, color, and motion.

By allowing the user to choose his/her own pace and path, the program automatically adapts for differences. By providing information in a variety of modalities, providing a context for the information, and allowing multiple paths through this knowledge, the system allows the learner to select information in the format or formats best suited to his/her learning style, ability level, and pace.

REFERENCE MATERIALS

Because of their interactive nature, reference materials on CD-ROM have really taken off. Encyclopedias, dictionaries, atlases, and almanacs have found their way to the electronic realm. Content-specific CD-ROMs are also available in science and social studies.

ELECTRONIC LEARNING TOOLS (cont.)

MULTIMEDIA ENCYCLOPEDIAS

In recent years, companies like Grolier, Compton, Britannica, Future Vision, and Microsoft have developed interactive multimedia encyclopedias on CD-ROM. A full set of traditional encyclopedias can now be stored on one CD-ROM with the addition of full color photographs, animation, sound, and movie clips. Computerized search mechanisms allow the user to search by title, subject, keyword, and a number of different indexes. Most will automatically outline articles so that the user can quickly find whether or not an article contains the information necessary.

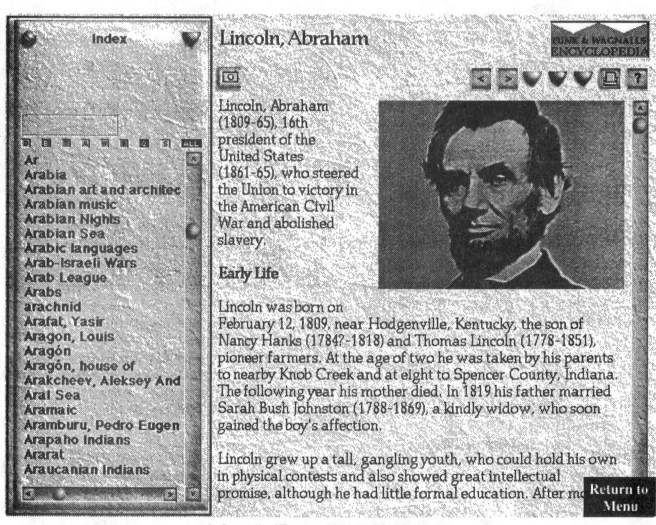

Infopedia (Future Vision Multimedia)

Classroom Usage

There are many classroom uses for encyclopedias on CD-ROM. They are valuable resources for students or teachers researching topics related to curriculum. They can provide the media needed for classroom published reports and presentations. Although encyclopedias are easy to use, they do force the student to use the logic skills involved in searching for information.

ELECTRONIC LEARNING TOOLS *(cont.)*

DICTIONARIES

When using dictionaries on CD-ROM, looking up a word is as easy as creative spelling. After each letter is typed, the search program will show what part of the dictionary you are in, narrowing the search after each subsequent letter. Once the correct word is found, a number of things can be done.

CD-ROM dictionaries give you access to any media related to the word in the form of hyperlinks (buttons on the screen that, when clicked with the mouse, display media). The word can be pronounced through audio links by a recorded human voice. Pictures are sometimes included to further define the word. Synonyms, antonyms, and other related words are linked with hypertext (text that acts as a button linking other screens or media) and are simply a click away. Finally, most dictionaries provide an electronic notepad in which you can store information and anecdotes while researching a subject.

aq·ue·duct 🔊

aq·ue·duct (ăk′wĭ-dŭkt′) *noun*
1. **a.** A pipe or channel designed to transport water from a remote source, usually by gravity. **b.** A bridgelike structure supporting a conduit or canal passing over a river or low ground.
2. *Anatomy.* A channel or passage in an organ or a body part, especially such a channel for Ɪnveying fluid.

Click here to view picture

[Latin *aquaeductus* : *aquae*, genitive of *aqua*, water. See aqua + *ductus*, a leading. See duct.]

Microsoft Bookshelf, American Heritage Dictionary, Microsoft Corporation

Classroom Usage

Because of their speed, electronic dictionaries can shorten the amount of time needed for students to look up words required for spelling and vocabulary skill building. Media included in this resource can be copied and pasted into reports or other writing. Finally, thinking skills are reinforced with the use of search tools built into the program.

ELECTRONIC LEARNING TOOLS *(cont.)*

ATLASES

Geography is not only the study of the physical and political mapping of the world, it is also concerned with the movement of people and how they adapt. With an electronic atlas, students or teachers can search maps by names, latitude and longitude, or by visual location. Once there, users can see photos and movies of the people and their customs, view their political symbols, and see pictures of the area. Do the maps in your classroom still show the former Soviet Union? With electronic atlases available on CD-ROM for as little as $30.00, schools can afford to stay current.

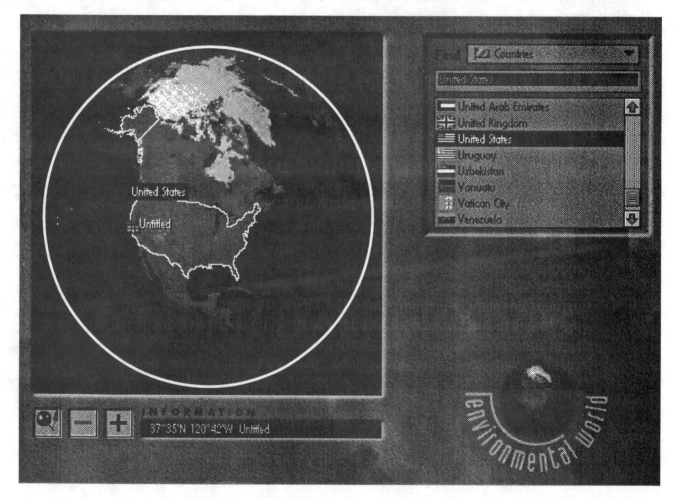

3D Atlas, Electronic Arts

Classroom Uses

Electronic atlases are very useful when teaching geography and social sciences. Geography skills can be introduced or reinforced using the atlas as a teacher presentation tool (see large screen projection in the Hardware section). Students can demonstrate knowledge of geography facts and skills using the electronic atlas. Student research, such as state and country reports, can be enhanced with media included with the program.

ELECTRONIC LEARNING TOOLS *(cont.)*

ALMANACS

Historical and cultural resources are very easy to obtain using almanacs on CD-ROM. These are equipped with high powered search engines. Like multimedia encyclopedias, these search engines allow you to find information by subject, title, name, era, year, and keyword. Most almanacs have multiple years on one CD-ROM, which makes comparisons of historical events very easy to do.

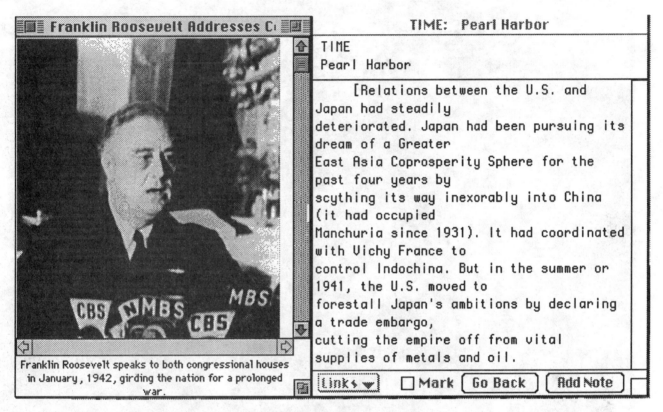

Time Almanac, Time Publishing, Inc.

Classroom Uses

Almanacs provide a rich resource of easily accessible historical and cultural information. Media libraries included with these programs can be used in student writing and presentations. Since multiple articles can be seen at the same time, comparison and contrast of events, eras, or people can be easily accomplished. Research of historical events becomes less time consuming and tedious, and in turn, more enjoyable.

CONTENT SPECIFIC REFERENCE

Many companies are releasing content specific, interactive science and social study titles on CD-ROM and laserdisc. Social studies discs are rich with text and graphics that depict different eras of history. Science discs show clips of observations and experiments that could never be recreated in the classroom. These learning tools are often inexpensive and easy to use. A content-specific program can be used as the centerpiece of a unit of study or simply a supplement to it.

ELECTRONIC LEARNING TOOLS *(cont.)*

CD-ROMs offer the ability to take media and text resources for use in computer generated reports. They are very interactive, allowing the user to capture information. Below is an example of a CD-ROM on space flight. The user can explore areas of the shuttle simply by clicking the area chosen with the mouse.

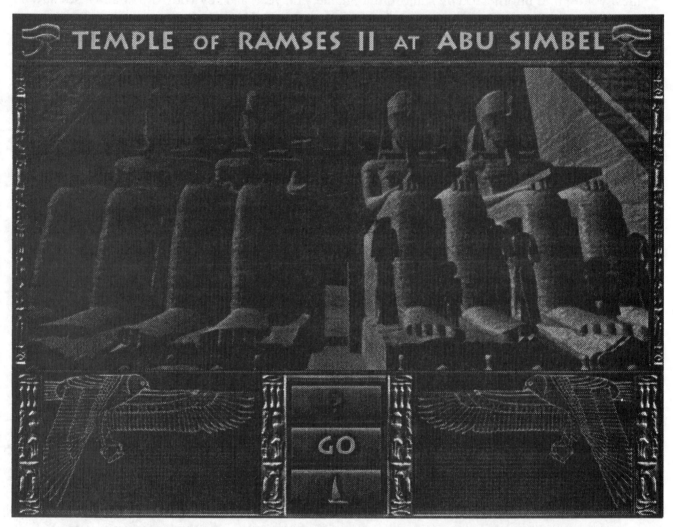

Nile, Passage to Egypt (The Discovery Channel Multimedia)

There are many content resources available on laserdisc, as well. Laserdiscs are much like VCRs, only much more interactive and versatile. (See page 77.) Information is accessed via the remote control, bar code reader, or computer aided video control (CAV).

Classroom Uses

Because these programs are related directly to curriculum, there are many uses in the classroom. Teachers can use the programs as media to present lessons. The computer can be a station for student research or individualized learning. Students and teachers can also use the media resources for printed reports and/or presentations.

ELECTRONIC LEARNING TOOLS *(cont.)*

SIMULATIONS

The next best thing to being there is to simulate it. Teachers have for years simulated a moment in history or an experience of a scientist. Technology assisted simulations take these one step further. These programs provide the students with audiovisual representations of the experiences so that they have a sense of what it is like to be in the role represented in the simulations.

A good example of this is Tom Snyder Productions' *The Great Ocean Rescue*. This laserdisc driven simulation of scientists working on environmental disasters provides the students with clues to solve a two part mystery. Groups of four students are given expert identities as oceanographers, marine biologists, geologists, and environmental scientists. They each do research on their jobs using expert booklets that come with the program. Once the research is completed, a video clip is played that describes the problem and gives clues based on the four identities. Part one requires the students to find the location of the disaster, while part two requires the students to help solve it. Because it is interactive, student's decisions result in different video clips being shown describing different consequences.

The Great Ocean Rescue (CD-ROM), Tom Snyder Productions

ELECTRONIC LEARNING TOOLS *(cont.)*

The Great Ocean Rescue, as well as other simulations, are available in CD-ROM and Laserdisc. Laserdisc versions can be connected to a TV and interacted with the aid of a remote control or bar code reader. It can also run as computer aided video (CAV). In this case a computer controls the laserdisc. The advantage to this is that the computer gives instructions about the sequence of the activity, keeps score, and controls the video clips, playing the correct clip on your command.

Other simulations come on CD-ROM or disks. These can be projected (see large screen projection in the Teacher Tools section) for a whole class experience, or be used as a station for smaller groups.

Classroom Usage

Simulations can be run as a whole class, cooperative learning activity, or as a small group activity. Because of their interactive nature, the media in simulations can be viewed out of context and used for reports or presentations.

ELECTRONIC LITERATURE

Multimedia computers and CD-ROM have made it possible for literature to be easily accessible by computer. Many of these units not only have the literature pieces, but supplementary information and media clips too. Many have either text-to-speech simulation (the computer translates text to speech) or recorded readers of the book. This aids students with reading difficulties and comprehension on difficult pieces of literature.

ELECTRONIC LEARNING TOOLS *(cont.)*

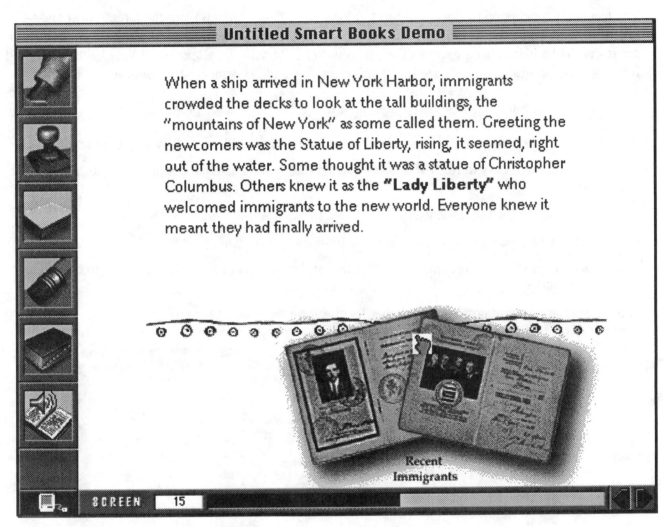

Untitled Smart Books Demo

When a ship arrived in New York Harbor, immigrants crowded the decks to look at the tall buildings, the "mountains of New York" as some called them. Greeting the newcomers was the Statue of Liberty, rising, it seemed, right out of the water. Some thought it was a statue of Christopher Columbus. Others knew it as the **"Lady Liberty"** who welcomed immigrants to the new world. Everyone knew it meant they had finally arrived.

Recent Immigrants

SCREEN 15

If Your Name Was Changed at Ellis Island, Scholastic

Scholastic's Smart Books are one example of electronic literature which incorporates all the components mentioned above as well as electronic research tools. The book can be electronically highlighted and stamped to draw attention to passages that are important. Electronic sticky notes can be placed for anecdotal notes, which can be written or audio recorded. Hypertext links (text that act as buttons linked to media) within the text can be clicked to give the reader more information about the passage. This information can be in the form of audio, video clips, or still pictures.

Classroom Usage

These electronic literature pieces can be fully integrated units of study. Teachers can use large screen projection to present the unit to the whole class. (See page 23.) A computer station can also be set up with tasks individualized for each student or group of students. Teacher written or audio recorded task notes can be imbedded in the program so that when a student reaches a certain point in the text he/she are asked to carry out a task related to it.

ELECTRONIC LEARNING TOOLS *(cont.)*

DRILL AND PRACTICE

The teacher's conception of how to use technology has changed much from the largely drill and practice mentality of the 80s. However, the baby shouldn't be thrown out with the bath water. There are many drill and practice programs that are beneficial for skill development. Many of the math and language arts programs available today are high interest and do wonders for building basic skills.

Here are a few questions to answer while evaluating drill and practice programs.

1) Is the program flexible? Will it allow you to choose the skill you are working on in class?

2) Is the program easy to run? If it takes a manual to make changes, it's probably not going to be used much.

3) Is it engaging for the students? Do they like to use the program?

4) Does the program give positive feedback for correct answers?

5) Does the program correct mistakes after the student has had ample time or trials to complete the problem?

6) Does the program provide the teacher feedback on the student's progress?

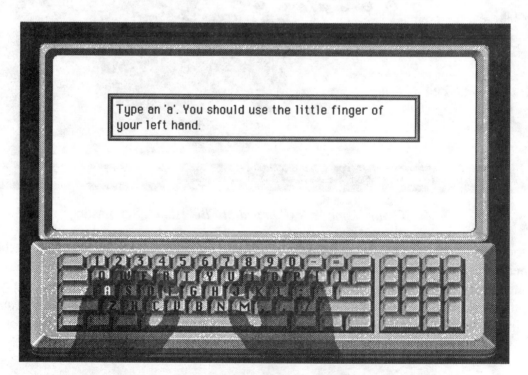

Type an 'a'. You should use the little finger of your left hand.

Mavis Beacon Teaches Typing, The Software Toolworks

Classroom Usage:

Drill and practice programs should be used primarily as individualized skill building activities. Many of the math and language skill building exercises can be used with the entire class as an introductory lesson using large screen projection. (See page 23.)

ELECTRONIC LEARNING TOOLS *(cont.)*

THINKING GAMES

Many of the thinking games available for computers help students develop logical thinking skills. Although usually a supplement to curriculum, these mind building and entertaining games are good for teaching memory, cognitive skills, strategies, and creativity.

An example of a thinking game that has merit as a math supplement is *The Factory* by Sunburst Communications. *The Factory* is built around the premise of an assembly line. On this assembly line, called a factory, students must use several strategies to build or predict products.

The Factory has three different modes:

1. **Experiment**—Test a machine or factory

2. **Predict**—Predict a product from a predetermined factory

3. **Challenge**—Build a factory that will make a given product

In the Challenge mode students must analyze a premade product and then put a series of machines in the assembly line that will duplicate it. This involves the development of many of the higher level thinking skills needed to solve visual and spatial problems.

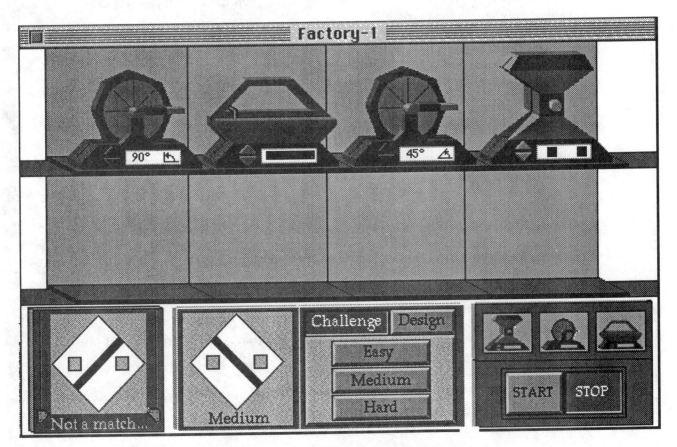

The Factory, Sunburst Communications

ELECTRONIC LEARNING TOOLS *(cont.)*

TEACHING THE TOOLS

At some point in every student's education, it was necessary to teach him/her to use a pencil, crayon, or dictionary. Technology is no exception. Students must be taught to use the tool in the correct manner if the teacher expects them to produce results using it. The good news is that kids have an intuitive nature about technology tools. They usually learn to use the electronic learning tools more easily than the teacher does. The second piece of good news is that these programs are usually the most user friendly.

Here are a few tips for teaching the tools:

1. Learn the program with a colleague or student.

   Spend ample time learning how to use the electronic learning tool. Remember, teachers don't know everything! Go to an inservice or sit down after school with a colleague or student and figure out the program. A student adept at computers will become a great resource for you.

2. Pass it on.

   Teach one student or group of students the program. Then have them pass on the knowledge to others in the class.

3. Pick one tool to teach at a time.

   Teach one tool and don't move on until most of your students have mastered it. The next tools will become increasingly easy to teach as skills are transferred.

4. Encyclopedias are great starting points.

   Because of their wealth of information and resources, encyclopedias are the most used electronic learning tool.

5. Devise fun assignments using the tools.

   Electronic scavenger hunts are great assignments to evaluate the students understanding of the tool. (See page 164.) These can be mini research reports on a topic being covered in class.

6. Two heads are better than one.

   Computer partners work very well when learning how to use a new program. If one doesn't remember how to use a function, the other probably will.

It is surprising how quickly students will learn to use electronic learning tools. In most cases they are off and running in a class period or two.

ELECTRONIC LEARNING TOOLS *(cont.)*

RECOMMENDED HARDWARE

With the exception of most of the Drill and Practice and Thinking Game software, most of the electronic learning tools on the market today are only available on CD-ROM. This is because of the abundance of resources available in each product.

Computer: Multimedia equipped computer including CD-ROM and speakers (usually built-in). Minimum 8 meg RAM.

Laserdisc: Remote controls are a minimum requirement. Bar code readers are preferable for easily moving from image to image. Many programs are available for operating laserdiscs remotely using the computer.

CHOOSING ELECTRONIC LEARNING SOFTWARE

1. Examine your curriculum to determine your needs.

2. Look through catalogs of educational software suppliers and match your needs with possible products.

3. Ask for demonstration copies of the products you choose. Disk products are usually in limited function demonstration copies. Full function CD-ROMs are often sent on a trial basis. You will sometimes be required to call the publishers for demonstration copies. Many companies will give 30-day trial periods.

Note: Apple Computer produces a CD-ROM twice a year that contains descriptions and demonstrations of nearly all the education programs available on the Macintosh. This is free to educators.

Note: Educational Resources also produces CD-ROM catalogs with detailed descriptions of both IBM Windows and Macintosh programs available through them.

4. Try out each for easy use, quality and quantity of information, and relation to curriculum before settling on one.

5. Once you have chosen a software title, shop around. Prices can range as much as 25%.

ELECTRONIC LEARNING TOOLS

RECOMMENDED SOFTWARE
Reference
Encyclopedias

Compton's Interactive Encyclopedia, Compton's, CD-ROM

Infopedia, Future Vision Multimedia, CD-ROM

Microsoft Encarta, Microsoft, CD-ROM

The New Grolier Multimedia Encyclopedia, Grolier, CD-ROM

Dictionaries

Macmillian Dictionary for Kids, Macmillian, CD-ROM

MerriamWebster's Dictionary for Kid's, Mindscape, CD-ROM

Atlases

3D Atlas, Electronic Arts, CD-ROM

MAC or PC USA, Broderbund, Disk

Picture Atlas of the World, National Geographic, CD-ROM

USA Geography, MECC, Disk

World Atlas, Mindscape, Disk

Almanacs

Time Almanac, Time, CD-ROM

Content Area

There are literally hundreds of content titles from which to choose.

Simulations
Disk

Social Issues: *Decisions, Decisions Series,* Tom Snyder Productions
Social Studies: *Interactive Government,* Pride in Learning
Geography: *Expedition USA,* SVE Software
Science: *Operation Frog,* Scholastic
Innerbodyworks, Tom Snyder Productions

CD-ROM

Social Sciences: *Sim City 2000,* Maxis

Laserdisc

Science: *The Great Ocean Rescue,* Tom Snyder Productions
Science: *Science Sleuths,* Videodiscovery

ELECTRONIC LEARNING TOOLS *(cont.)*

ELECTRONIC LITERATURE

Every year more and more literature titles are being computerized. Look for titles that you already use in your teaching. Use the electronic versions as supplements.

20,000 Leagues Under the Sea, Orange Cherry, CD-ROM

History of American Literature, Clearvue, CD-ROM

Huckleberry Finn, Bookworm, CD-ROM

Knights and Kings, Entrex, CD-ROM

Thinking Games:

There are also many thinking games from which to choose. Remember to ask yourself, "In what thinking skills are my students weak?"

Building Perspective, Sunburst Communications, Disk

The Factory, Sunburst Communications, Disk

Memory Master, Heartsoft, Disk

Mindcastle, Lawrence, Disk

Shopping Strategies, Gamco

Where in the World is Carmen San Diego, Broderbund, Disk and CD-ROM

Drill and Practice

Math

Decimal and Fraction Maze, Great Wave, Disk

Math Ace, Magic Quest, Disk or CD-ROM

Math Blaster 2, Davidson, Disk

Mathblaster Mystery, Davidson, Disk or CD-ROM

Language Arts

Essential Punctuation, Gamco, Disk

Spell It Plus, Davidson, Disk and CD-ROM

Word City, Magic Quest, Disk and CD-ROM

Word of Words, Randolph Educational Systems, Disk

WRITING AND PUBLISHING TOOLS

WHAT IS WORD PROCESSING?

Word processing is any software program that allows electronic writing and correcting of documents. Correcting and editing tools make word processors the single most used computer application in the world. With the addition of graphic insertion capabilities, the newer word processing programs have become an even more useful tool.

WHAT IS DESKTOP PUBLISHING?

Desktop publishing programs are used to produce high quality printed documents. What makes them different from word processing programs is their ability to manipulate the look of text and graphics. Interesting effects and ease of graphic placement make these programs powerful tools for creating a polished document.

HOW DO YOU USE THEM?

Teachers

It is extremely important for teachers to communicate in writing with parents, administrators, colleagues, and students. The problem in the past has been the amount of time that teachers must invest in a document in order for it to convey information in a professional manner. Word processors and publishing tools can help a teacher create the many different documents in an efficient, informative, and professional way. Here are a few ways teachers use these tools.

newsletters	grade reports	informal assessments	notes home
bulletin boards	signs	documentation	handouts
worksheets	IEP's	lesson plans	proposals

Efficiency is built into the process. Once a teacher has made a document, it becomes a template for the next.

Example: A newsletter can be preformatted with title, columns, margins, and any other information that remains the same for each separate document. The new date can be automatically inserted when the document is opened. All that remains for the teacher to do is type in the text. If you did the same unit or activity last year, just electronically cut and paste the text from last year's newsletter into this year's.

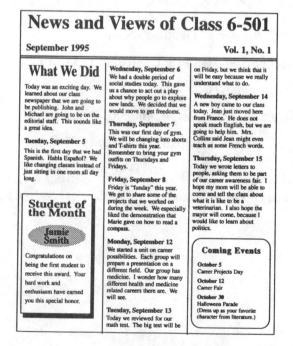

News and Views of Class 6-501

September 1995   Vol. 1, No. 1

What We Did

Today was an exciting day. We learned about our class newspaper that we are going to be publishing. John and Michael are going to be on the editorial staff. This sounds like a great idea.

Tuesday, September 5
This is the first day that we had Spanish. Habla Español? We like changing classes instead of just sitting in one room all day long.

Wednesday, September 6
We had a double period of social studies today. This gave us a chance to act out a play about why people go to explore new lands. We decided that we would move to get freedoms.

Thursday, September 7
This was our first day of gym. We will be changing into shorts and T-shirts this year. Remember to bring your gym outfits on Thursdays and Fridays.

Friday, September 8
Friday is "funday" this year. We get to share some of the projects that we worked on during the week. We especially liked the demonstration that Marie gave on how to read a compass.

Monday, September 12
We started a unit on career possibilities. Each group will prepare a presentation on a different field. Our group has medicine. I wonder how many different health and medicine related careers there are. We will see.

Tuesday, September 13
Today we reviewed for our math test. The big test will be

on Friday, but we think that it will be easy because we really understand what to do.

Wednesday, September 14
A new boy came to our class today. Jean just moved here from France. He does not speak much English, but we are going to help him. Mrs. Collins said Jean might even teach us some French words.

Thursday, September 15
Today we wrote letters to people, asking them to be part of our career awareness fair. I hope my mom will be able to come and tell the class about what it is like to be a veterinarian. I also hope the mayor will come, because I would like to learn about politics.

Student of the Month

Jamie Smith

Congratulations on being the first student to receive this award. Your hard work and enthusiasm have earned you this special honor.

Coming Events

October 5
Career Projects Day

October 12
Career Fair

October 30
Halloween Parade
(Dress up as your favorite character from literature.)

WRITING AND PUBLISHING TOOLS *(cont.)*

Students

Aside from the pride students shows in a computer generated report, they learn valuable communication skills. Getting their point across using not only text, but pictures, drawings, tables, and graphs teaches them to communicate effectively.

Example: Along with the student's writing, a report on The Civil War could include a picture, a timeline, or a graph that illustrates certain points made in the report.

The Civil War

by Gary

The American Civil War was the most bloody conflict in American history. It claimed more American lives than any other war the that the United States fought in before or since. It was so bloody because both sides were Americans. You see civil wars are conflicts between people in the same country.

In the 1860's the Southern United States had major differences with the North. The South believed that the states should have more say in how they ran themselves. The major difference was slavery. The South believed that each state should be able to decide if slavery was legal or not. The North believed that the national government should have the power to impose laws on the st... Many people in the national government, includi... Lincoln, believed that sl...

The Children's Writing and Publishing Center, The Learning Company

WHAT CAN WRITING AND PUBLISHING TOOLS DO?

Word Processing

Word processing software will be your most frequently used tool in your software arsenal. All word processing programs work essentially the same way with minor differences in the way the they set up and edit documents. Text is typed into a white screen that is made to simulate a paper page. The power of a word processor is in the editing features. Below is a list of features most word processors support.

WRITING AND PUBLISHING TOOLS *(cont.)*

Cut, copy, and paste: Pictures or text can be cut (removed) or copied and pasted into different areas of the document. This also works between different documents as well as different programs.

Find and Replace: This editing tool allows you to find words, phrases, sentences, punctuation, etc. and remove or replace them throughout the document.

Make Templates: If a document produced with the same layout frequently, such as a newsletter, a template with that layout can be made to your specifications and saved for later use.

Insert Options: Pictures and graphics can be inserted into the document.

Style: Many style options are available including: font (what the text looks like), type size, alignment, and even color.

Layout: Paragraphs, tabs, columns and other layout features can be changed on portions of or the entire document at once.

Proofread: Spelling and grammar checkers, as well as thesaurus tools, are built into many word processors.

Draw: Several drawing tools like line, square, and circle makers are built into many programs.

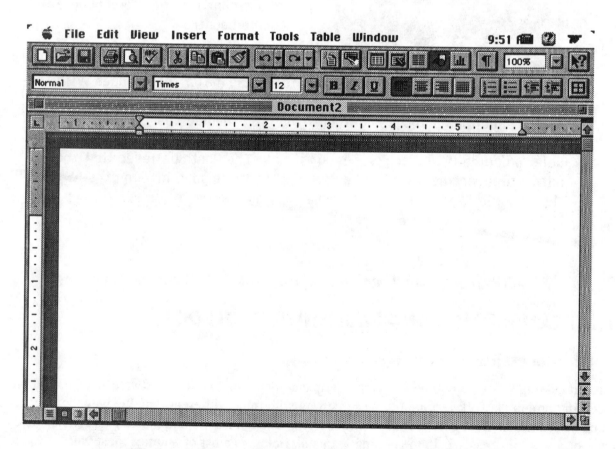

Microsoft Word screen page (Microsoft Corporation)

WRITING AND PUBLISHING TOOLS *(cont.)*

Buttons or menus are used to customize the document. Although word processing programs allow you to electronically paste in graphics or draw pictures right on the screen, they are more useful when manipulating text. Once the document is finished it can be printed and/or saved for later editing, or for use in another application, such as a presentation or a desktop publishing document.

INTEGRATED WORD PROCESSORS *("Works" Programs)*

Integrated Word Processors are fully functional word processors with the addition of spreadsheets, databases, communications, and drawing programs. Each of these works with the other to create useful documents. In other words, within these types of programs a student could write a report with the word processor, insert a self-made graph from the spreadsheet, keep track of research in the database, draw a picture and insert it in the report, and send the report to another computer using the communications package.

See the Data Analysis section page 78 for an in depth look at databases and spreadsheets.

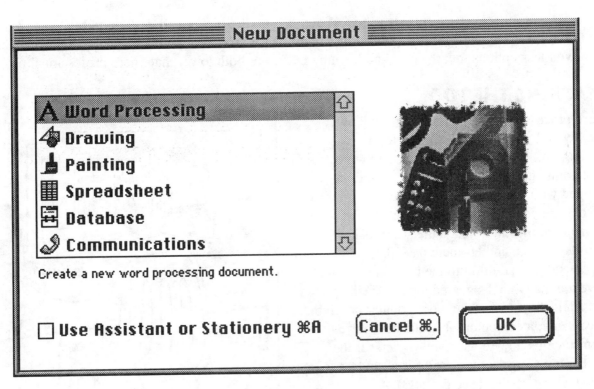

ClarisWorks (Claris Corporation)

WRITING AND PUBLISHING TOOLS *(cont.)*

DESK TOP PUBLISHING

Desktop publishing software allows the user to easily manipulate layout of text and graphic items in a document. These high power applications usually come with higher price tags, overkill for most teacher uses with the exception of yearbook or newspaper layout. There are many lower power (and lower cost) programs that allow the user to do a number of different layouts. These programs are not as flexible as the more professional programs, but they are certainly adequate for classroom use. Here are a few of the functions that desktop publishing programs can carry out.

Size: Graphics can be sized to any proportion.

Move: Text and Graphics can be moved from place to place in the document.

Style: Size, font, alignment, and style of text can be easily changed.

Rotate: Items can be rotated to different angles.

Import: Text can be imported from a word processor or other program. This is very useful, as desktop publishers lack many of the editing and proofreading tools that word processors have.

Teachers can use desktop publishing programs for creating bulletin board displays, newsletters, and teaching aids. Student uses include books, newspapers, yearbook production, as well as graphic art production.

Note: Except for school newspaper and yearbook layout, the higher end desktop publishing programs are usually overkill. Many of the publishing programs for kids have premade layouts built in. These leave you less options, but the cost and learning curve are both lower than more professional programs.

TEACHING THE TOOL

Word processing tools can be taught relatively quickly and without much impact to the curriculum. Most of the more popular word processing and desktop publishing programs are shipped with built-in tutorials. These step-by-step lessons are computer-driven and self-paced. It is normally sufficient to teach the students how to start the tutorial and let them pace themselves with supervision. In addition to the built-in tutorials, there are many books geared toward teaching kids and adults how to use the more popular programs. If available, a computer lab is the best place to train students how to use the program. If the teacher uses large screen projection, students can follow along easily. (See page 23).

WRITING AND PUBLISHING TOOLS *(cont.)*

RECOMMENDED SEQUENCE FOR GROUP INSTRUCTION OF WORD PROCESSING

If the teacher chooses to do group instruction to teach word processing and publishing tools, the following sequence works well. This may be done in as little as a period or spread out over several periods.

1. Have the students start the program. Many Mac or Windows programs have picture icons that represent the program. Double clicking this icon will start the program.

2. Begin with a new document. These documents are untitled and unsaved at first.

3. Save the blank document. This involves giving the document a name and placing it where it can be found. System software differs in how this is done. Refer to manuals for information about saving.

4. Word processing is most efficient when all the text is entered before editing for style. Have all students type a title and press return (on Apple) or enter (on IBM Compatible) twice. Have the students notice that the program enters a line each time this is done. This is very important during the editing phase.

5. Have the students type a paragraph. Return or enter should not be pressed until the paragraph is finished. Have the students notice that the words automatically wrap around at the margins.

6. Teach the students how to highlight a word with the mouse. Have them highlight and then retype another word to replace the original.

7. Highlight all the text and change the font (type style).

8. Highlight the title and change the size; make it bold and underline it.

9. Use the cut or copy and paste function to move text around in the document. This is done by highlighting the word(s) that is going to be cut (removed) or copied and choosing the cut or copy command, usually from the edit menu. Then to paste the word(s), place the cursor where you want the word(s) and choose the paste command.

10. If the program has a spell checker, spell check the document.

11. Teach the students to save the document often. In most programs the Save command is in the File menu. Power outages or mistakes can cause a loss of information if not saved.

12. Save the document and quit the program. Then restart the program and teach the students to find and open the document again.

13. If the program is capable of importing pictures, place a picture in the document.

14. Print the document. The Print command is nearly always found in the File menu.

15. Save the document and quit the program.

WRITING AND PUBLISHING TOOLS *(cont.)*

TIPS FOR TERRIFIC LOOKING REPORTS

Limit the amount of fonts to **one** or **two**. Too many fonts make a paper look cluttered.

DON'T USE ALL UPPER CASE FOR THE BODY OF THE REPORT. Upper and lower case is much more readable.

Use colored text only to add accents or bring attention to certain areas. Too many colors distract the reader.

Pictures should add meaning to the paper. They should be placed near the text that they are supporting or that support them.

When possible, wrap text around pictures. This helps avoid loss of space and is pleasing to the eye.

Too many pictures are distracting. More than three pictures per page is usually overkill.

Use columns only when appropriate. Newsletters and multiple subject papers lend themselves to the use of columns.

Tabs and margins should be aligned throughout the document. Spacing should be uniform.

Don't over-use italics. Italics should only be used to bring attention to something in the paper.

Finally, remember your audience. Your layout should reflect the mood you wish to create for your reader.

WRITING AND PUBLISHING TOOLS (cont.)

Lovely Layouts

THIS IS AN EXTREME EXAMPLE OF A REPORT THAT BREAKS MANY OF THE RULES OF EFFECTIVE PUBLISHING. *Italics are not used effectively and* fonts are changed and with no **THOUGHT** as to the reason.   Spacing varies and margins don't align. Pictures have no relationships to text and aren't placed effectively.

Great Example

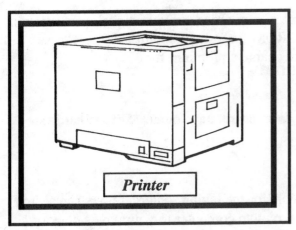

Printer

This, on the other hand, is a great example of how to publish an effective, easy to read report. THE FONT IS ONLY CHANGED TO DRAW ATTENTION TO SOMETHING IMPORTANT. Line spacing is uniform throughout the document. Pictures are inserted that relate to the meaning of the report and are close to text that they relate to. *Italics are used to draw attention to something important like a caption.* Mixed case (UPPER and lower) makes the writing more readable. Remember the ideas are the important part of the paper, but if it doesn't look good, no one will want to read it.

WRITING AND PUBLISHING TOOLS *(cont.)*

TIPS FOR CAPTURING PICTURES

One of the strengths of new computers is their ability to capture and manipulate digital photography. Students and teachers use these pictures to bring more meaning to their writing. But how do you get digital photos that relate to your curriculum? Here are several ways.

Photo Collections

Several software manufacturers like Adobe market photo collections on CD-ROM. These royalty free collections can be quite expensive and tend not to have exactly what you want.

Screen Capture Programs

There are several freeware (free to the public), shareware (full version given free with documentation that tells you where to send a fee if you like the program) and retail screen capture programs available for both IBM and Macintosh compatible computers. These programs allow the user to "capture" any picture that can be displayed on the screen and save it as a digital photo for use in any type of document. Freeware and shareware can be found through online services, on the Internet, or at some smaller software retailers.

Digital Cameras

Cameras like the *Apple Quicktake*, the *Connectix Quickcam*, and the *Kodak DC* are tools that can be used to take pictures just like regular cameras. The only difference is that they don't have film. The digital pictures are shown on the computer. The pictures can then be used in documents, presentations, or just printed. These cameras range from less than $100 for a tethered, black and white model to over $800 for an exceptional quality color portable.

Digital Developing

Several photo processors like Kodak and Seattle Film Works (mail order) provide digital developing of 35mm film. Pictures can be placed on disks or photo CD-ROM for a small additional fee. Classes will not require the professional quality images that developers charge a premium for.

Scanners

Scanners can be used to digitize photos and other images from nearly any source. See the hardware section page 26 for a detailed description.

The Internet

The Internet has millions of photographic resources available for the taking. Internet users can search for media by subject then download (copy a picture from a remote computer to yours) by a click of a mouse button.

Copy and Paste

Many educational programs like encyclopedias allow the user to copy non-copyrighted images from their programs. Consult your software documentation for instructions on how to do this.

WRITING AND PUBLISHING TOOLS *(cont.)*

WORD PROCESSING AND THE WRITING PROCESS

Word processing skills help students become better communicators because of the increased student motivation they create. They are able to concentrate on communication as a process because word processors allow them to experiment with different ways of saying something. Since the students don't have to rewrite the entire paper each time they revise it, there is more motivation to make changes that make the writing clearer. Planning and drafting become more important to the student. Writing becomes an active process. The following are some suggestions for using word processing tools throughout the writing process.

Prewriting:

Students should be given time to think about and research the subject about which they are writing. Word processors can be used in brainstorming sessions. After the words or concepts are entered into a document they can be easily cut and pasted into an outline or draft. Outlines can be expanded with new ideas or compressed by removing ideas. Rearranging the outline to provide a better sequence is also easily done using a word processor.

Drafting:

Using the word processor in the draft phase of the process is the most time consuming for young writers but the most beneficial. This initial investment in time reaps benefits in the revision and proofreading phase. This phase should be a free flow of ideas. Students should be encouraged to use inventive spelling and not be bogged down with vocabulary that might slow the flow of ideas.

Revising:

Word processors become the most valuable during revision. Have the students read their writing back to themselves or a partner. Encourage them to make changes in the document that add to the overall understanding of the piece. Use the electronic thesaurus to replace overused words. If parts of the report don't seem to be in the right order, cut and paste the portions until the sequence is right.

Proofreading or Editing:

The many editing tools included in word processors can make short work of proofreading chores. Spelling programs find many misspelled and will give options of what was most likely meant. The student must then find the correctly spelled word from the list. This reinforces basic spelling skills during editing. Grammar checkers available on many programs can be set to check for punctuation, verb usage, mixed tenses, and agreement, as well as other functions. Each time corrections are suggested. It is the student's task to decide whether the correction makes sense.

Publishing:

Most word processors written for students come with easy publishing options like picture placement and premade templates. This can be the most exciting part of completing the student's project. Printing a document that they have seen through the process is very satisfying.

One of the keys to good student writing is organization throughout the process. The Report Writing Checklist (page 56) and the Final Draft Checklist (page 58) are pages that can be reproduced so that your students can keep track of their projects through the process. The Outlining handout (page 57) can act as a guide for organizing the body of the report.

WRITING AND PUBLISHING TOOLS *(cont.)*

REPORT WRITING CHECKLIST

The subject of my report is_____

The topic of my report is_____

The report must include these sections. Put a check mark by each required section.

_____ cover

_____ title page

_____ table of contents

_____ outline

_____ bibliography

_____ note cards

_____ other _____

_____

_____

_____

Types of research materials I will use:

1.

2.

3.

The report will be graded with the following point scale.

Criteria	Amount of Points Possible
_____	_____
_____	_____
_____	_____
_____	_____

WRITING AND PUBLISHING TOOLS *(cont.)*

Name: _____ Date: _____

OUTLINING

Outlining is a way of organizing the information in your report. Below is a sample outline. The topic is divided up into several subtopics. A subtopic is something specific about the topic. Each subtopic must have details that prove what the subtopic says.

Use the word processor to organize your information about the topic into an outline. Subtopics start with Roman numerals and are aligned with the left margin. Press return or enter at the end of the subtopic to start a new line. Press tab to indent your supporting details under the subtopic. Start details with capital letters. Indenting details helps show that they belong to the subtopic above them.

Title

   I. Introduction

  II. First Subtopic

        A. Supporting details

        B. Supporting details

        C. Supporting details

 III. Second Subtopic

        A. Supporting details

        B. Supporting details

        C. Supporting details

 IV. Third Subtopic

        A. Supporting details

        B. Supporting details

        C. Supporting details

  V. Conclusion

Tech Tip:

If you want to change the order of your outline, don't delete everything and retype it. Cut and paste the parts of the outline until it is in the order you want.

WRITING AND PUBLISHING TOOLS *(cont.)*

Name: _____ Date: _____

FINAL DRAFT CHECKLIST

Put a check mark next to each item when you've completed it in your report.

Completeness

Check that your report includes:

_____ cover

_____ title page

_____ table of contents

_____ text of the report

_____ bibliography

Title Page

Check that the title page includes:

_____ title

_____ your name as author

_____ name of the person assigning the report

_____ name of the class

_____ date

Table of Contents

_____ Are all the main section headings (subtopics) included?

_____ Are the page numbers correct?

Text

_____ Do the sentences make sense?

_____ Are headings uniform in text style?

_____ Are all your pictures, drawings, and charts near the text they go with ?

_____ Are your quotes accurate?

_____ Are your pages numbered correctly?

_____ Is the punctuation and capitalization correct?

Bibliography

_____ Did you include all of your sources?

_____ Did you include enough sources?

WRITING AND PUBLISHING TOOLS *(cont.)*

CHOOSING WORD PROCESSING AND PUBLISHING SOFTWARE

1. Examine your curriculum to determine your needs.

2. Check to see if your site or district has established a standard program for word processing. Since many word processors are not compatible with one another, organizations usually set standards. It is also important that not only the brand name be the same, but that the version be the same also. For example, *Microsoft Works 3.0* will not read files written using *Microsoft Works 4.0*. However, newer versions will normally read older versions. If your school does not have a standard, check to see what the office staff uses. Secretaries are great resources for help with word processing.

3. There are many student-oriented word processing and publishing tools, such as *The Student Writing Center* by The Learning Company. The advantages to these programs are their ease of use. Many have tutorials as well as teacher lesson plans built in to help young writers quickly master the program. The disadvantage is that these programs can duplicate the jobs that your word processors do. They also do not have the many features that standard word processors have built in. Teachers must weigh the pros and cons and determine the best course of action.

4. Check with your district or county offices of education. Many larger organizations can or have negotiated licenses with the software companies. These "pay per computer" licenses usually discount the purchase price over 50%. Many times these licenses also extend to your home computer as well.

5. Look through catalogs of educational software suppliers and match your needs with possible products.

6. Ask for demonstration copies of the products you choose. Disk products are usually in limited function demonstration copies. Full function CD-ROM's are often sent on a trial basis. You will sometimes be required to call the publishers for demonstration copies. Many companies will give 30-day trial periods.

Note: Apple Computer produces a CD-ROM twice a year that contains descriptions and demonstrations of nearly all the education programs available on the Macintosh. This is free to educators. For a free CD-ROM call 1-800-800-2775.

Note: Educational Resources also produces CD-ROM catalogs with detailed descriptions of both IBM Windows and Macintosh programs available through them. Call 1-800-624-2926 for a free CD-ROM sampler.

7. Try out each for ease of use and amount of useful features.

8. Once you have chosen a software title, shop around. Prices can range up to 25%.

Tech Tip: Set up a software show in a lab. Have each piece of software running on a separate computer. Invite other teachers and administrators to try each and give you an informal evaluation.

WRITING AND PUBLISHING TOOLS (cont.)

SUGGESTED WRITING AND PUBLISHING SOFTWARE

Here is a listing of publication programs, their publishers, type, suggested grade level, and platforms in which they are supported. Platform refers to the type of computer and operating software needed to run the program. (See the software appendix for a more detailed description and pricing.)

Software Title	Publisher	Type*	Suggested Grade Level	Platform
Microsoft Works	Microsoft	IWP	All	Mac and Windows
Word	Microsoft	WP	All	Mac and Windows
Pagemaker	Aldus	DP	All	Mac and Windows
Publish It	Timeworks	DP	All	Mac and Windows
Print Shop Deluxe	Broderbund	DP	All	Mac and Windows
Writing Center	Learning Company	WP/DP	2-12	Mac
Claris Works	Claris	IWP	All	Mac

*WP refers to word processing, IWP refers to integrated word processing, DP refers to desktop publishing

OPTIONAL HARDWARE

There are many hardware products that help in the publishing of documents reports. Many of these help gather graphics to insert into published documents.

Equipment	Description
Scanner	Scans text or picture documents and digitizes them for use in documents and presentations.
Portable Word Processor	Many companies are marketing portable word processors for around $300.00. These battery-operated, notebook-size machines can be typed on at a desk, then connected to a computer and downloaded to a word processor. This saves valuable computer time.
Digital camera	takes pictures digitally and feeds them to your computer for use in documents and presentations.
Laser Printer	High quality printer.
CD-ROM	Many pictures and clipart available on CD-ROM.

Art Tips

There are many publishers who produce very affordable disk and CD-ROM collections of clip art. This premade art can be inserted into student-generated documents. Adding this artwork gives students pride in their work. Many writing programs come with several graphics built in. Buy CD-ROMs, if possible, so that the resource can be shared within the class and between classes. Make sure the students get in the habit of naming the sources of graphics, as well as text, that they use in their reports.

CREATIVITY AND PRESENTATION TOOLS

WHAT ARE CREATIVITY TOOLS?

Creativity tools are programs that allow *students to display their knowledge or skills* with new and challenging compute-raided media. These high interest tools fall into two families: *paint programs* and *presentation programs*. The division between these families are not always clear though, as many paint programs have presentation capabilities and most presentation programs have paint programs built in. Paint programs are typically not as flexible when presenting information and, likewise, presentation programs are not as powerful in their art abilities.

WHY USE CREATIVITY TOOLS?

As much as we sometimes hate to admit it, our students are changing. Due to many factors, not the least of which is television, children have learned to process information in short, interactive, colorful bursts. All one has to do is watch a music video in order to witness this change. From the time that our children are infants they have grown up with crib toys which are based upon these quick bursts of learning (push this button a mirror appears, another and a bell rings). As adolescents, these same children watch music videos and play interactive computer games. Even educational television shows such as *Sesame Street* and *Bill Nye the Science Guy* have adopted formats that deliver information in these quick sensory bursts. We can argue the positives and negatives of this phenomenon, but it does not change the fact that it is happening and will surely continue.

Creativity tools allow students to receive and deliver the information they have learned in creative and thought provoking ways. Instead of turning in a paper to display knowledge, students can now use the computer or television screen. No longer limited to the two dimensions of the page, students explore sight, motion, sound and interactivity. Because of the interactive nature of these programs, the delivery of this information is always at the user's pace (which is usually much slower for teachers than students).

CREATIVITY AND PRESENTATION TOOLS *(cont.)*

PAINT PROGRAMS

What is a paint program?

A paint program, like crayons, water colors, pencils, or clay, is just another medium for students to express themselves through art. The difference is that this medium uses a computer and monitor instead of paint and canvas. By manipulating different built-in tools, the student can "paint" pictures on the screen. These pictures can then be printed, electronically pasted into written projects, or used in presentations.

(*Kid Pix 2,* Broderbund)

How do you use a paint program?

Teachers:

Paint programs can be used for whole class instruction of all curriculum areas using large screen projection. The computer essentially becomes your chalkboard allowing you to prepare drawings or photographs to display during class. Using the slide show option that most paint tools have built in, teachers can easily show progressions that are much more difficult or impossible with a blackboard.

CREATIVITY AND PRESENTATION TOOLS *(cont.)*

One example would be helping students find patterns. A physical map of the bottom of the Pacific Ocean in the first slide, the occurances of volcanic erruptions as an overlay in the second, and occurances of earthquakes as an overlay in the third slide would help students make generalizations about plate tectonics of the area.

Paint programs also help the teacher create original artwork, diagrams, maps, graphs, tables, which can be inserted into written documents. Graphics can be developed for insertion into worksheets, bulletin board displays, newsletters, or professional documents.

Students:

Students use paint programs to draw illustrations for original stories or reports, make science observations, explore visual math and mapping skills, produce creative time lines, and experiment with CAD (Computer Aided Design).

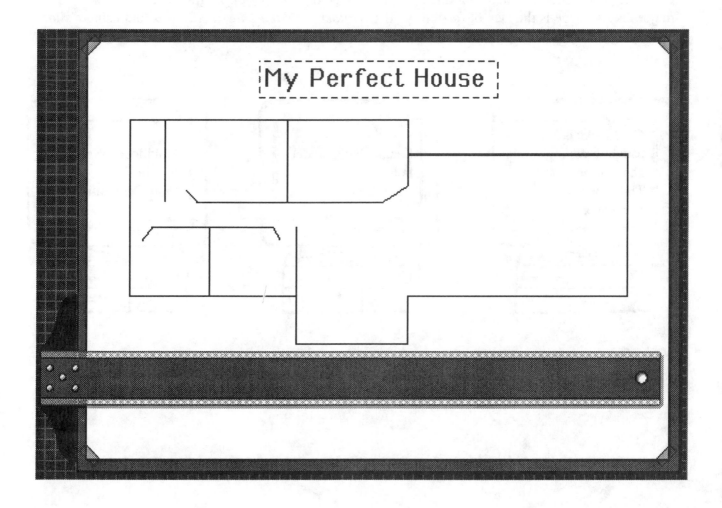

CREATIVITY AND PRESENTATION TOOLS *(cont.)*

WHAT IS A PRESENTATION PROGRAM?

A presentation program allows the student to use multimedia (text, art, sounds, graphics, animation, and video) to demonstrate their knowledge of a subject. Instead of pages in a written report, the student creates screens that are linked to one another. The user places on these screens any media that conveys the ideas he/she wish to communicate. Although the output can be printed, these presentations are meant to be viewed with an interacting audience using the computer.

There are two types of presentation programs: slide show or linear presentation programs and hypermedia programs.

SLIDE SHOW PROGRAMS

These creativity programs allow students or teachers to display media in a linear format. That is, screens on the computer are linked in a straight line series from first to last, much like a conventional slide carousel. These can be set to automatically show screens at predetermined time intervals or be advanced by the user one slide at a time. An advantage of this type of program is ease of use. The major disadvantage is the lack of flexibility. If *Goldilocks and the Three Bears* was told using a slide show program, it would look something like this:

CREATIVITY AND PRESENTATION TOOLS *(cont.)*

HYPERMEDIA PROGRAMS

Although a little harder to master, the flexibility and creativity that hypermedia programs afford make them well worth the extra investment in training time. Hypermedia not only allows the user to present information in a linear fashion, it also allows for more interactivity. The audience not only views the report, but decides the order in which the report will be viewed. Using hypermedia, *Goldilocks and the Three Bears* might look something like this:

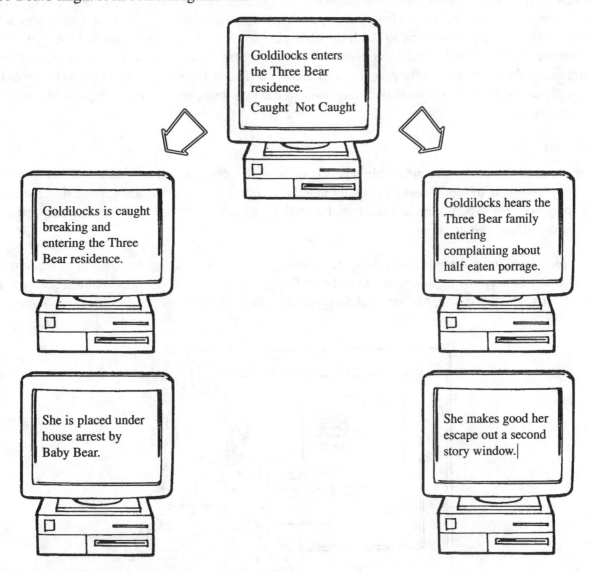

HOW TO USE A PRESENTATION PROGRAM

Teachers:

The chalkboard is an invaluable tool for teachers. Its drawback is that it is limited to static, two-dimensional drawings and text. Presentation programs allow the teacher to go beyond the chalkboard to present lessons that come alive with pictures, drawings, animation, movies, speeches, sounds, and text. The computer becomes an electronic chalkboard full of color, motion, and sound.

CREATIVITY AND PRESENTATION TOOLS *(cont.)*

Example: Imagine teaching a unit on the Civil War. Your lesson for the day is about Abraham Lincoln's role in the conflict and the decisions he had to make. Using the computer displaying its image on a TV, you present a time line of the events that lead up to the war. Each time you choose an event by clicking it with the mouse the class hears a speech or piece of music, views a picture or short movie clip, or a combination of any or all of these.

Because of their interactivity, presentation programs can be used for customized, individual instruction. Small groups or individuals can view or interact with teacher developed lessons at a computer station. If the teacher uses a presentation to teach the class certain skills, he/she can then use the presentation at a computer station for independent, individualized instruction of students who were absent during a lesson or for those needing more practice with the skill. This allows all the students to be served more efficiently as the teacher is able to continue on with the next lesson while the computer offers the remediation.

Students:

After the teacher becomes comfortable with using the technology, it is a natural transition to begin to teach students how to report using computer aided presentations. Reports are given using the computer to display not only typewritten information, but audio and videotaped research, animation, full colored photos, drawings, and graphics.

Example: Imagine a student researching the effects of ocean currents on weather. The student explains this concept using animation that shows the interaction between water and air, he/she found in an interactive encyclopedia, and text he/she typed in, using a book from the library as a source.

CREATIVITY AND PRESENTATION TOOLS *(cont.)*

HOW DO YOU BUILD A PRESENTATION?

Most presentation programs work with the same basic method. You build a workspace on the screen to convey the ideas that you want to present using whatever media you feel appropriate. Each program has a different name for the workspace on the screen. Some programs use a workspace that resembles a large index card and others use a paper-like page configuration.

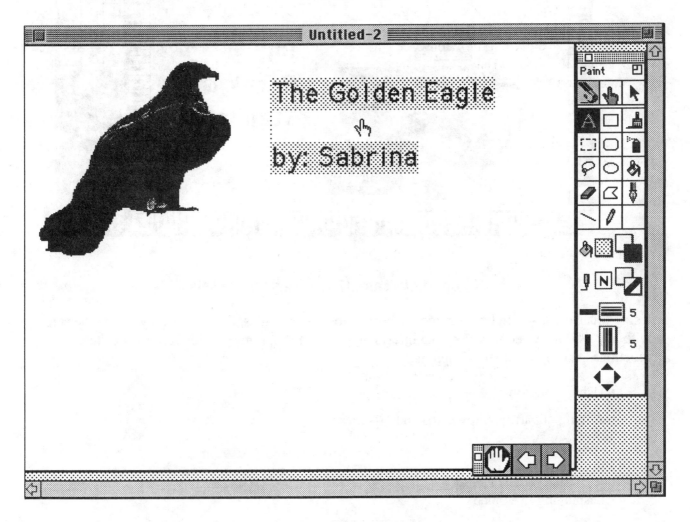

(*Digital Chisel screen,* Pierian Springs Software)

CREATIVITY AND PRESENTATION TOOLS *(cont.)*

(*HyperStudio* card, Roger Wagner Publishing)

Using this workspace and several tools that the program provides, the user simply builds the screen(s) with any media needed to convey the information. Most programs provide for many different functions. Some include these options:

- Using paint tools

- Adding clipart (predrawn art) and graphics

- Adding text

- Playing digital video

- Displaying live video

- Playing animation

- Playing sounds

- Controlling a laserdisc player

- Playing audio CDs

- Advancing to another screen

- As well as many other practical or special effects

CREATIVITY AND PRESENTATION TOOLS *(cont.)*

Here is a picture of a student-made *HyperStudio* presentation that incorporates many of the capabilities listed on the previous page.

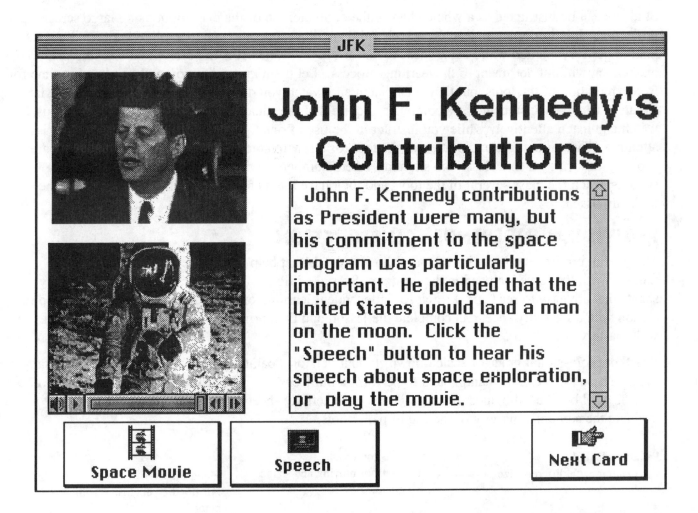

CREATIVITY AND PRESENTATION TOOLS *(cont.)*

TEACHING THE TOOLS PAINT PROGRAMS

Paint programs can be taught to the whole class directly or individually in an independent station.

WHOLE CLASS INSTRUCTION

Students can be instructed as a whole class in the computer lab or the classroom using large screen projection. It is important to teach one tool and then allow students time to explore with it. Students tend to get very excited while using these tools for the first time. It is important to allow this excitement without detriment to the learning process. Let them know that you will be allowing time for free exploration of the tools, but they must listen and watch you demonstrate first. If you are in a lab situation where each student has a computer, require that the students place their hands in their laps, watch and listen attentively while you instruct in the use of one tool. Do this quickly if everyone is attentive. Then allow free exploration of the tool for a few minutes, observing to make sure they are showing mastery. If in a classroom situation where computers will be used after instruction or in stations, teach the class several of the tools and then have them create a drawing that uses all of the tools discussed.

INDIVIDUAL INDEPENDENT INSTRUCTION

Many paint programs come with easy to follow tutorials that help the novice digital artist become familiar with the tools included in the program. School editions of the programs come with activity sheets that are easy to read and written for independent learning of the program. Students assigned to a station with an activity sheet can complete the lesson and then print out the result for evaluation of skill mastery.

Whether professional grade or scaled-down student versions, paint programs have essentially the same tools. These tools can be manipulated to perform a number of artistic tasks. Below is an example of a typical "tool box" used in most paint programs. Use activity sheet page 71 "Painting the Town" to evaluate the student's mastery of the use of paint tools.

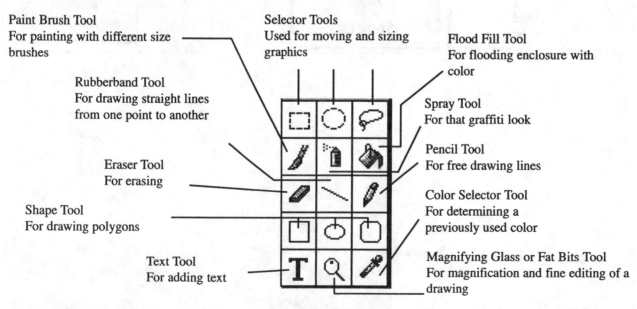

Paint Brush Tool
For painting with different size brushes

Rubberband Tool
For drawing straight lines from one point to another

Eraser Tool
For erasing

Shape Tool
For drawing polygons

Text Tool
For adding text

Selector Tools
Used for moving and sizing graphics

Flood Fill Tool
For flooding enclosure with color

Spray Tool
For that graffiti look

Pencil Tool
For free drawing lines

Color Selector Tool
For determining a previously used color

Magnifying Glass or Fat Bits Tool
For magnification and fine editing of a drawing

CREATIVITY AND PRESENTATION TOOLS *(cont.)*

PAINTING THE TOWN

Name: _____ Date: _____

Directions: Reproduce the following picture using a paint program. The tools that were used to draw the picture are named for you. When you are finished, print the picture, attach it to this paper, and turn it in.

Note: Use the pencil, paint brush, eraser, and magnifying glass to clean up any mistakes.

CREATIVITY AND PRESENTATION TOOLS *(cont.)*

TEACHING THE TOOLS

Because paint programs are important components of most presentation programs, many of the same methods can be used to teach these tools. However, much more time should be allowed for the mastery of using different media in presentations. Functions such as adding video or sound to a presentation take a few minutes to teach but must be practiced more to master. The following is a recommended sequence for teaching the use of a presentation program.

1. Teach students how to start the program and view examples of student projects done using the program. (All presentation programs come with project examples.)

2. Teach students how to start a new document.

3. Teach students how to use the paint tools to do original artwork.

4. Teach students how to add both typed and pasted text to the screen.

5. Teach students how to add and manipulate pictures and clip art.

6. Teach students how to add digital video from CD-ROMs or other sources.

7. Teach students how to move from screen to screen within their presentations.

8. Teach students how to plan and organize presentations.

Once the students have mastered the basics, start a **Tip of the Day** time. These can be a combination of teacher and student-generated tips on the use of the program. Art tips, design advice, as well as using more advanced functions, can be subjects covered during extra time before a break.

SINGLE COMPUTER

Working in pairs, have the students use the tutorials that come with most presentation programs to explore the use of the program. Give each pair a 30-minute block of time to work on the computer. Many computers have built in alarm clocks that can be set to go off after an allotted time. If your computer does not have one, use a timer. Use the sequence above and the tutorials as a guide. Assign one or two students who are adept at the program as computer tutors. These students can help when difficulties are encountered. This will limit interruptions in the classroom and empowers students to work together and problem solve.

POD OF COMPUTERS

When working with two or more computers in the classroom, set up stations through which the students rotate. Have a different task set up in each station so that you can work with students at the computers or in other groups. Using large screen projection to introduce the use of parts of a program prior to the use of stations, thus limiting difficulties with independent work at the computers.

THE COMPUTER LAB

This is the easiest setting for teaching the use of presentation programs, since most labs have enough computers for each student to be involved either individually or in pairs. In the lab, reward active listening with plenty of time to explore the program. If students are listening closely, make instructions short and concise. Then allow the students to explore the use of the program.

CREATIVITY AND PRESENTATION TOOLS *(cont.)*

WRITING AND ORGANIZING COMPUTER AIDED MULTIMEDIA REPORTS

Multimedia reports, not unlike traditional reports, involve using a process. If you teach students how to write effective reports, then producing a multimedia report is simply an addition to this process. The addition is the gathering of different media to be used to enhance the written report. Below are tips for teaching the process of producing a multimedia report.

CHOOSE A TOPIC

This sounds trivial, but it is probably the most important step in the process. Students must ask the following questions: Is the topic relevant to the subject being taught in class? Is the topic too narrow/broad? Are there sufficient resources available for the topic? (e.g. books, audio tapes, computer media, online information, etc.)

Research the Topic

Use resources like a text book, library, CD-ROMs, or the Internet to find sufficient information and media to complete the report. Is the information found relative to the topic? Does the media chosen fit the topic?

Break the Topic Down into Subtopics

What is going to be presented about the topic? Do the subtopics fit the topic? Are they logical and sequential? Will the audience be interested in the information?

Organize the Information

Use an outline or other prewriting tool to organize the information into a logical sequence. Is the report in an order that makes sense to the reader? Does the information answer probable questions that the reader might have?

Rough Draft

Write the rough draft. Is the content of the report accurate? Does the writing make sense?

Editing

Remove any writing mistakes from the rough draft.

Storyboard (See Hypermedia Planning Sheet page 74)

Plan the multimedia report using papers or index cards which describe different screens. If interactive, how will the user interact with the report (buttons, choices, etc.)? If sequential, map the sequence. Describe backgrounds, clip art, or graphics used. Where will the text be located?

Create Report

Use the computer or laser disc to create the report. Test all buttons or media. Does the report work? Is the text readable? Does media work properly? Is it easy to interact with the report?

PRESENT REPORT AND SELFEVALUATE

Present the report by displaying it or allowing individuals or groups to interact with it. What do people like about your report? Was it easy for the group to follow? Was it easy for the individual to interact with it?

CREATIVITY AND PRESENTATIONS TOOLS *(cont.)*

COMPUTER HYPERMEDIA PLANNING SHEET

Name(s): _____ Date: _____

Topic: _____ Screen Number: _____

Directions: Complete one of these sheets for every screen in your multimedia report. Draw the screen as you want it to look. Indicate the placement of graphics, drawings, buttons. Answer the questions below.

Notes

File   Edit   Move   Tools   Objects   Colors

1. Describe the background of the screen. What, if any, graphics or drawings will you use? What source(s) will you use for the graphics (clip art libraries, paint tools, scanner)?

2. Describe the use of text on this screen. Will the text be in a text block? Where will the text be located?

3. Describe any buttons on this screen. What actions will the buttons carry out (e.g., play digital movies, animation or sounds, link to other scans, etc.)?

CREATIVITY AND PRESENTATION TOOLS *(cont.)*

LASERDISC MULTIMEDIA REPORTS

What is a laserdisc player?

A laserdisc or video disc player is a piece of hardware that works much like a video tape player. Instead of a video tape, the LD player plays a nonrecordable laserdisc about the size of an old long play record. This plastic disc can contain still and motion pictures complete with sound. There are two advantages of the LD player over a VCR. The first is its facility for accessing pictures easily. The user simply inputs the picture number into the remote control or uses a bar code reader to scan a bar code that advances the player to the desired picture. The second is the LD player's ability to show a still image. Using pause on most VCR's causes the picture to flutter and jump. This does not occur with an LD player.

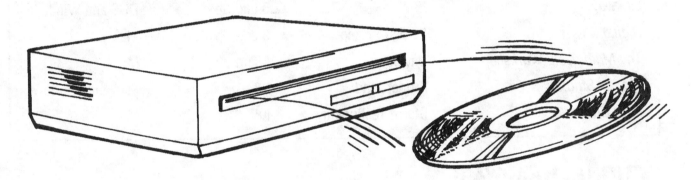

Laserdisc Aided Multimedia Report

Laserdisc Aided Multimedia Reports are easy to create if there are LD resources available on the topic. After creating the written report, the student simply attaches bar codes or frame numbers, that correspond to the LD images, to the margins or within the written report. The reader or presenter then simply reads the report, scanning the bar code with a bar code reader or inputting the frame numbers as they come to them. The LD player automatically plays the clip or displays the picture on a television.

Interactive Anything

With an LD player and the appropriate discs, nearly any assignment can be enhanced with interactive multimedia. Bar codes or frame numbers can be attached to time lines and maps. Creative writing can have attachments that show pictures of characters. Science projects can show not only the end product but the experiment in progress or related subjects. Students can tell the stories of important events in history while showing pictures that help relate the story.

CAV (Computer Aided Video)

Although LD players play on televisions, similar to VCR's, many models can be controlled by a computer. In this way the computer becomes a fancy remote control, allowing the user to sequence otherwise random pictures on the laserdisc. Laserdiscs that include this type of software are catagorized as level 3. Many programs such as Roger Wagner Publishing's *Hyperstudio* and Apple *Hypercard* allow the user to easily set up slide shows of images on any laserdisc.

CREATIVITY AND PRESENTATION TOOLS *(cont.)*

SUGGESTED PRESENTATION SOFTWARE

Here is a listing of presentation programs, their publishers, suggested grade levels, and platforms in which they are supported. Platform refers to the type of computer and operating software needed to run the program. (See the software appendix for a more detailed description and pricing.)

Software Title	Publisher	Suggested Grade Level	Platform
HyperStudio	Roger Wagner	5 and up	Mac and Windows
Hypercard	Apple	5 and up	Mac
Linkway	IBM	5 and up	DOS and Windows
Digital Chisel	Pierian Spring	5 and up	Mac
The Multimedia Workshop	Davidson	5 and up	Mac
Kid Pix Studio	Broderbund	K8	Mac and Windows
Kid's Studio	Storm Technology	K8	Mac

OPTIONAL HARDWARE

There are many hardware products that enhance the building of multimedia presentations and reports. Many of these peripherals facilitate the gathering of graphic images to insert into presentations and published documents. Other hardware is used to allow large screen display and VCR recording of presentations. (See the hardware appendix for a more detailed description.)

Equipment	Description
Scanner	Scans text or picture documents and digitizes them for use in documents and presentations
Digital camera	Takes pictures digitally and feeds them to your computer for use in documents and presentations
Modem	Allows the computer to communicate with others via the telephone lines to share text or graphics
CD-ROM	Many graphic, sounds, and movies are available on CD-ROM
AV card	A circuit card that is inserted into the computer to allow capturing of images from a video source like a VCR or camcorder
LCD Panel	A panel that projects the computer image on to an overhead projector.
TV interface	A box that allows your computer to be connected to a TV for large screen display.

CREATIVITY AND PRESENTATION TOOLS *(cont.)*

SUGGESTED LASERDISCS

Laserdisc Title	Publisher	Suggested Grade Level	Level*
GTV	National Geographic	5 and up	Level 3
Windows on Science	Optical Data Corporation	5 and up	Level 1
The Visual Almanac	Voyager	5 and up	Level 3
Images USA	Scholastic	5 and up	Level 1
The National Gallery of Art	Voyager	5 and up	Level 3
Science Slueths	Videodiscovery	5 and up	Level 3
Understanding Weather and Climate	SVE	5 and up	Level 1

*Level refers to how the laserdisc can be controlled. Level 1 means that the laserdisc can be accessed with the use of a remote control or bar code reader. Level 3 means that a computer program is available in addition to the barcode reader and remote control.

DATA ANALYSIS TOOLS

WHAT ARE DATA ANALYSIS TOOLS?

In order to make informed decisions, draw conclusions, or make generalizations, it is important for students and teachers to have not only enough data, but also the ability to sort, compare, and analyze that data. Data analysis tools give one the ability to break down large amounts of information into manageable reports. Data analysis tools used in schools fall into two different families: databases and spreadsheets.

Databases

Database tools allow you to sort, search and print a collection of related information known as a database. You can use a database to analyze information that you consider significant (e.g., class lists, address books, inventories, lists of skills mastered, etc.).

Category	Title	Price
Business	Feast and Famine	$22.95
Business	Inside the Banking System	$28.95
Computers	Easy Computer Graphics	$9.50
Computers	Computing Glossary	$14.95
Cooking	Surfing the Microwave	$12.50
Cooking	Art and Artichokes	$6.50
Fiction	Diamond Murders	$18.50
New Age	You, Me, and Uncle	$19.95

Records: 11
Sorted

Spreadsheets

Spreadsheets will allow you and your students to organize numbers, make calculations, and graph. You can also add graphics and headings in order to make your data easier to understand (e.g., complex math computations, science data, etc.).

Workbook1

Student Attendance – 1996–97

Student Names	Days in School	Days not in School
Amy Wright	162	18
Andy Horning	175	5
Ashley Ryan	171	9
Brian Stone	160	20
Dennis Smith	179	1
Donald Brock	175	5
Jan Harper	169	11
Jane Helewell	135	10
Jimmy Whittman	165	15
Joe Hiney	180	0
Johnny Adams	172	8
Keith Berglund	177	3
Kevin Basmadjain	161	19
Lee Margolis	165	15
Meg Harrison	168	12
Missy Heyert	178	2
Nancy Holly	177	3
Sara Pugh	171	9
Steve Dana	160	20
Tracey Dana	169	11
Willy Green	180	0

Why Use Data Analysis Tools?

Every day we are asked to make important decisions. The more informed we are about these decisions, the better the chance we will make the correct decisions. Therefore, we must give our students tools that can help them break down and analyze larger and larger amounts of information. Spreadsheets and databases help students visualize the big picture and ask the question, "What if?"

DATA ANALYSIS TOOLS *(cont.)*

WHAT IS A DATABASE?

Databases are used to sort large lists of information by categories that the user sets up. Databases are extremely useful for finding groups of information that have similar attributes.

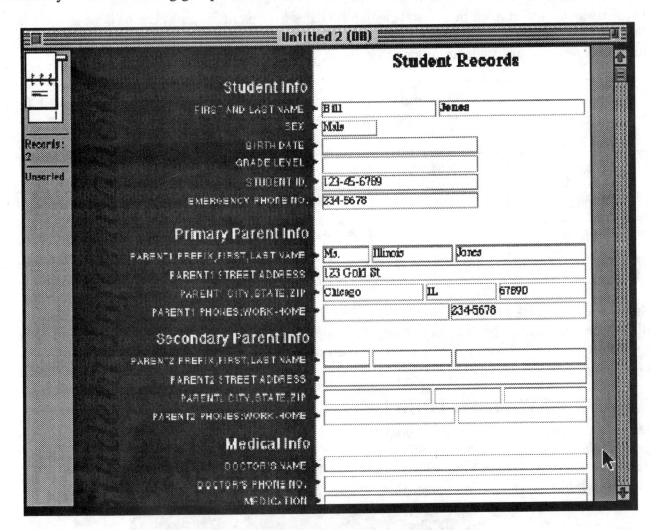

Claris Works by The Claris Corporation

Here are a few ways that a database can assist you:

- maintain address lists and have them automatically inserted onto letters, envelopes or labels
- keep track of important information like experiment results or whether or not a student has turned in a permission slip, then sort to find similarities
- catalog an inventory of items in your home and compare it to other databases
- create lists to sort like bibliographies
- catalog collections like books, software, and equipment
- find similarities and differences within large lists of information

DATA ANALYSIS TOOLS *(cont.)*

Databases are great teacher tools. Start a database of all your students at the beginning of the year. Include all useful information about each student, such as: name, parent's name(s), phone number, address, medical information, tested levels in academic areas, book numbers, notes to be returned, etc. With this information in a database many of the classroom clerical duties become routine. If the teacher wants a report of all the students with birth dates in September, a sort can be done in seconds. Students who have not turned in notes can be tracked quickly. Letters can be automatically addressed to parents of individual students, groups of students, or the entire class.

Last Name	Fist Name	Phone Number	Book Number	Field Trip
Bush	George	555-1234	E8	x
Clinton	Hillary	555-4856	E6	x
Marcos	Imelda	555-7346	E14	
Washington	George	555-1126	E21	x

Sample Database Report

Students can also use databases. Science experiments that involve finding attributes that are similar or different are good uses for databases. Since the student must set up the database to find what they are looking for, the higher level thinking skills are used without the drudgery of the student doing each comparison.

WHAT DO DATABASES LOOK LIKE?

Databases are like card files on your computer. Each card in a card file contains information about one person, place or thing. In a database these are called records. The sum of all the records makes up the database. Each record may have several headings called "fields". A field is a single piece of information like first name, last name, phone number, etc.

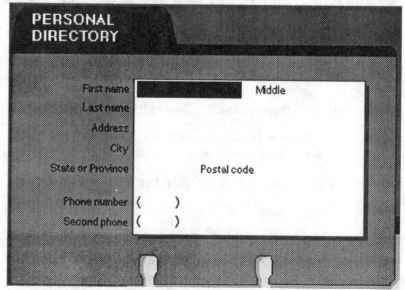

DATA ANALYSIS TOOLS *(cont.)*

Once you have designed the fields in the database, you can enter information, called "field entries" for each record.

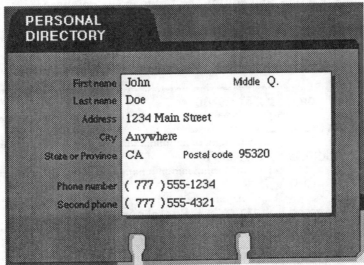

Once the records have been entered into the database they can be viewed in several ways:

Data View:

The data view is used for entering, editing, and viewing one record at a time.

List view:

List view is for designed for entering, editing, sorting, and viewing several records at a time.

	First name	Middle	Last name	Address1	City	State	Postal code	Area code	Phone1
	John	Q.	Doe	1234 Main Street	Anywhere	CA	95320	777	555-1234

DATA ANALYSIS TOOLS *(cont.)*

Design View:

Design view is for adding, deleting, and editing the fields in the database.

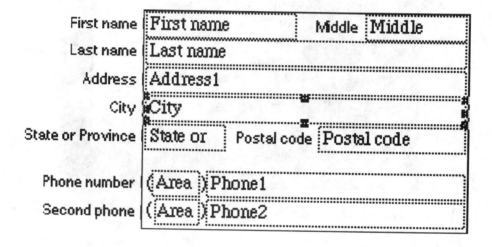

TEACHING DATABASE TOOLS

Teaching students how to use a database tool is best done when some type of product will result: an address book, a classroom inventory, a comparison or contrasting of outcomes in an experiment or historical events. See Lesson Plans section page 241 for an introductory lesson on using databases.

WHAT IS A SPREADSHEET?

Spreadsheets are powerful calculating tools that work much like an accountant's ledger. However instead of manually calculating columns or rows of numbers, the user inputs a formula that gives the desired calculation. Spreadsheets also graph the numbers in order to give a more visual representation of the data. The following are a few classroom uses for spreadsheets:

* develop budgets for math simulations

* analyze science data

* maintain a checkbook

* manage grades

* schedule class projects

* chart growth

* keep track of fund raisers

DATA ANALYSIS TOOLS *(cont.)*

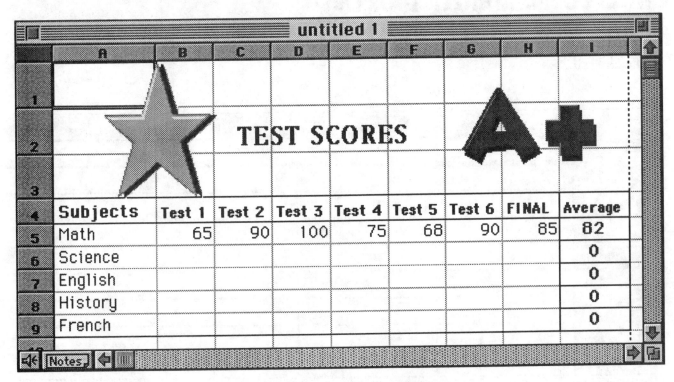

untitled 3

	aluminum cans	glass bottles	plastic bottles	
TAKING CANS AND BOTTLES TO THE RECYCLING CENTER?				
cash/lb at recycling center	$0.82	$0.05	$0.38	
number of pieces to equal 1 lb.	24	2	7	
value of one container	$0.03	$0.03	$0.05	
number of pieces you collected	100	100	100	
cash from recycling center	$3.42	$2.50	$5.36	
AMOUNT OF MONEY WE NEED =	$200.00			
AMOUNT OF MONEY COLLECTED SO FAR =	$11.27			
AMOUNT OF MONEY STILL NEEDED =	$188.73			

The Cruncher by Davidson

Let's use a classroom management example to illustrate how spreadsheets work. **Example:** You would like to average test grades to get a handle on how individual students and the class as a whole are doing. This can be done with a spreadsheet as shown in the example below.

untitled 1

TEST SCORES

Subjects	Test 1	Test 2	Test 3	Test 4	Test 5	Test 6	FINAL	Average
Math	65	90	100	75	68	90	85	82
Science								0
English								0
History								0
French								0

The Cruncher by Davidson

DATA ANALYSIS TOOLS *(cont.)*

If you need a visual representation, perhaps perhaps a graph of student progress for a parent conference, you can have one with a few clicks of the mouse. Because the program is integrated, the spreadsheet or graph can also be inserted into a word processing document.

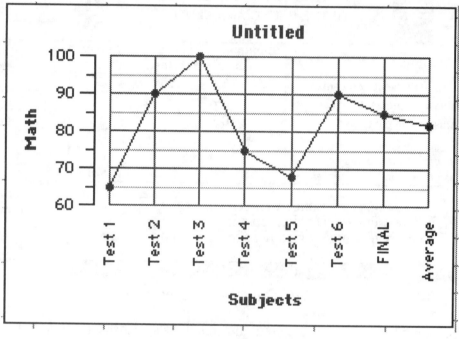

The Cruncher by Davidson

WHAT DO SPREADSHEETS LOOK LIKE?

Spreadsheets appear on the computer screen as a grid of columns and rows. Columns are lettered; rows are numbered. The combination of a column letter and a row number corresponds to a box that is called a "cell."

	A	B	C	D	
1					
2					
3					
4					
5					
6					
7					
8					
9					
10					

DATA ANALYSIS TOOLS *(cont.)*

Columns and rows can be labeled with headings.

Untitled1 (SS)

	A	B	C	D	E
1		Red Hair	Blond Hair	Brown Hair	Total
2	Fourth Grade				
3	Fifth Grade				
4	Sixth Grade				
5	Seventh Grade				
6	Eighth Grade				
7					
8	Total				
9	Percentage				
10					

Data can be entered in the form of numbers, dates, or times.

Untitled1 (SS)

	A	B	C	D	E
1		Red Hair	Blond Hair	Brown Hair	Total
2	Fourth Grade	4	13	27	
3	Fifth Grade	7	22	19	
4	Sixth Grade	12	12	22	
5	Seventh Grade	3	18	23	
6	Eighth Grade	6	8	31	
7					
8	Total				
9	Percentage				
10					

Formulas are entered so that calculations can be done.

B8   =Sum(B2:B7)

Untitled1 (SS)

	A	B	C	D	E
1		Red Hair	Blond Hair	Brown Hair	Total
2	Fourth Grade	4	13	27	44
3	Fifth Grade	7	22	19	48
4	Sixth Grade	12	12	22	46
5	Seventh Grade	3	18	23	44
6	Eighth Grade	6	8	31	45
7					
8	Total	32	73	122	227
9	Percentage	14.10%	32.16%	53.74%	100.00%
10					

DATA ANALYSIS TOOLS *(cont.)*

Finally, charts and graphs can be created using the graphing feature built into spreadsheet programs.

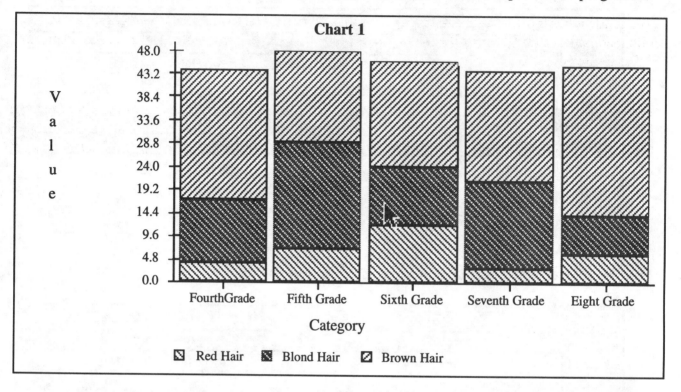

Like databases, teaching students how to use a spreadsheet tool is best done when some type of product will result, such as a questionnaire, budget, or science data collection. See the Lesson Plans section page 241 for an introductory lesson on using spreadsheets.

DATA ANALYSIS TOOLS *(cont.)*

SUGGESTED DATA ANALYSIS SOFTWARE

The following is a list of data analysis tools that are appropriate for the middle school classroom. The title, publisher, type of program, and platform supported are provided for ease of selection. Platform refers to the type of computer operating system that is needed to run the software. See Hardware section page 10 for a detailed description of operating systems.

Software Title	Publisher	Type of Program	Platform Supported
Microsoft Works	Microsoft Corporation	Integrated word processor, database, spreadsheet, draw and communications	Mac, DOS and Windows
Microsoft Excel	Microsoft Corporation	Spreadsheet	Mac, DOS and Windows
Fox Pro	Microsoft Corporation	Database	Mac, DOS and Windows
The Cruncher*	Davidson	Spreadsheet	Mac and Windows
Claris Works	Claris Corporation	Integrated word processor, database, spreadsheet, draw and communications	Mac and Windows
FileMaker Pro	Claris Corporation	Database	Mac and Windows

*The Cruncher is extremely good for use with middle school students.

TELECOMMUNICATIONS TOOLS

The next five years will radically change the way our schools relate to the world. The information superhighway has become a reality. From your school, district office, or home you will be able to travel all over the world to gather information. As more people travel this electronic highway, maps to find information and rules to keep traveling safe become vital to successfully completing the journey.

It would be possible to devote this entire notebook to telecommunications tools and the Internet. However, many of the tools have not made their way to the realm of the novice computer user. Therefore, this section will deal with the easiest to use and most educationally significant of these tools.

WHAT IS TELECOMMUNICATION?

Telecommunication is probably the single most important advance in computer technology in the last two decades. It is the ability for computers to exchange information over distance. This is usually done with a piece of hardware called a "modem." Modems translate the digital information that a computer uses into analog or sound information that can be transmitted over telephone lines. Once transmitted, a computer equipped with a modem at the other end of the line receives the analog information and translates it back to digital.

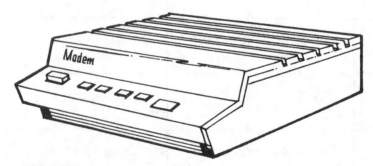

WHAT IS A NETWORK?

A network is any two or more computers that are linked so that they can communicate with each other. Networks are usually "hardwired", meaning they do not need modems to communicate. A local area network (LAN) is the connection of computers at a common site, like a school. These LANs can be attached to a wide area network (WAN), like a district or county network. Many districts have begun to attach their networks to the Internet.

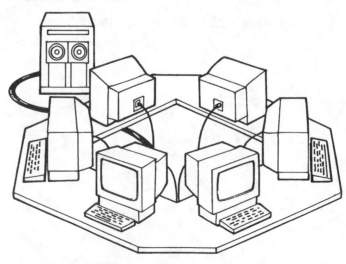

TELECOMMUNICATIONS TOOLS *(cont.)*

WHAT IS THE INTERNET?

The Internet is a worldwide connection of computers that can communicate. It is a global technology network made up of many smaller contributing networks. Essentially, it is the network that connects networks. They all speak the same language (TCP/IP). This system gives immediate access to information. It's like being able to open any book in any library from your computer. You can look at (and print out) articles, documents, and pictures, and review current facts about news, weather, and sports that you may use in your classes.

The Internet was created in 1983 with 100 networks and has grown by leaps and bounds. By 1993 there were approximately 10,000 networks attached to the Internet. Most experts believe the amount of networks attached to the Internet is in the hundreds of thousands and that this number is increasing at the rate of about 15% a month. Since each of the connected networks can be as many as tens of thousands of computers; the total number of individual users of the Internet is most likely in the millions.

WHY SHOULD I USE THE INTERNET IN THE CLASSROOM?

The Internet gives teachers and students access to information of a quality and quantity never seen in education. Using the Internet allows the user to bring information, media and even software from all over the world almost instantly. This allows students, teachers, administrators, or anyone using this tool to have this valuable information for individual or cooperative projects.

TELECOMMUNICATIONS TOOLS *(cont.)*

Gathering information is merely one aspect of the power of the Internet. Communications is the other. Once you have access to the Internet, you have access to all the users of the Internet: teachers sharing and collaborating with other teachers, students with other students, scientists and business people, everyone. Distance, class, race, and culture are no longer barriers to the sharing of ideas. People simply communicate.

HOW DO I GET ON THE INTERNET?

There are three ways to access the Internet; dial up, direct connect, and SLIP or PPP. To locate the nearest network provider call the Consortium for School Networking at (202)-466-6296.

DIAL UP

Most people access the Internet by dial up. This requires a modem. A modem translates the computer's digital information into an audible sound so that it can be transmitted over the phone line to a service provider. This service provider in turn gives you limited access to the Internet, usually just storing the most popular Internet site's resources on their computer for you to access.

There are commercial service providers, like America Online, Prodigy, Compuserve, and eWorld, as well as smaller local companies, who will charge you a monthly fee for access to their network as well as the Internet. This option is preferable to most consumers at this time because of the ease of use. These businesses also provide many other consumer-related services. Most commercial providers have special rates and plans for schools. Approximate cost for hardware and software, not including the PC or the cost of the phone call, is $100 to $800 plus a monthly fee of approximately $30 depending on usage.

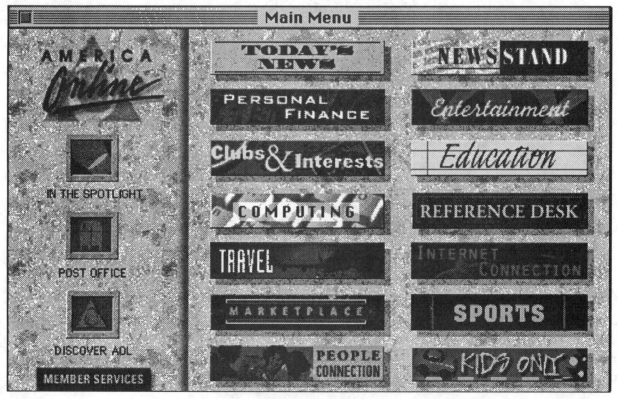

(America Online)

TELECOMMUNICATIONS TOOLS *(cont.)*

Most online services have education areas that in themselves are very valuable. America Online, for example, has an area run by teachers in their "spare time" called the Electronic Schoolhouse. In this area you will find lesson plans, student projects, and many class projects in which classes all over the world work together. Postcard Geography is one such project. To participate, the teacher simply downloads a list of classrooms participating in the project and has the students send postcards describing their community to each of them. In return the class receives postcards from everyone on the list. Many classes receive hundreds of postcards, each describing an area of the U.S. or world.

DIRECT CONNECT

The second option for accessing the Internet is "direct connect." "Direct connect" allows you to bypass the service provider to obtain direct access to the Internet, doing away with the need for a modem. The advantage to this option is the speed at which you can access the network. Your computer becomes part of the network at all times. When you want information from across the campus, across the country, or across the globe you have nearly immediate access. The disadvantage is that the cost of the hardware to connect to the network is out of the reach of most schools. However, many states have begun to develop the infrastructure so that schools can attach to the Internet directly. The approximate cost depends on many variables such as the amount of materials and labor involved in hardwiring the school, partnerships with phone companies, amount of hardware needed, etc.

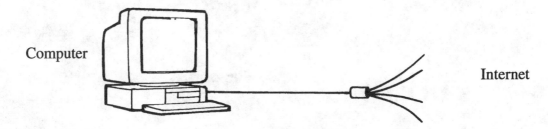

Computer   Internet

SLIP OR PPP

The third option is SLIP or PPP, which gives you full access to the Internet at slower speeds. SLIP stands for Serial Line Internet Protocol and PPP stands for Point to Point Protocol. Like dial up services you will need a modem, but your service provider gives you access as if you were directly connected. You will need a computer with SLIP or PPP software, telecommunications applications software (to allow you to use telnet and FTP File [Transfer Protocol] see page 95), which is compatible with your dial up service. The approximate cost, not including the PC or the cost of the phone call, is $100 to $800 plus a monthly fee from $20 to $60. The advantage to this option is that the cost is relatively low. The disadvantage is that the slower speed at which you can retrieve information makes downloading large files, such as those associated with video and audio, time consuming.

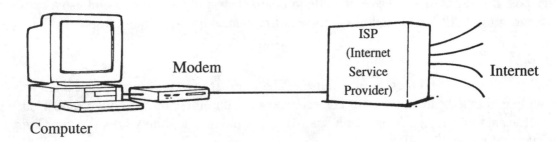

Modem

ISP
(Internet
Service
Provider)

Internet

Computer

TELECOMMUNICATIONS TOOLS *(cont.)*

If you are using either direct connect or SLIP/PPP you will need to purchase Internet software. There is a variety of software, each of which does a slightly different job. If you are a beginning Internet user, start with a graphical interface program. These software packages integrate nearly all the functions that you would wish to use. Graphical interfaces allow you to navigate to the information for which you are searching by pointing and clicking the mouse on certain pictures or words. These descriptions are buttons that automatically route you to where the information is. You may be retrieving a picture in New York and text from New Foundland in the same session. The most popular browser programs are *Netscape* by Netscape Communications Corporation and *Mosaic*. See software index for more information. Many dialup services like America Online and Compuserve include net browsing software as part of their package.

Netscape (Netscape Communications)

OKAY, WHAT DO I DO WITH IT ONCE I GET IT?

There are four things that Internet access will allow you to do: send and receive electronic mail (E-mail), post messages to an electronic bulletin board (newsgroups), log on and use a computer at a remote location (TELNET), and bring copies of resources back to your computer (FTP).

E-MAIL

E-mail is the easiest and most common use of the Internet. Once you have an e-mail account number, you will be able to send and receive correspondence with others on the network. It is also possible for Internet users to exchange e-mail with users of other independent networks such as CompuServe, America Online, and Prodigy.

TELECOMMUNICATIONS TOOLS *(cont.)*

In addition to the exchange between single users, e-mail can be sent to or received by lists of people who subscribe. These subscriptions, unlike newspapers or magazines, are interactive. A subscriber can discuss problems, share solutions, and argue issues.

The following are some educational uses:

E-pals: Become cyberspace pen pals with other students around the world. You not only correspond, but cooperate on research and share projects.

Electronic Expeditions: Students can ask questions and/or read reports from a wagon train going west, the space shuttle, the Iditorad, or a South American bike expedition to name a few.

Request Information: There are many resources in which students and teachers can request information for research they are conducting.

In order to send e-mail, you must have access to e-mail software like Eudora. Commercial online services such as Compuserve and Prodigy provide e-mail services that are integrated into their software packages. Once you have the software, simply start the program and choose the "create a message" option. In the "To:" box, input the e-mail address of the person you are writing to, e.g. **pgardner@school.k12.ca.us.** Finally type your text and choose the "send" option.

Although it is customary to make E-mail short and concise, it is not without its whimsical side. It is customary to add characters that express emotions to E-mail. These are normal type characters that look like faces on their sides. A few are listed below.

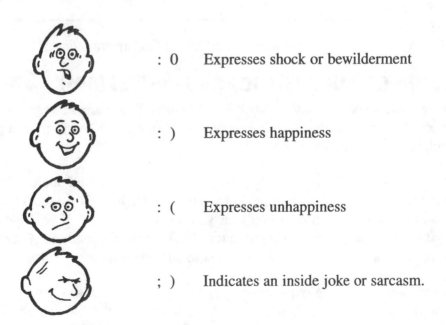

: 0   Expresses shock or bewilderment

:)   Expresses happiness

: (Expresses unhappiness

;)   Indicates an inside joke or sarcasm.

TELECOMMUNICATIONS TOOLS *(cont.)*

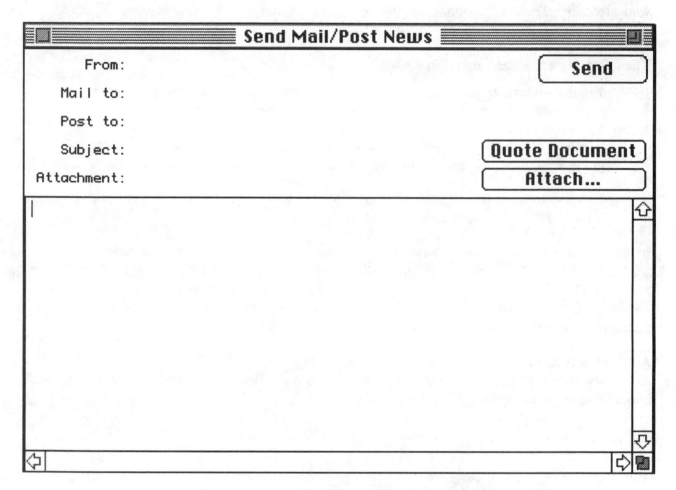

Netscape e-mail (Netscape Communications)

NEWSGROUPS OR BULLETIN BOARD SERVICES (BBS)

Newsgroups are subject specific, interactive bulletin boards. When at a newsgroup, the user can read the postings and post responses to them. This is similar to pinning up a message on a public bulletin board and then having others pin up responses.

There are currently over 10,000 newsgroups and you will be able to find one on almost any subject. Many of these newsgroups are not appropriate for students due to their subject matter or academic level. Some Internet providing services don't carry all the newsgroups. If you find out about a newsgroup that might be of interest to you, request that your provider add it. Providers are usually very open to these requests as there is no additional cost to add a newsgroup.

There are two ways to use newsgroups: logging on to a computer that has newsreader software or using one's own newsreader software. It is suggested that novices use Web browsing software like *Netscape* or *Mosaic*. These extremely user-friendly programs integrate most of the software needed.

TELECOMMUNICATIONS TOOLS *(cont.)*

TELNET

TELNET allows you to enter another computer and explore its resources. Your computer acts as a terminal attached to the remote network. In fact, if you logged on to the computer at the actual site you would see the exact same screens. It doesn't matter if the site is across campus or across the globe, the information can be accessed at nearly the same speed. The amazing thing is that there is usually no charge to use this information.

Here are a few uses for TELNET.

Libraries: Many libraries including The Library of Congress, many university libraries, as well as many public libraries have set up TELNET access to card catalogs and other services.

News Services: Get up-to-the-minute information on breaking news, some of which never makes the newspapers or TV.

Using Telnet in a graphical environment is extremely easy. You simply follow the instructions given by the software, usually pointing and clicking on pictures that lead you through the instructions of use. If your school uses a text-based Telnet account, it will be necessary to get specific training in how to search for and access Telnet sites.

FTP

File Transfer Protocol (FTP) allows you to easily search the world for reports, photographs, film clips, sounds, and programs and bring them back (download) to your computer. It is also possible to give (upload) files to an FTP site. This is similar to Telnet, however, the user is limited to searching for and transferring files. These files can be inserted into written reports or presentations.

Many networks have set aside portions of their machines to offer files for anyone on the Internet to retrieve. Since you do not need to have an account to access these, they are called anonymous FTP sites.

Once again, if you are using a graphical interface such as *Netscape* or *Mosaic*, FTP is as easy as pointing and clicking text or media that opens up a box in which you type the FTP site address. If your interface is strictly text, you will need to receive training specific to your software in order to use FTP.

Some uses might include the following:

Educational Resources: Get thousands of lesson plans, ideas, and research.

Student Research: Students can find information on nearly any subject they wish to research. Not only text, but graphics, sound, and video files are available as well.

Free and Inexpensive Software: The state and federal governments have funded many software packages that then become public domain. These programs can be transferred for use on your computer for free. Shareware authors also place their software on the Internet. These programs can be downloaded and used before being paid for. If you like them, just follow the instructions for payment. The fees are usually low, between $5 and $10.

TELECOMMUNICATIONS TOOLS *(cont.)*

THE BEST PLACE TO START

The World Wide Web (WWW)

You can't turn a page in a magazine or a channel on television these days without receiving an invitation by businesses, government, and educational institutions to visit them at the World Wide Web. But what is it?

The World Wide Web (also known as WWW or the Web) is the fastest growing segment of the Internet. The reason for the Web's success is its ease in navigating. Early Internet explorers had to input long strings of text that directed them to their destination. Once there, they were hampered by continually typing commands to retrieve information. Developers of the WWW agreed upon a graphical interface called "hypertext" and "hypermedia". They are simply words and pictures that when clicked, route the user to the destination or information they want. These hypermedia buttons are often called "hyperlinks" because they link you to other sites on the web.

In order to access the WWW, you must have a Web browsing program. The most popular browsing programs are *Netscape* and *Mosaic*. However, if you are connected to a commercial service provider like America Online or Compuserve, they usually have their own web browser. Some tools will allow the downloading of sounds and motion pictures that others do not.

Web browsers have also integrated all the older Internet navigation tools like e-mail, FTP, Telnet, as well as other information search tools into one software package. This has made using the Internet simple for even the most novice of users.

Each web homepage (the screen you see when you electronically arrive at a site) has a Universal Resource Locator or URL. This is a techy's way of saying "address." There are several ways to get to homepages that contain information you want to see. One way is to simply enter the URL of a homepage into the Web browser and click the search button. These URLs are not hard to find. All one has to do is to peruse magazines or watch television these days to find dozens of them. The URL to the Whitehouse, one of the most visited homepages, is http://www.whitehouse.gov/WH/Welcome.html

However, before using any activities, it is strongly recommended you verify the suggested sites. Web sites frequently change addresses or become unavailable for a myriad of reasons. Teacher Created Materials attempts to offset this ongoing problem by posting changes of URL's on our Web site. Check our home page at *www.teachercreated.com* for updates on this book.

What do the URLs stand for?

TELECOMMUNICATIONS TOOLS *(cont.)*

If you don't know the URL of a site or are just looking for sites about a special topic, Web browsers have special search tools to help you find your way. For example, to find the Whitehouse homepage you might enter the word "whitehouse" into a search screen. The software searches the Internet for occurrences of the word "whitehouse" and returns with a list of the sites it finds. Then, it is simply a matter of clicking the name, and you arrive at the site.

Once at a homepage, it is just a matter of pointing and clicking to the areas that are of interest to you. When you click these hyperlinks, you can be transported to other pages on the same computer or even to other computers anywhere in the world. Most Web pages have links to other pages on other computers with related information. For example: If you were searching for information about ocean animals you might enter the URL that takes you to a homepage in San Diego, California. On that page you might find a hypertext button that instantly links you to a homepage in Sidney, Australia, and from there you might be transported to other related information in Miami, Florida. Since your Internet link is a local phone call, the cost of this world wide expedition in search of knowledge is no more than talking to a friend across town.

Below is a picture of a typical "Home Page."

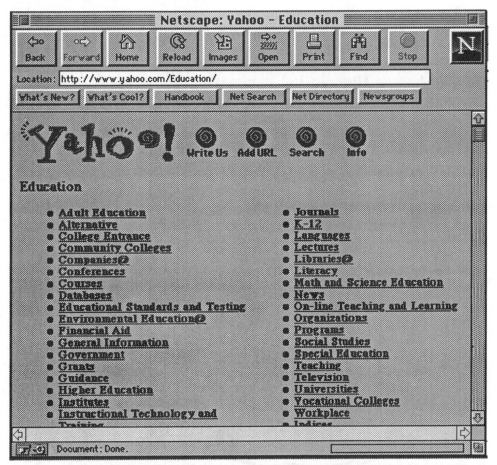

Netscape (Netscape Communications)

Pages 104–109 are devoted to giving you a look at some of the more popular Web sites and their possible use in the classroom.

TELECOMMUNICATIONS TOOLS *(cont.)*

GOPHER

You may have a student in class who you like to send to the office or other classrooms to get information for you. You send this student because you know that you can count on getting the information somewhat reliably. The Gopher Internet tool is much like this enthusiastic student. The gopher goes for information. Gopher sites are arranged in easy to use menus dealing with a diverse pool of information.

If your Internet connection is the easy-to-use graphical, point-and-click type, Gopher sites are easy to navigate through. You simply choose the menu that matches the subject you are interested in, point the mouse at it, then click. Each menu narrows until you reach the information that you are looking for. For instance: If you are looking for lesson plans for a unit you teach on the Civil War, your search may look like this:

Education

    K-12

        Lesson Plans

           Middle School

             History

               Wars

                 Civil War

Once you arrive you may find a hundred lesson plans dealing with the Civil War.

TELECOMMUNICATIONS TOOLS *(cont.)*

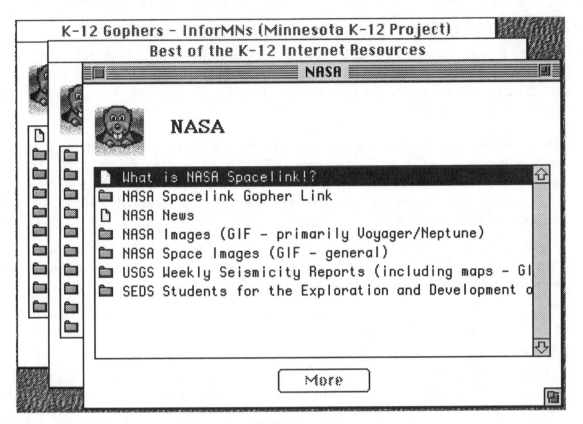

OTHER INTERNET SEARCHING TOOLS

There are many other Internet searching tools that can help users find the information they are looking for. These tools search computers all over the world looking for information that you request. For example, if you wanted to see information about K-12 education, you would simply enter this information into the search tool by typing the keywords "K-12 education" into a search box. It is suggested that, because of ease of use, the novice Internet explorer should make every attempt to use a Web browsing program like *Netscape* or *Mosaic*, as these programs allow them to take full advantage of most of these search tools in a graphic, point-and-click environment.

Some of the search tools that are associated with Gopher are listed below.

Veronica: A search tool that allows the user to input a keyword to search the entire Internet.

Jughead: Like Veronica, Jughead searches for information using a keyword but on a single site or area of the Internet.

Archie: Archie is much more specific. You will have to know at least part of a file name that you are looking for.

WAIS (Wide Area Information Search): Yet another way to search for specific information. WAIS is used for very specific searches. In WAIS the user enters the specific information needed, such as "recent research dealing with." WAIS then searches looking for information dealing with this subject.

TELECOMMUNICATIONS TOOLS *(cont.)*

THE BOTTOM LINE

If you can point and click with a computer mouse, you can explore the Internet using the newer, more graphical environments available in telecommunications software today. These tools will enable you to do your job better and in less time than you thought possible. Here are a few tips for making your Internet journey a smooth one:

1. If your school does not have access to a telecommunication service, try one of the commercial services like America Online, CompuServe, or Prodigy. All these services provide free introductory offers, usually 10 hours of online time. In addition to the wealth of services these provide, many now have access to the Internet. You'll need a dedicated phone line, a modem, and the service's software package.

2. If your school is unwilling to provide teachers with these tools and you have a home computer, subscribe to a service at home. You'll find that the services provided are worth the cost of membership to your family, as well as your professional growth.

3. If your school has an older, non-graphical Internet access, ask that these connections be upgraded. It is usually not a cost factor, just a lack of information, that keeps schools from upgrading.

4. If your school is making a commitment to telecommunications, urge them to invest in direct connect, SLIP, PPP, or a commercial online service. These options will give the use of the graphical point and click navigating tools.

5. If you are not ready to make the telecommunications plunge yet, keep watching. Most experts feel that computer telecommunications will become as common as televisions within the next five years. In fact, many of the phone companies, computer companies, and even cable TV companies are banking on it.

I've heard there's a lot of bad stuff on the Internet. How do I keep my kids out of what I don't want them to see?

Because the Internet is public domain, free speech is not only the right, but the rule. Therefore nearly anyone can publish nearly anything on it. We must acknowledge the fact that there are inappropriate materials on the Internet and then do everything we can to actively avoid them. We cannot weed out all of the materials that are unacceptable for academic purposes, but it should be clearly understood by all students that access to such material in any form is strictly forbidden.

In order to make the responsibility of using this tool clear, many educational institutions have developed Acceptable Use Plans or AUPs. These AUPs usually include a contract that is quite clear about the responsibilities of the student and must be signed by the students, as well as their parents or guardians.

Although the actual percentage of unacceptable materials is small, it is a cause for concern for students, parents, and teachers. If a student stumbles onto the information while doing legitimate research, contact your teacher or person responsible for technology at your school.

TELECOMMUNICATIONS TOOLS *(cont.)*

THE BOTTOM LINE (cont.)

There is no fool-proof way of keeping students out of areas that they should not be in. Here are a few general rules of thumb when students are surfing the net:

1. Supervision, supervision, supervision.

2. Send an agreement home, for parents to sign, that explains the benefits and risks of Internet research.
   (See the sample agreement in appendix.)

3. Make students aware of, "Netiquette"; the rules of using the Internet. (See page 102.)

4. Create a list of Internet sites that are safe. Require that the students only visit those areas. (See the list of popular Internet sites listed in the appendix.)

5. If directly connected, talk to administrators about creating their own Home Page. These directories can be customized with links to Internet sites that are proven safe and educationally sound.

The Internet can be an educational gold mine of information, not only for your students, but for you as well. It is the way people will receive most of their information in the future. With a few precautions, teachers and students can reap the benefit of this vast network of information.

DOWNLOADING WEB SITES

One method of cheating the fickle nature of the Web is to use a Web "whacking" program, such as *Web Buddy*, produced by DataViz. *Web Buddy* will allow you to "whack" or download a single Web page or even an entire Web site, including the links and graphics. It stores the Web pages on your hard drive where they can be accessed with your browser at a later date-even if the page or site has disappeared! Students can enjoy the Web-based activities without the associated wait times during peak Internet hours, or the dreaded "Not Found" error. Teacher Created Materials publishes *Web Buddy,* a book filled with classroom projects and tips on using the *Web Buddy* software which is included on a CD-ROM. It is available for $39.95 by calling (800) 662-4321.

TELECOMMUNICATIONS TOOLS *(cont.)*

NETIQUETTE

Just as there are behaviors which are acceptable at school, students need to learn the correct procedures and rules for using the Internet. Before beginning to use these exciting research tools, it is important to understand the many consequences of the new computer connections that will be made. It is important to understand that this powerful educational tool is a privilege. It can provide countless hours of exploration and use, but like a driver's license, it is a privilege that can be taken for breaking the rules.

The following is a list of helpful rules when using the Internet:

You're Not Dealing with Computers, You're Dealing with People.

When interacting with someone on the Internet, be careful about what you say. Your writing has to be much more clear than your conversation to avoid misinterpretation. Sending a message that is strongly critical is called a "flame". To avoid "flaming", never say anything to someone that you would not say to him/her in person. Avoid the use of sarcasm and be careful with humor. Without voice inflections and body language, remarks can be misinterpreted.

Don't Post Personal Information About Anyone

The Internet is becoming a very crowded place. Like society as a whole, there are nice people and there are not-so-nice people. Do not give out your home phone number or your address to anyone.

Be Brief

More people will read your information if it is short and clear. This also helps conserve disk space on computers.

Do Not Harass Users

If someone asks that you in no way contact them, you must stop all contact immediately. You may feel you have the right of freedom of expression, but others have the right to be free from harassment.

Be Careful with Copyrights

Cut and paste functions make electronic media extremely easy to use when communicating one's own, as well as others' ideas. As long as you are using an article for educational purposes and not selling it, you may use the information. It is important, however, to cite all references.

Double Check Downloads

There are many software products available on the Internet. Many of these products are offered free of charge. Be sure the software product you are downloading is not a commercial product that has been distributed illegally. Most commercial software products have a title screen with a copyright statement.

TELECOMMUNICATIONS TOOLS *(cont.)*

SUGGESTED SOFTWARE

It seems that there is a different software tool for nearly every job needed to be done using the Internet. The beginning level user of the "Net" can be mind-boggled by all the choices. There is an answer, though. The graphical interfaces of today have opened the telecommunications door to the most beginning of computer users. Below are the most popular of the graphical interfaces.

Title	Platform	Connection Needed
Netscape	Macintosh and Windows	Direct Connect, SLIP, or PPP
Mosaic	Macintosh and Windows	Direct Connect, SLIP, or PPP

SUGGESTED ONLINE SERVICES

If you or your school is considering a dial up service, the following is a list of recommended commercial service providers.

Service	Phone Number	Platform	Internet Connection
America Online	(800)827-6364	Macintosh and Windows	Graphical
Classroom PRODIGY	(800)PRODIGY	Macintosh and Windows	Graphical
CompuServe	(800)848-8990	Macintosh and Windows	Graphical
EWorld	(800)775-4556	Macintosh and Windows	Graphical

SUGGESTED HARDWARE

Hardware	Description
Modem	If you are using a dial up or SLIP/PPP connection you will need a modem to connect your computer to the phone line. If you will be using a graphical interface (*Netscape*, *Mosaic*, or an online service) your modem should be not less than 14,000 baud. This baud rate refers to the speed at which the modem transmits and receives information.
Network Card	Computers that are directly connected to a network will need a network card. This is an integrated circuit board that is installed into your computer. It allows your computer to communicate with the network.

TELECOMMUNICATIONS TOOLS *(cont.)*

POPULAR WWW SITES FOR EDUCATORS

(The White House Home Page)

Internet Address (URL):

http://www.whitehouse.gov/WH/Welcome.html

Description:

This Web site is maintained by the Office of the President of the United States and contains information about the first family and the executive branch.

Curriculum Ideas:

1. Take a virtual tour of the Whitehouse. You can do this by clicking the "Tour" button on the page.

2. E-mail the President or Vice President a letter convincing them to support or not support some type of current legislation.

3. Collect media for a report or presentation on the First Family. With a Web browser such as *Netscape* you simply click the picture you want to save.

4. Research the Executive Branch of government. Simply click the button on the home page and you get a complete description of the duties of the Office of the President.

TELECOMMUNICATIONS TOOLS *(cont.)*

The Library of Congress Homepage

Internet Address (URL):

http://www.loc.gov/

Description:

The Library of Congress presents information about and materials from its collections over the Internet. Its online information and services include: schedules of exhibits and events, a menu of services provided, a substantial digital library of various text and media, an online catalog system, information on Congress and the government, as well as links to related WWW sites.

Curriculum Ideas:

1. Research the branches of government by searching for information about our political system.

2. Collect media for presentations by pointing and clicking on the media desired.

3. Get e-mail addresses of the members of Congress and write them about important issues.

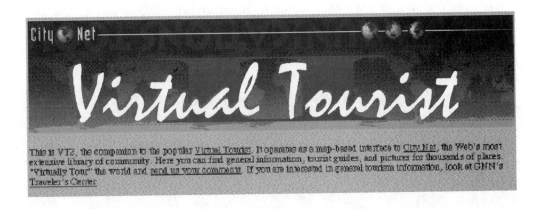

Internet Address (URL):

http://www.vtourist.com/

Description:

The Virtual Tourist is an electronic map of the world, with each section being a hypermedia link: obtain general information and thousands of pictures of places all over the world.

TELECOMMUNICATIONS TOOLS *(cont.)*

Curriculum Ideas:

1. Use the media collected from this site to make pamphlets advertising places all over the world.

2. Play an online geography scavenger hunt. Have students collect pictures and text about different countries that you assign.

3. E-mail tourist information offices in different countries requesting information.

Internet Address (URL):

http://aws.com/

Overview:

The Nationwide School Weather Network is a system whereby students record weather information and transmit it to schools all over the United States. This, in addition to real time satellite images, allows students to closely study the data they collect.

Curriculum Ideas:

1. Become a national school weather site. Students involved with this program collect data, from a weather station that they put together, and report the data back to the network. They then view their results, and that of others from all over the country, along with up-to-date satellite images, to make comparisons between the two.

The JASON Project

Bringing the thrill of exploration and discovery live to students around the world as they participate in an amazing electronic field trip

Internet Address (URL):

http://www.jasonproject.org/

TELECOMMUNICATIONS TOOLS *(cont.)*

Description:

Founded by Dr. Robert D. Ballard in 1989, the JASON project is an interactive electronic field trip in which students and teachers follow research expeditions live on the Internet via satellite. In the past the JASON project has discovered the first hydrothermal vents in the Mediterranean, examined war ships sunk in the War of 1812, studied the effects man has on the environment in a rain forest and had students drive a remote vehicle to collect samples at the foot of a volcano.

Curriculum Ideas:

Take part actively in the project or simply follow the results via an e-mailing list and the Jason project home page. This project actively involves students in the discoveries made.

Internet Address (URL):

http://forum.swarthmore.edu/mathmagic/

Description:

MathMagic is a project in which groups of registered students work together to solve math challenges appropriate to their grade level. The students use the computer to collaborate with other students in different parts of the world in order to solve the challenges.

Curriculum Ideas:

1. Join the program and have groups of your students collaborate with others around the world to solve the problems.

2. If you have limited computer resources, divide up the class and solve the challenges on your own.

Internet Address (URL):

http://www.cjsspecialties.com/camden/kidspage.html

TELECOMMUNICATIONS TOOLS *(cont.)*

Description:

The Kid's Page is a directory of appropriate K-12 Internet sites that have proven to be of high educational value and interest to students. Each one of the sites listed are hypertext linked to the actual site. This means that by clicking on the name site, your computer is automatically routed to that site.

Curriculum Ideas:

1. Because this is a directory, it can be a starting place for students practicing the skills needed for exploring the Internet.

2. Use this site as a base for an Internet scavenger hunt.

Internet Address (URL):

http://server2.greatlakes.k12.mi.us/explorer/

Description:

The Explorer Homepage is a directory of resources including lesson plans, video and audio clips, and free software in the area of math and sciences. All the resources are cataloged by curriculum, description, grade level, and skills.

Curriculum Ideas:

Because this is a depository for hundreds of teacher resources and lesson plans, ideas abound here.

TELECOMMUNICATIONS TOOLS *(cont.)*

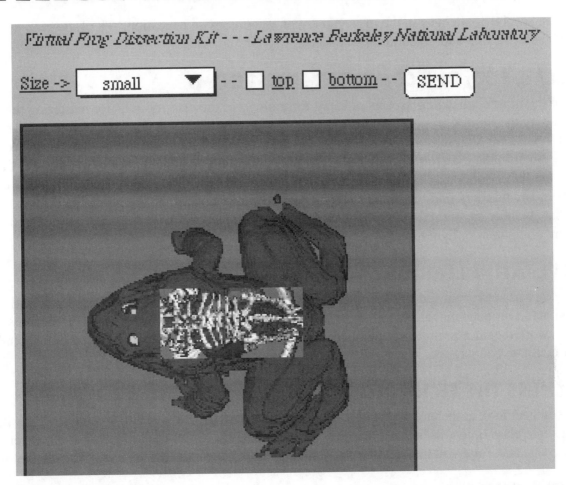

Internet Address (URL):

http://george.lbl.gov/vfrog/

Description:

The program allows interactive dissection of a frog. Students can rotate the frog, remove organs, and even view the skeleton. The dissection kit is available in a number of languages.

Curriculum Ideas:

This activity is a perfect supplement to a unit on body systems. Have the class compare the frog's anatomy to that of their own. Does the frog have the same systems? How are they different?

MANAGEMENT CHALLENGES

There are several challenges in the management of technology in education. The following outlines the challenges which are addressed in this section.

THE LAB, POD, ONE COMPUTER CLASSROOMS

One of the most challenging aspects of using technology in the classroom is not mastering the tools, it is managing the limited computer resources usually found there. Ratios of kids to computers range from 1:1 to 1:100 with most schools falling somewhere in the middle. Many teachers must work with one computer in the classroom, trying to teach the curriculum and computer use at the same time. Others are lucky enough to have a pod (mini lab) either under their control or shared by other classes. Finally, many teachers find themselves scheduled into computer labs or library/media centers. Each of these has its inherent strengths and challenges. Pages 111-128 deal with the management of these different computer configurations.

COOPERATIVE LEARNING WITH TECHNOLOGY

Technology has also changed the way we work, creating a world of people who cooperate and collaborate. Our educational system must reflect a change in the same direction. Our students must learn to work together in order to complete a project or goal. Technology can be a tool that students use to facilitate cooperation. Page 119 deals with cooperative learning with technology.

TEACHING THE TECHNOLOGY

Many teachers look at technology as just one more thing to teach. This is, to some extent, a valid point in that some class time will be used teaching the students how to use the technology. However, the increased on task time will make up for the time instructing the class on the use of the technology.

OBSOLESCENCE

Teachers must also deal with equipment that is out-dated or sometimes obsolete. Many of our schools jumped on board the first educational computer revolution in the 1980s, but somewhere along the line, they either fell off the boat or were forced off by other financial priorities. Many schools are dealing with computers that were developed 20 years ago, eons in the world of technology. This challenge can be overcome by utilizing older technology alongside the newer.

TEACHER TECH TOOLS

Most teachers enter the profession to TEACH. The profession is much more than teaching, however. Teachers must be secretaries, psychologists, and analysts to name but a few roles. Technology tools can help increase teacher's productivity, freeing up more time for developing and implementing better lessons. Pages 143-159 are overviews of several teacher productivity tools.

ONE-COMPUTER CLASSROOM

THE LONE COMPUTER

Having a single computer can be very nerve-racking if your goal is to have every student have access every day. Even if you had the students for the entire day without interruption, each student would only have approximately ten minutes of computer contact time. The management of rotation schedules alone would drive a teacher off the deep end. So how can we utilize a single computer in a class of 30+ students during the time allotted to class each day?

CLASSROOM ADMINISTRATION

Like the superhero of the old west, the lone computer can be a savior. Having a single computer in the classroom has the advantage of convenience. The job of classroom administration (See Teacher Tech Tools pages 143-159) of grades, portfolios, newsletters, and student handouts is easy because the computer is there to be your aid.

LESSON ENHANCEMENT

Presentations

The computer can also help make presentations that can captivate your students and make your lesson easier to follow. The easiest way to achieve this is to simply make transparencies. Using the computer and printer equipped with a word processor, paint, or desktop publishing program, you can simply print on transparency film. These can be displayed on an overhead projector. If a color printer is available, create full-color transparencies.

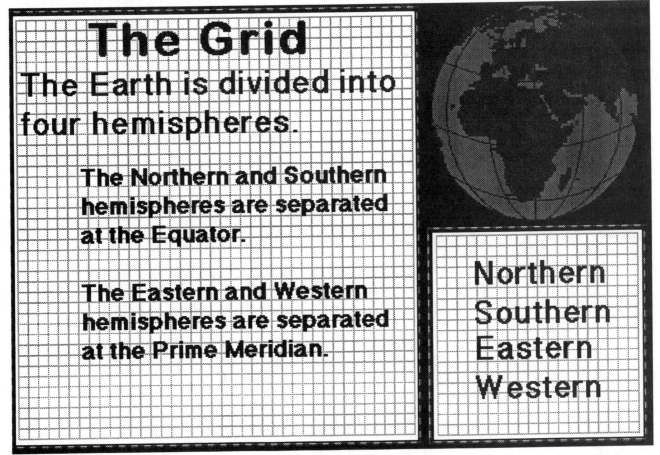

ONE-COMPUTER CLASSROOM *(cont.)*

Another way of using the computer for presentations is to use a device to project the computer screen onto a larger screen. (See Large Screen Projection Devices, page 23.) In this way the computer becomes a chalkboard. Whatever is seen on the monitor is seen by the class. Unlike the chalkboard, the computer can project in full color with motion and sound, allowing the teacher to take explanation to another level.

Multimedia encyclopedias, atlases, and content-related software are great for presenting audio/visual clips, charts, maps, and diagrams that give the students a better understanding about what is being taught. Presentations can be customized by the teacher by using a program like *Hyperstudio, Kid Pix Studio*, or *Power Point* to capture and sequence multimedia. The teacher can create a custom slide show that follows what is being taught. On page 209 there is a blank storyboard that will help you sequence a typical presentation.

COMPUTER AIDED SIMULATIONS

There are several computer aided simulations that lend themselves to a one-computer classroom. Tom Snyder Productions and Video Discovery offer several simulations that motivate, inform, and help develop higher level thinking skills. These simulations usually begin by outlining some type of problem that the group faces. Managing these simulations is easier as student teams must use the computer to find what problem faces them and clues for solving the problem. They then return to their seats and begin researching to gain a better understanding of the problem and its possible solutions. After coming to a consensus about how to solve the problem, they return to the computer and choose a solution. If they are correct they go to the next level. If wrong, they continue to work on the same problem until it has been solved.

CLASSROOM MANAGEMENT METHODS

One of the most challenging aspects of using a single computer in the classroom is getting students to have individual or small group time on the computer. Allowing the students time to create projects and do research can be like trying to get a square peg into a round hole. Time and class numbers usually dictate how well this can work. Here are few ways to maximize the amount of access that your students have on the computer.

ONE-COMPUTER CLASSROOM *(cont.)*

TRADITIONAL METHOD

If your day consists of more traditional 40-50 minute blocks, the amount of computer access time will be limited. In order to get the most out of this time constraint, you will probably need to use the computer for lesson enhancement through presentations and simulations. You will have to limit the amount of time allowed for student use.

The following illustrates a one period schedule for the use of a single computer in the classroom.

Time	Teacher's Action	Computer Use
15 minutes	Teaching whole class how to outline information for a report.	Teacher uses a presentation program like *Kid Pix Studio* or *HyperStudio* to illustrate the steps for creating an outline.
25 minutes	Teacher moves about the class assisting students with the outlining of details for individual reports. Students use information from library books and the computer to compile information.	Selected students are using multimedia encyclopedias like *Grolier* and *Compton's* to find and print articles about their topics.
10 minutes	Teacher brings closure to the activity by sharing successes, pointing out common mistakes, reviewing the skill.	Students who continue to have trouble with the skill, review the presentation at the computer.

ONE-COMPUTER CLASSROOM (cont.)

ROTATIONAL STATION METHOD

If your schedule permits longer, more flexible periods, a single computer can be utilized as one of several learning stations in the classroom. Cooperative learning is the key to using a single computer in this type of configuration. Grouping students so that a team utilizes the computer as a tool to carry out a task can actually give you more one-on-one contact with students. The computer becomes one of several stations in which the group works in order to develop a project. To illustrate how this works in the classroom, look at the schedule and diagram below.

The students in this class are divided into six cooperative groups. The class is set up into six stations, each of which has a different activity that relates to the topic in which they are working. This activity is based splitting a longer block of time into three parts and extending the activities over two days so that all the groups have access to all the stations. This can be adjusted based on the amount of students in the class and time period available. Activities should be thoroughly explained at the beginning of each period and reviewed between rotations. Task cards for each activity help reinforce the directions and keep groups on task.

	Group 1	Group 2	Group 3	Group 4	Group 5	Group 6
Station Number	1	2	3	4	5	6
	6	1	2	3	4	5
	5	6	1	2	3	4
Day 2						
Station Number	4	5	6	1	2	3
	3	4	5	6	1	2
	2	3	4	5	6	1

WHERE DO I PUT IT?

Where you put your one computer will depend entirely on two things, how you use the computer and where the plugs are. The second concern is probably more important than the first. If there is no power where you would like to put it, there is no need putting it there. If power is not a problem, think about how the computer will be used the most. If the computer is primarily a tool for you to manage your classroom, you will need it to be close to the materials you use to plan and organize your classroom. See page 143 for suggestions. If you use the computer as a student work station, see page 116. If you use the computer more to present information, see page 115.

Tech Tip: If you would like to utilize the computer in a number of ways, a mobile cart would be a good investment. The computer can then be repositioned and utilized in a number of ways.

ONE-COMPUTER CLASSROOM *(cont.)*

THE LONE COMPUTER
Diagram 3 (The Presenter)

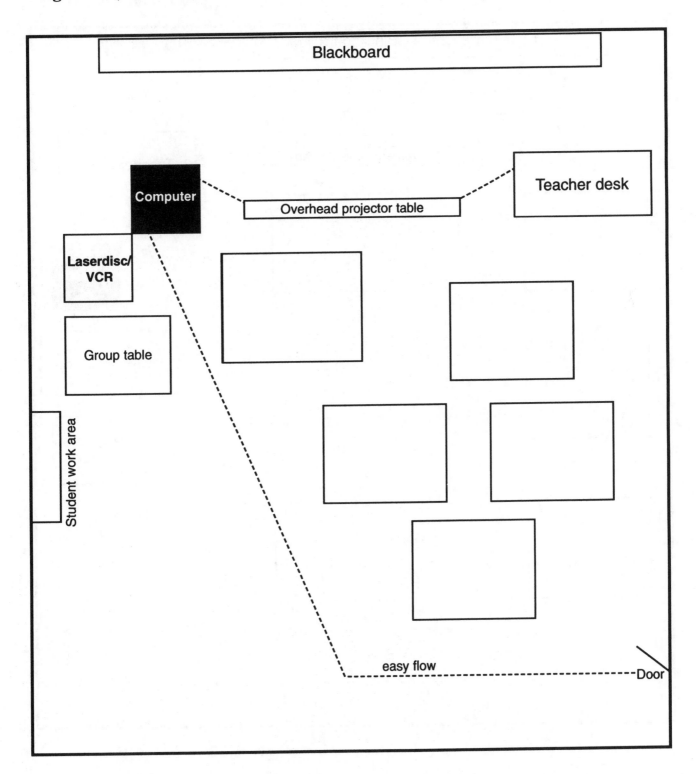

ONE-COMPUTER CLASSROOM

THE LONE COMPUTER
Diagram 2 (The Work Station)

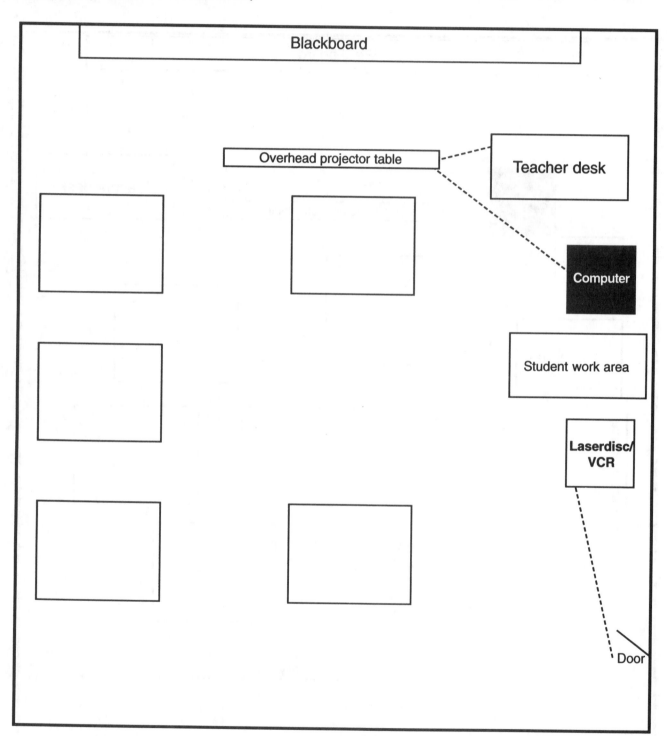

ONE-COMPUTER CLASSROOM *(cont.)*

THE LONE COMPUTER

Diagram 1 (The Teacher Assistant)

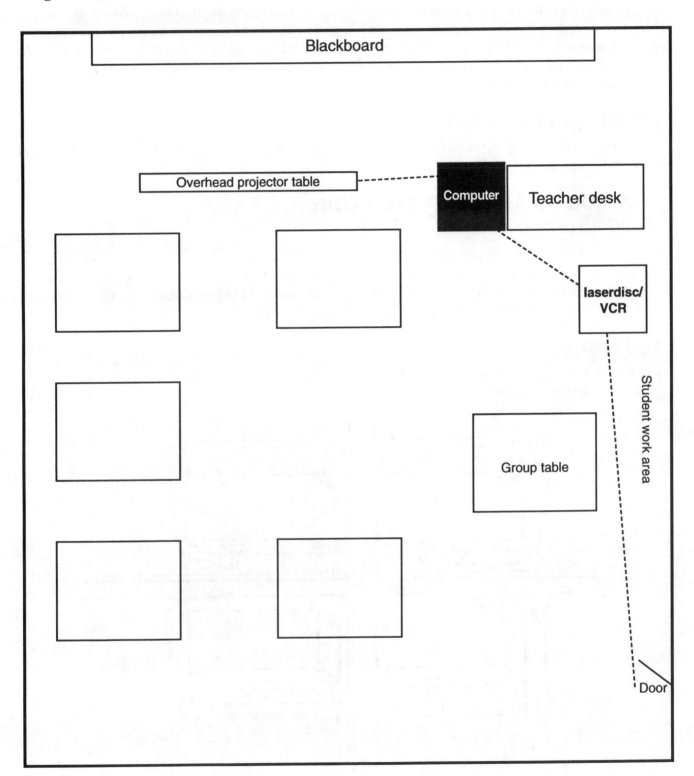

THE COMPUTER POD

CLASSROOM ADMINISTRATION

The pod is a wonderful way to give all the students access to computers, but don't forget your needs. Teacher's administrative tasks can be streamlined with the use of teacher tech tools. (See page 143–159.) Keep one of the computers on a mobile cart in order that it may be easily transported to your work area. Since the computer will be used by both teachers and students it is important to invest in security software in order to keep gradebooks and other sensitive documents away from the wandering mouse (see page 146.)

LESSON ENHANCEMENT:

Keep one computer on a cart or in position to use as a presentation station. See Lesson Enhancement in the One-Computer Classroom, page 111.

CLASSROOM MANAGEMENT METHODS
Modified Traditional Method

If your schedule is a more traditional day divided into 40-50 minute periods, a modified traditional method works very well. Students are divided into three multi-level groups. The teacher works with one group while a second group works independenly and the third uses the computer pod. This rotates each day so that students work through all the stations in three days.

THE POD

The pod is an arrangement of more than three computers within a classroom or shared between a limited number of classrooms.

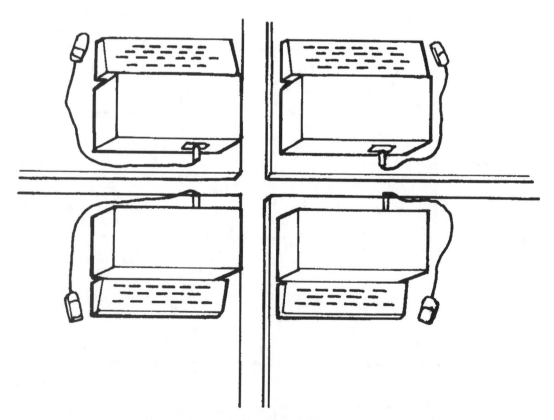

THE COMPUTER POD *(cont.)*

ROTATIONAL STATION METHOD

If your schedule allows more flexible scheduling, a rotational station method can be used. The advantage to this arrangement is that students have increased computer contact time. This configuration facilitates the production of student projects. The best way to use this arrangement is through the use of stations. by dividing the class into three to four manageable groups and working on different tasks that relate to the curricular area, not only facilitates the use of the technology, it also frees teacher time for individual and small group instruction. Once the students are trained in the use of the program, very little teacher time is required to keep this station on task.

The best way to manage a station activity is to divide the amount of time that the students are in your class by the amount of groups there are in the class. Then divide the project into activities to be completed in each station. Here is an example.

Time/Activity	Gathering research or media for the report	Writing rough drafts of reports	Building multimedia presentation screens on computers
8:30–9:00	Group 1	Group 2	Group 3
9:00–9:30	Group 3	Group 1	Group 2
9:30–10:00	Group 2	Group 3	Group 1

If you have a limited time period, simply spread the activity over three days. Each group works at a different station each day.

COOPERATIVE WORK GROUP METHOD

If the classroom can accomodate the separation of the computers into different parts of the room, cooperative work grouping is another method. In this system students are grouped at tables with a computer at each group. The class can be instructed as a whole and then use the computer and other materials to complete the assignment. Students within the group must take on roles that facilitate the completion of the task.

THE COMPUTER POD *(cont.)*

WHERE DO I PUT IT?

Like the lone computer, the classroom computer pod must be placed in proximity to electrical connections as well as network connections if your school is networked. If there is only one electrical outlet, talk to your administrator or maintenance person about the size of the circuit. Is the circuit heavy enough to support the computers you wish to connect? Finally, always use a surge suppresser when connecting computers to an electrical circuit. These relatively inexpensive extension cords suppress electrical surges that occur during power outages and electrical storms. For an investment of between five and twenty dollars you can save months of work and hundreds of dollars in computer repairs.

Tech Tip: Always number or name each computer and assign students to their computers. This way if something happens to the computer you will be able to ask the proper questions to a limited number of students to find out what happened. Labeling any wires used to connect the computers will also be helpful when disconnecting and reconnecting them.

Using pods can also save money in that they allow network possibilities. It is not necessary for computers in proximity to each other to have printers for each. Six computers can be set up to print at one printer for an average cost of about $30 per computer.

The diagrams on pages 121 and 122 illustrate possible placements of the computer pod within a classroom. The first facilitates the use of computers as a presentation tool, while the second allows students to work on projects without disturbing other stations.

THE COMPUTER POD *(cont.)*

Diagram 1

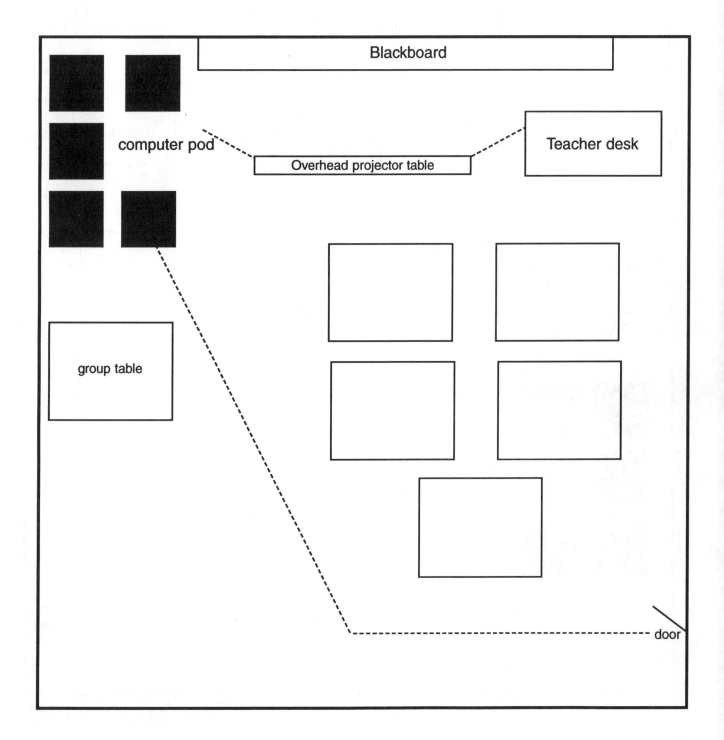

THE COMPUTER POD *(cont.)*

Diagram 2

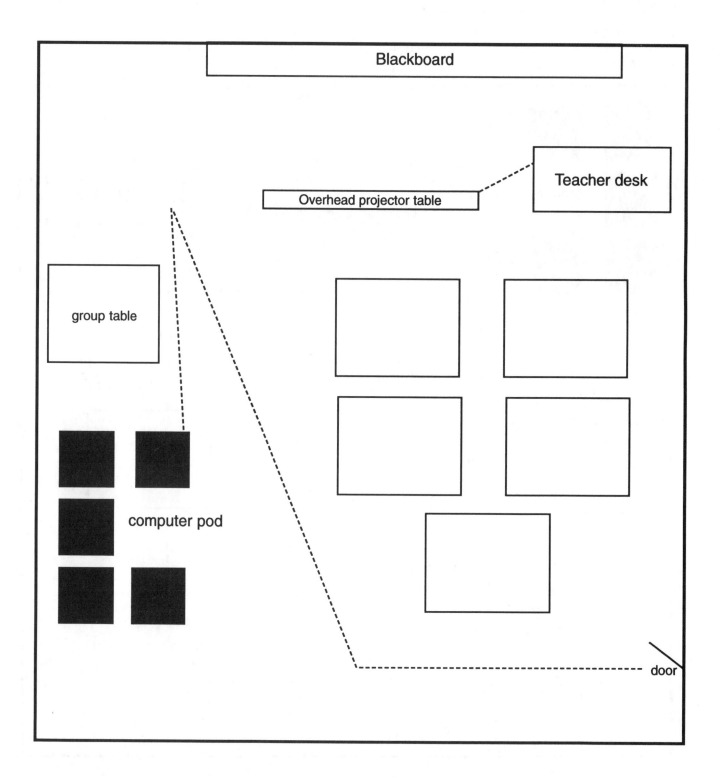

THE LAB/MEDIA CENTER

THE PAST

During the first computer revolution in education, schools placed most of their technology resources into lab settings. These classrooms were usually run by a person whose main job was supporting the teacher with skill building activities in the form of games. These skills were usually taught in isolation with no real connection with the curriculum. In addition, the time spent in the lab was limited to just a few hours a month. The rigid scheduling of the lab was one contributing factor to its isolation from the curriculum.

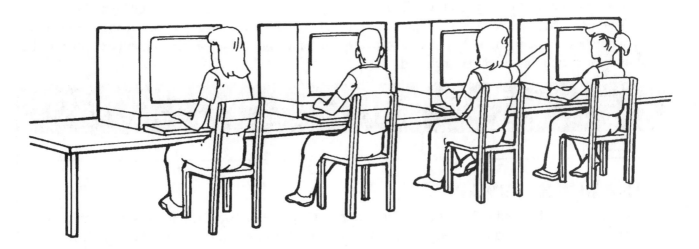

THE PRESENT

The computer labs of today have evolved to become part of the library. By combining these resources under the name Media Center, schools have found that the computer lab can become an extension of the classroom rather than isolated from it. The computer lab portion of the Media Center is used to teach students the skills they need to create projects and then provides the means to create them. The library becomes a research area helping teachers and students gather the information needed to complete projects.

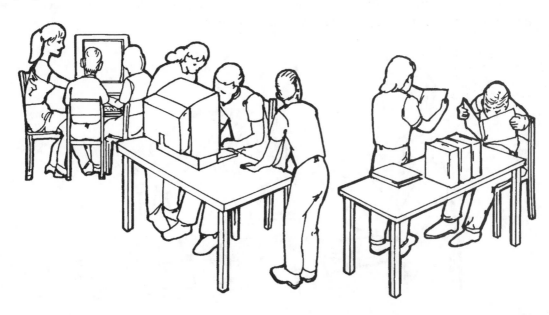

THE LAB/MEDIA CENTER *(cont.)*

LAB ADMINISTRATION

A lab/media center creates several unique management challenges, some of which the computers themselves can help manage. Here are a few tips for helping the lab run smoothly.

KEEPING TRACK OF SOFTWARE

Because many labs are the software checkout center as well as a classroom, it is imperative for a lab teacher to keep track of not only titles that he/she uses but other titles as well. This is also very important for copyright documentation. Be sure to register all copies of software and keep the documentation. Number each copy of software for which you are in charge. Create a software list using a database to help you keep track of software titles and sign outs. Here is a good example of the type of information that might be included.

Software Title	Date Purchased	Publisher	Serial Number	School Number	Total Copies	Registered On	Checked Out to

MANAGING HARDWARE

Databases can also be used to keep track of hardware. This type of documentation is invaluable for maintenance, upgrading, and warranty repair. This is some information that might be included:

Hardware Type	Serial Number	Amount of RAM	Amount of Storage	Service Records	Warranty Good Until

Just keeping track of cables and what they hook up to can be a nightmare. Use tape to label cables so that if you have to disassemble the lab, assembly can be done with minimal effort.

Use a maintenance program like *Norton Utilities* (Symantec) to periodically check machines for errors, optimize performance, repair damaged disks, and backup files.

THE LAB/MEDIA CENTER *(cont.)*

SOFTWARE DOCUMENTATION

All the software manuals should be kept in the same place so that they are easily accessible to teachers and/or students when a question arises. Organize these by tool type: electronic learning, word processors, presentation, data analysis, telecommunications, etc. Make sure that you teach students to use the contents, indexes, and glossaries of these books to find answers to their questions quickly and easily.

LESSON PLANS

Keep technology lesson plans in an area that is easily accessible to teachers. Sources for technology lesson plans include: the Internet, colleges, resource books like this one, and those written by teachers at your school. Many school versions of popular educational software have books full of lesson plan ideas.

BULLETIN BOARDS

Schedules, sign-up sheets, project progress sheets, and other administrative paperwork should be posted where they are easy to read and are accessible to both students and teachers. Rules and consequences should be posted and reviewed occasionally with students. Frequently used technology related vocabulary should be displayed and reviewed occasionally with students. If there are vocabulary and skills that are specific to a certain type or brand of software, make sure that you put these up on a special bulletin board so that students can refer to them when needed. Keep teachers apprised of new technology ideas, hardware, software, and happenings by using one board for teacher information.

STUDENT WORK

Finally, like the classroom, student work should have a prominent place in the lab. Students should take pride in the projects that they have completed. A few ideas for displaying student work include these:

- Print copies of reports and other writing and put them on bulletin boards.

- If the students have created presentations like a slide show, videotape the presentations and keep them in a library to be viewed by anyone who would like to see them.

- Display storyboards and rough drafts with the final project in order for passers-by to appreciate not just the finished product, but the process as well.

- If your school has interconnected TV cable, display videos of projects on a closed circuit TV system to all classes who want to tune in. You can also use a video camera to create your own school news channel. Surprisingly, for most systems, this can be done by simply connecting a VCR to the source of the cable entering the school. Check with your cable company and/or school maintenance supervisor to see if this can be done at your school.

THE LAB/MEDIA CENTER *(cont.)*

WHERE TO PUT IT

The placement of computers in the lab can be a crucial part of management. The following is an effective lab configuration for student project production. Yours will differ depending on the size and shape of the room and the amount and type of technology resources available. It is important to consider traffic flow and lines of sight when setting up your lab.

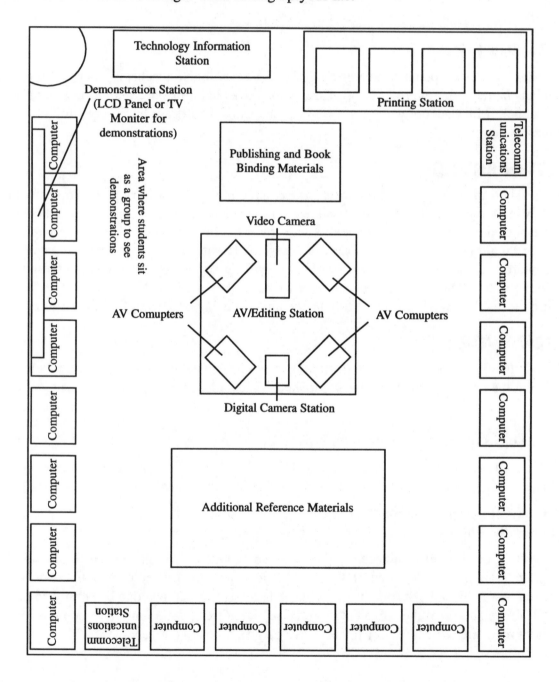

Audio visual computers can be used for student projects, but when possible, these computers should act as stations for students who need to digitize video, audio, and photographs.

THE LAB/MEDIA CENTER *(cont.)*

SCHEDULING

If your school has decided to use the computer lab as a project-based learning center, the scheduling of the lab will have to reflect this shift in thinking. Students will probably require a longer period of time spread over two to three weeks. This will mean scheduling may need to be more flexible than has been practiced in the past. Before the schedule is made, however, it is best to ask a few questions.

- What will the students do in the lab/media center?

- How long will the students need to do it?

- What resources will be needed?

- How many students can the lab/media center accommodate?

- Is your school day divided into short or long blocks of student contact time?

When these questions are answered, you will have a good idea of how much time each class will need to complete a single project in the lab/media center. This information will be needed in order to decide which one of the following scheduling strategies will be the best for your school.

FIXED SCHEDULE

A fixed schedule allots lab time in a consistent way.

"Mrs. Jones' class gets the lab from 9:00 until 9:50 on Mondays, Tuesdays, Wednesdays, and Fridays and 9:50-10:40 on Wednesdays and Fridays this year."

Time	Monday	Tuesday	Wednesday	Thursday	Friday
9:00-9:50	Jones	Jones	Jones	Julius	Jones
9:50-10:40	Feldman	Julius	Jones	Preez	Preez
10:40-11:30	Feldman	Pittman	Pittman	Pittman	Preez
11:30-12:00	Santelli	Terry	Preez	Terry	Terry
12:00-12:50	Alexander	Terry	O'Boyle	Oxford	O'Boyle
12:50-1:40	Minter	Minter	Minter	Minter	O'Boyle
1:40-2:30	Cornell	Oxford	Oxford	Alexander	Cornell
2:30-3:10	Bryant	Bryant	Bryant	Bryant	Byrant

This is a very equitable way of distributing the lab time, but it is not very inflexible and lends itself more to the use of computers for individualized skill reinforcement rather than project-based learning.

THE LAB/MEDIA CENTER *(cont.)*

ROTATIONAL FIXED SCHEDULE

This type of schedule allows each class to get the lab for several days in a row when working on a project.

"Mrs. Jones' class will have the lab from 9:00 until 10:00 every day during the months of November and February."

In this type of schedule, the time is equitably distributed into larger blocks during preset times of the year. Teachers can plan projects with these times in mind, and there is sufficient time to complete them without interruption.

Time	Monday	Tuesday	Wednesday	Thursday	Friday
9-10	Jones	Jones	Jones	Jones	Jones
10-11	Smith	Byrant	Smith	Byrant	Smith
11-12	Oxford	Oxford	Jerry	Oxford	Jerry

TEAM TEACHING SCHEDULE

If your school is departmentalized by subject, grade level, or teaches in cross curricular teams, you may want to divide the time between teams.

"The Math/Science team gets the computer lab during the months of October and May."

The team, in turn, determines the distribution of the computer time.

"Mr. Smith's and Ms. Patterson's classes will work on the physical science multimedia reports from 9:00 to 10:00 every day."

Time	Monday	Tuesday	Wednesday	Thursday	Friday
9-10	Smith/Patterson	Smith/Patterson	Smith/Patterson	Smith/Patterson	Smith/Patterson
10-11	Cornell/Jones	Cornell/Jones	Cornell/Jones	Cornell/Jones	Cornell/Jones
11-12	Feldman/Mintor	Feldman/Mintor	Feldman/Mintor	Feldman/Mintor	Feldman/Mintor

EXTRA TIME

Time not scheduled during the day can be available for entire classes through sign ups. Using the lab sign up form on page 141, have teachers sign up for unused times during the day. In order to facilitate larger blocks of time, it may be necessary to limit the number of classes that can sign up during a set time period, like a week or month. This way teachers can sign up for several unused blocks in a row.

A lab pass system can also work very well. Make laminated lab/media center passes that have the time slots that the lab is available printed on them. Distribute an even amount to each teacher, letting them send one student per pass. These times can include before and after school, recesses, and lunch periods.

TEACHING THE TECHNOLOGY

PLANNING

The most challenging aspect of running a lab is planning. If you have decided to use the lab/media center as a project-based learning center, it will be important that the lab teacher coordinate a project that is an extension to the learning that is happening in the class. This should not be an isolated area where students go for "computer recess" or game playing. The classroom teacher and the lab teacher must be able to plan weeks, sometimes months, in advance of the time that students will be in the lab/media center in order to make sure that curriculum and prelab activities are enhanced by the computer time.

COLLABORATION

As soon after the schedule has been made as possible, the teacher and the lab teacher should meet to discuss what type of experience the classroom teacher wants from the lab. The lab teacher's role is to give suggestions, but the classroom teacher should have the final word as to the experience, since he/she is ultimately responsible for his/her students' growth. Below is a dialogue of a productive planning meeting between teacher and lab teacher. It is given as an example of one type of collaborative model.

Lab Teacher: Your lab time is next month, and I thought we should get together to plan your class project.

Classroom Teacher: Great! We have just started a unit on ancient civilizations. What can you suggest we do for a project?

Lab Teacher: That sounds very interesting. Do the students normally do any type of creative or informational writing in conjunction with the unit?

Classroom Teacher: Yes, they do. Each of my groups produce a report about different civilizations, and then we compare them to one another.

Lab Teacher: Wow! That gives us several options then. We could use a publishing program to create individual reports for each with photographs and maps, a presentation using all different types of media, or we could do a combination of both.

Classroom Teacher: That sounds exciting. I think that the combination of a written report and a multimedia presentation would be fantastic. What would I need to do in class to prepare the students for the computer time?

Lab Teacher: Well, aside from what you normally do to write the report, the students will have to storyboard the presentation, design each of the presentation screens, and select the media they want to include in both the written report and the presentation. All in all it should take them about 12 class periods to complete. You'll probably want them to present their reports to the class, so figure another two periods for that.

TEACHING THE TECHNOLOGY *(cont.)*

Classroom Teacher: OK, I'll work these activities into my lesson plans. Where do we start?

Lab Teacher: I have a few handouts that you can use to do the in-class activities. First, let's talk about these reports the kids do. Do you have any samples from last year?

As you can see, the lab teacher adapted the tools available in the lab to what the teacher had found was successful in the class. In this way the lab enhanced the teaching of the unit and didn't replace it. Each tool discussed in this book can be adapted in the same way. The list below will help you to make the curricular ties necessary in the lab.

Electronic Learning Tools: Use these to strengthen skills and research units being taught in class.

Writing and Publishing: These tools should be adapted to produce writing that reflects what is being studied in the classroom.

Presentation Tools: If oral reports or just more creative uses of communication are needed, suggest these tools.

Data Analysis Tools: Are complex comparisons and visualizations needed for something being taught in class? These tools are perfect for that type of job.

Telecommunication Tools: If you are set up for this, students can enhance their in-class learning in several ways, from gathering information to communicating with others all over the world.

TEACHING THE TECHNOLOGY *(cont.)*

STRATEGIES FOR TEACHING TECHNOLOGY TOOLS

Tech Tutor Team

Let's face it, many times students learn to use technology tools much faster than adults. So why not exploit their natural abilities by establishing a Technology Tutor Team. Take a group of students who have a talent with the technology and divide them up into specialties. One student may become an expert on word processing and publishing, another may become an art expert, and still another may have a talent in using different hardware such as CD-ROM, laserdisc, video, or scanners. This team of students is then able to teach other students how to use different software or hardware and help students who are having trouble. This frees up more time for you to work with students in a one-on-one and small group setting.

Parent Partners

Technology has caused the growth of the home office. Many more parents are skipping the commute in favor of the telecommute (sending files back and forth to offices using the computer). Many times these parents have a lot of computer experience and flexible work schedules, a perfect combination for becoming a Parent Partner. These parents can be used to teach students the use of technology tools as well as add a career component to your classroom.

Many parents have the time and enthusiasm to help in the classroom, but lack the computer experience. Take these parents to computer training inservice days or spend time learning a program together with them. These parents will be invaluable as helpers and will appreciate learning along with the students.

TEACHING THE TECHNOLOGY *(cont.)*

TECHNOLOGY TEAM TEACHING

We all have our teaching strengths. Find a teacher who has a technology talent that you lack and vice versa. Team up to teach a unit using different technology tools. For example: Teacher A's students use writing and publishing tools to create super reports, while Teacher B's students find a lot of information on the Internet. Pair the students from the different classes to create written reports using the Internet as a research tool. Each student benefits from the other's talents. At the same time, each teacher gets exposure to another tool in a curriculum rich environment.

PASS IT ON METHOD

In the one-computer classroom, it is especially time consuming to teach the use of specific software. This method lessens that burden by turning the students into teachers. Using this method, the teacher instructs a single student or group of students in the use of a program, usually dividing it into small sub-skills. Once they have shown mastery of the computer skill, the original student passes on the skill to the next student. The teacher still needs to monitor the progress ocassionally, as the teaching tends to degrade with every successive teacher. But this tends to free the teacher from continually reteaching students in the use of the program.

TEACHING THE TECHNOLOGY *(cont.)*

There's Still Juice in That Old Apple or IBM or Tandy or . . .

Many schools invested large amounts of money over the past 15 years in computers that were, at the time, state-of-the-art. It would now cost more to dispose of these computers than it would to purchase them (if you could still purchase them). So how does a school or district keep up? The answer is probably, "It doesn't." The power of computer technology doubles every 18 months while the price of technology declines at the same rate. (Gordon Moore, 1995). Given this fact, the best education can do is to stay as close to state-of-the-art as financially possible. So, as districts upgrade technology, older machines are going to find themselves next to newer machines. Fret not, they all have a place in education.

The pillar of educational computers in the 1980s was the Apple II series and to a lesser extent, IBM DOS machines. These computers were often put into computer labs and were utilized for drill and practice games and word processing. Now that schools have begun to upgrade there labs to the more modern Macintosh and IBM computers, these older computers have found their way into the classroom. So what do you do with them when you get them?

- First, raid every cabinet that might house software. Review each software title you find to see if it matches the curriculum you teach.

- If you don't already have one, find out if there are any printers available that work with the computer.

- Set up the computer so that it can be viewed using a television. The computer and TV, in effect, become an electronic chalkboard, allowing you to teach how to use program, play whole class games and simulations, and even video tape presentations. (See large screen projection, page 23.)

Suggested Apple II Software

The following is a list of suggested software that works well in the middle school setting.

Software Title	Publisher	Curriculum Area
Children's Writing and Publishing Center for Children's Writing and Publishing	The Learning Company	Language Arts
Combo Pack of additional pictures	CenterCreative Pursuits	Language Arts
Ace Reporter	Mindplay	Language Arts
Fraction Munchers	MECC	Math
Hands On Math 2	Ventura	Math
Science Giants	MECC	Science
The Rainforest	Toucan	Science
Timeliner	Tom Snyder Productions	Social Studies
Carmen San Diego series	Broderbund	Social Studies
Teacher Tool Kit	Hi Tech of Santa Cruz	Teacher Utility
Bannermania	Broderbund	Teacher Utility
Print Shop	Broderbund	Teacher Utility

TEACHING THE TECHNOLOGY *(cont.)*

INDIVIDUALIZED LEARNING WITH TECHNOLOGY

Students learn in a variety of ways. One of the things that computers do well is help students learn skills and content by addressing many modalities including, auditory, visual, and kinesthetic. Although the model of using technology in the classroom has changed, computer skill-building exercise still remains an effective use of the tool. Because of the engaging way that computers deliver instruction, students tend to work harder and longer on skill-based curriculum than they do with traditional strategies.

Since using the computer for individualized learning removes it from the use of the rest of the class, one of the challenges is deciding when to and when not to use it in this way. Here are a few instances when the use of computers is a good option.

- **Writing:** Some students have a very hard time with penmanship. Use typing tutors like *Mavis Beacon Teaches Typing* to teach the student keyboarding. Set up a ten minute period every day for the student to practice. Allow this student to use a word processor on written assignment.

- **Language Arts:** There are several programs that build language and communication skills. Some include *Essential Grammar* and *Punctuation* by Gameco and *Word City* by Magic Quest.

- **Spelling:** Some students, like many adults, have a very hard time with spelling. The spell checking mechanisms in word processors allow this individual to have a free flow of ideas without being hampered by spelling. Since the spell checkers scan the document and return the misspelled word with a list of possible replacements, this actually becomes a spelling lesson in itself. The student must choose the correctly spelled word, adding a visual recognition component.

- **Math:** The teaching of math computational concepts is also a good use of individualized computer time. Many students need many repetitions to learn math algorithms. The key is to select software that can be customized to teach the concepts that you are teaching in class. The computer should act as a one-on-one tutor.

- **Critical Thinking:** Many students have exceptional academic abilities (you know, the ones who already know the concept or skill you are teaching before you teach it). There are several critical thinking games, like *The Factory* from Sunburst and *Sim City 2000* by Maxis, that challenge these students when you are working with the rest of the class.

Once you have decided how to use the computer to individualize instruction, the next question is how do you manage it? Here are a few ideas:

Remove the computer from the sight of the class if possible. This will cut down on the "I wish I were back there" syndrome.

MANAGEMENT HELPERS

Do not schedule time blocks for students. Most of the time this just leads to clock watchers who don't pay attention in class. Randomize the names of students who are to use the computer. This can easily be done by simply making a master list of the students and renumbering it each day. You simply tell the student who is number one that he is first. Then have the students set a timer to warn them when they're finished. Egg timers are fine, but most newer computers have alarm clock functions built in. This, in conjunction with a pair of headphones, create a great individualized learning center.

Change the program from time to time. If the novelty wears off, time on task will begin to wane too.

MANAGEMENT HELPERS *(cont.)*

TECHNOLOGY MATERIALS

Having the following materials in proximity to the computer station will help you manage the station, as well as cut down on the amount of time you will have to invest in the center.

- **Disks:** Each student should have two disks on which to save projects. Students should save frequently during a work session on their first disk to reduce the chance of data loss. The second disk will be a back-up of the first. Projects should be saved to this disk at the end of a work session. If either of the disks become damaged the other will become a back-up.

- **Disk File:** Plastic disk filing boxes are an inexpensive way to keep student's disks organized.

- **Document Holders:** These clips or stands are used to hold drafts so that students can easily read them while typing final drafts.

- **Paper:** Teach the students to reload paper into the printer and keep an extra supply.

- **Ribbons or Ink Jet Cartridges:** Keep extras near the printer and teach students how to properly change them. Color ribbons and cartridges are available for most printers but tend to be more expensive. Make sure that students only use these when color is needed.

- **Hand Cleaners:** If you do not have easy access to a sink, prepackaged hand cleaning wipes are a good alternative. Clean hands will help eliminate damage to the keyboard.

- **Software Manuals:** Keep all software documentation in a file near the computers. Many software producers print shortcut, quick start, or quick reference pages in their manuals. Make copies of these and place them in folders or indexed binders so that students can easily find answers to their questions.

COMPUTER LOG

"He always gets the computer!" is a familiar refrain in the one-computer classroom. It is very hard to be equitable with a limited amount of computer time. One way to keep track of this is the computer log like the one provided on page 140. Having the students log on and off of the computer can also help the teacher track down someone who may have knowingly or unknowingly caused the computer to malfunction. Tracing the steps that were taken by the student can sometimes save a lot of time in repairing problems.

SIGN-UP SHEETS

Sign-up sheets, like the one on pg. 141, can help the teacher divvy out extra time that is available on the computer. This is best done by priority rather than a first come, first-served basis. For instance, a student who needs to finish a report or presentation would have a higher priority than a student who wishes to play a game or just "mess around" on the computer.

MANAGEMENT HELPERS *(cont.)*

PROJECT LOG

A successful student project will have many components that need to be kept track of. This is not only necessary for grade and record keeping, but it teaches the students valuable organizational skills. The Project Log Sheet on page 142 can be customized to any project. Below is an example of a Status Sheet for a slide show project.

Project: _____   Due Date: _____

Status Sheet Slide Show Project Student Names										

Tech Tip: Most newer computers have a built in alarm clock that can be set to signal the user at a given time. These can be used to signal a student that his computer time is up.

MANAGEMENT HELPERS *(cont.)*

TROUBLE SHOOTING TIPS

The students are in their seats anxiously awaiting the amazing technology-assisted lesson that you have worked on for a week. You are ready to dazzle them with your lesson on ancient Egyptians that includes digital video clips of the pyramids and animation of the building of the Pharaoh's tomb when you turn to the computer and . . .

Problem	What Do I Do?
The computer won't turn on.	Check all the connections between the computer and the electrical circuit. Is everything on? Sounds silly, but it happens.
The mouse or keyboard won't respond or doesn't work properly.	Check all the connections between mouse/keyboard and the CPU. Clean the inside of the mouse by taking out the ball on the bottom and cleaning the lint or dirt from the rollers.
I can't find my file.	Both Windows based machines and Macs have Find File commands that will locate missing files.
The program won't run.	Make sure you don't have any other programs running at the same time. Restart your computer and try again.
The program runs, but the picture isn't very good.	Check to see if your computer is set for the correct amount of colors. On Windows and Mac there is a monitor control panel in the computer that operates this. Check the color settings on the monitor itself. These are usually buttons on the front or rear of the computer.
The printer won't print.	Is the printer on, plugged in? Are all the cables secure from the CPU to the printer?
The program won't save to a disk.	Is the disk unlocked? On the plastic 3.5" (8.75 cm) disks, this is done by sliding the switch in the corner so that you can see through the hole it covers. The 5.25" (15.6 cm) floppy disks are locked when a piece of adhesive tape is placed over the notch in the corner. Is the program saving to the hard disk drive instead? Choose "Save As" and direct the program to save onto the disk.

MANAGEMENT HELPERS (cont.)

LAB SCHEDULE MASTER

Week of: _____

Days/Time	Monday	Tuesday	Wednesday	Thursday	Friday
9-9:30					
9:30-10					
10-10:30					
10:30-11					
11-11:30					
11:30-12					
12-12:30					
12:30-1					
1-1:30					
1:30-2					
2-2:30					
2:30-3					

MANAGEMENT HELPERS *(cont.)*

COMPUTER LOG

Name	Date	Time On	Time Off	Project

MANAGEMENT HELPERS *(cont.)*

SIGN UP SHEETS

Name	Date	Project Needed	Date Due

MANAGEMENT HELPERS *(cont.)*

PROJECT LOG

Project: _____ **Project Dates:** _____

Student Name															

TEACHER TECH TOOLS

Teachers are inundated with task upon task that, although necessary, take time away from the most important job they have, teaching. In any given day, a teacher may have to write letters, calculate grades, create handouts, design lessons, write lesson plans, record attendance, document student behavior and progress, manage the classroom, produce incentives, decorate her room, etc., etc., etc. Every extra minute taken from one area is lost from another. This means that many times the craft takes a "back seat" to the secretarial tasks that must be completed.

One of the most important advantages of computers in the classroom is the increase of teacher productivity, creativity, and professionalism. Simply put, a computer can make your job easier and free up more time to teach.

Pages 144-159 are overviews of several tools that can increase teacher productivity, creativity and professionalism. These tools fall into the following four categories:

Information: Anything related to the acquisition of information related to teaching. Research, locating and gathering classroom resources, as well as news and communication are included.

Management: Anything related to the management of the classroom, including record keeping, physical arrangement of the classroom, and attendance.

Publication: This includes correspondence and documentation.

Presentation: Anything that has to do with the presentation of information, including simulations and lesson presentation.

Tech Tip: Remember, all technology tools have a learning curve. This means that there is an initial investment of time to reap the many benefits later. Some tools' learning curves are steeper than others. You must evaluate whether or not the initial time investment is worth the benefits you will receive. Each of the tools listed in the following pages has one of the following learning curve notations to help you evaluate its usefulness to you.

> **Steep Learning Curve:** Means that there is a relatively high initial time investment.
>
> **Moderate Learning Curve:** Means that the initial time investment is moderate.
>
> **Flat Learning Curve:** Means that the initial time investment is low.

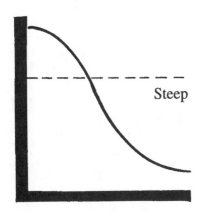

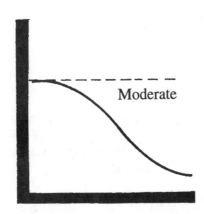

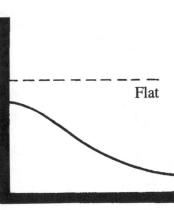

TEACHER TECH TOOLS *(cont.)*

ATTENDANCE AND RECORDS TOOLS

Teacher Task: taking attendance, viewing student records, student documentation

Learning Curve: Moderate

Suggested Software: *SASI* (Macro Educational Systems)

Advantages: Schoolwide programs like *SASI* are springing up everywhere. These extremely pricey programs do everything but tie your shoes. Most of them allow you to take attendance by clicking on the photograph of the student. All students needing readmit slips automatically pop on the screen the next day. This program works extremely well on a network, where the office gets all information transmitted to them. All administrative reports are automatically compiled for attendance. The usefulness for the teacher is in the classroom package. This package includes grade and portfolio management, student discipline and medical record access, and information reporting options. If your school doesn't have these tools now, the amount of labor required for attendance record keeping will probably force them to in the future.

Example:

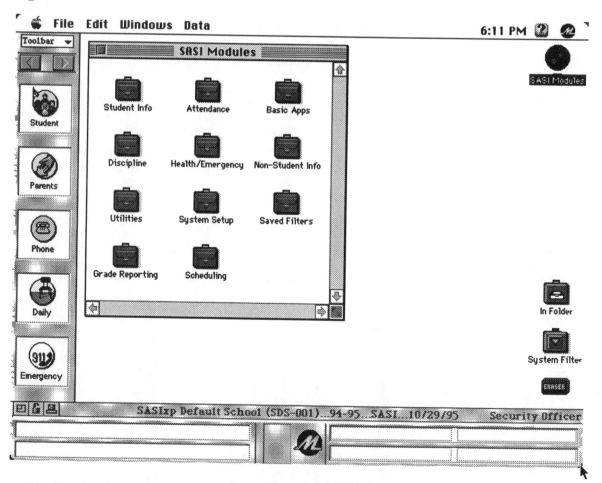

SASIxp (Macro Educational Systems)

TEACHER TECH TOOLS *(cont.)*

TELECOMMUNICATIONS TOOLS

Teacher Task: Researching information for lessons, sharing ideas with colleagues, networking with other educational professionals around the world

Learning Curve: Moderate to steep depending on the service

Suggested Software: *America Online, CompuServe, Prodigy, EWorld, Scholastic Network*, any Internet software and appropriate connection

Advantages: Telecommunications gives teachers access to a world of information. Most of the commercial online services have education areas where teachers can post questions on electronic bulletin boards, download lesson plans, take part in discussions, take professional growth classes, read periodicals, and participate in projects with other classrooms. Most of the topic areas are managed by experts in the fields. Teachers find that the e-mail alone is worth the cost of the service.

Example:

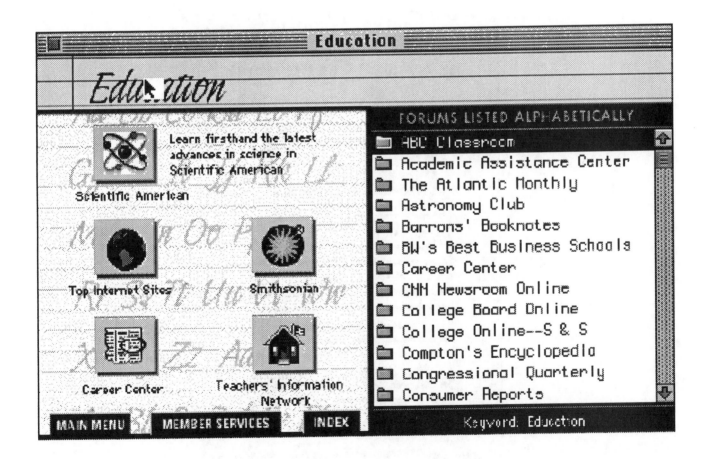

(America Online Education area)

TEACHER TECH TOOLS *(cont.)*

FILE AND DESKTOP SECURITY TOOLS

Teacher Task: Securing files that students should not have access to, making sure students don't accidentally erase files on the computer.

Learning Curve: Flat

Suggested Software: *At Ease*, *Fool Proof* (SmartStuff Software), *On Guard* (Power On Software), *KidDesk* (EdMark)

Advantages: Most computers in educational settings are used by a number of users in a given day. It is important to secure files from the occasional wandering mouse. File security programs allow the teacher to lock files and applications so that a password is required to access. Some other options include not allowing users to copy files and custom desktops for each user. *Fool Proof,* for example, allows the teacher to designate what programs a student can use, where his/her files can be stored, and what level of access they will have to the storage devices.

Example:

(*Fool Proof,* Smart Stuff Software)

TEACHER TECH TOOLS *(cont.)*

ELECTRONIC REFERENCE MATERIAL TOOLS

Teacher Task: gathering information and/or media for lessons and student projects

Learning Curve: Flat to Moderate

Suggested Software: *Grolier Multimedia Encyclopedia, Microsoft Bookshelf, Infopedia, Compton's Multimedia Encyclopedia, Macmillan Dictionary for Kids, Time Almanac*

Advantages: Electronic reference materials like encyclopedias, dictionaries, and almanacs on CD-ROM make research a snap. An entire set of encyclopedias with sound, photographs, and videos can be placed on one CD-ROM. The search tools included in these materials allow the user to search by name, subject, or title. Not sure what you're looking for? Type a keyword you think might be in the article. The computer will give you a list of articles in which the word occurs. Not sure how to pronounce a word? Most of the dictionaries will say the word for you. If you have the ability to project the image on a large screen, these reference materials become instant audio and visual aides.

Example:

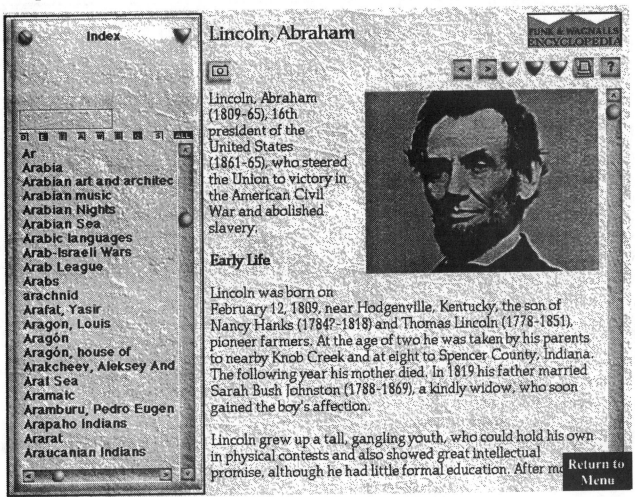

Infopedia (Future Vision Multimedia)

TEACHER TECH TOOLS (cont.)

PRESENTATION TOOLS

Teacher Task: Multimedia Presentation

Learning Curve: Moderate to steep depending on how involved you want to get

Suggested Software: *HyperStudio* (Roger Wagner Publishing), *Hypercard* (Apple), *Linkway* (Eduquest), *Kid Studio* (Storm), *Digital Chisel* (Perian Springs), *The Multimedia Workshop* (Davidson), *Kid Pix Studio* (Broderbund)

Advantages: The chalkboard is a valuable tool for teachers. Its drawback is that it is limited to static, two dimensional drawings and text. Presentation programs allow the teacher to go beyond the chalkboard to present lessons that come alive with pictures, drawings, animation, movies, speeches, sounds, and text. The computer becomes an electronic chalkboard full of color, motion, and sound.

Example:

*HyperStudio (*Roger Wagner Publishing)

TEACHER TECH TOOLS *(cont.)*

NEWSLETTER TOOLS

Teacher Task: Parent communication

Learning Curve: Moderate

Suggested Software: *Microsoft Works* (Microsoft Corp.), *Claris Works* (Claris), *Print Shop Deluxe* (Broderbund), *The Writing Center* (The Learning Company)

Advantages: Keeping communication lines open with parents is one of the most important jobs teachers must do. Parents are much more likely to be involved in their childrens education if they know what is happening in the class room. A newsletter is an easy way to keep those communication lines open. If you produce a classroom newsletter now or would like to, technology tools can make short work of it. Many word processors, like *Microsoft Works,* have pre-made newsletter layouts so that all you have to do is enter the text information. Once you have a layout you like, simply make it a template so that each newsletter is laid out the same way. If you repeat things year to year, save your newsletters on disk and then cut and paste any of the appropriate text into your new newsletter. This will save you even more time.

Example:

Microsoft Works 4.0 (Microsoft)

TEACHER TECH TOOLS *(cont.)*

GRANT WRITING TOOLS

Teacher Task: Obtaining funding for technology in the classroom

Learning Curve: Flat

Suggested Software: *Grant Writer's Assistant*

Advantages: Looking for some dough but tired of the bake sales? Why not try writing a grant for some of the millions of dollars in public and private money earmarked for technology? Grant writing programs like *Grant Writer's Assistant* can assist you in getting funding for technology by taking you step by step through the grant writing process. Since most grants for technology are similar, many times you can use the same information in each grant. There is an initial time investment, but it can pay big dividends. Remember, don't be discouraged if you don't get the first grant; it's a learning process.

Example:

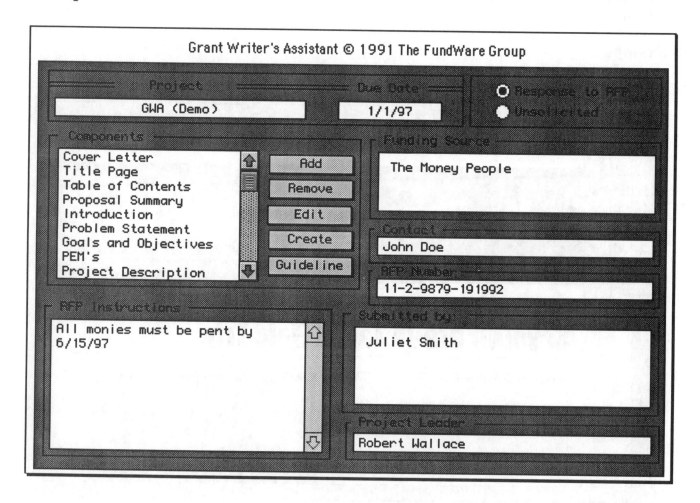

Grant Writer's Assistant (Fundware)

TEACHER TECH TOOLS *(cont.)*

CALENDAR TOOLS

Teacher Task: Creating calendars, staying informed of appointments and special events, time management

Learning Curve: Flat to Moderate depending on level of use

Suggested Software: *Calendar Maker* (CE Software), *Print Shop* (Broderbund), *Now Up To Date* (Now Software), Any word processor

Advantages: Teacher's lives are dictated by bells, whistles, and calendars. There are many different calendar programs, each with different levels of "functionality" built in. Some like *Print Shop* and *Calendar Maker*, simply make calendars that can be changed and printed. Others, like *Now Up To Date*, have more advanced features like audible warnings when appointments are due and "to do" lists that remain on calendars with daily reminders until they are done (very annoying but useful). Remember, if you're just making calendars for display or unit planning, better word processors have these templates built right in.

Example:

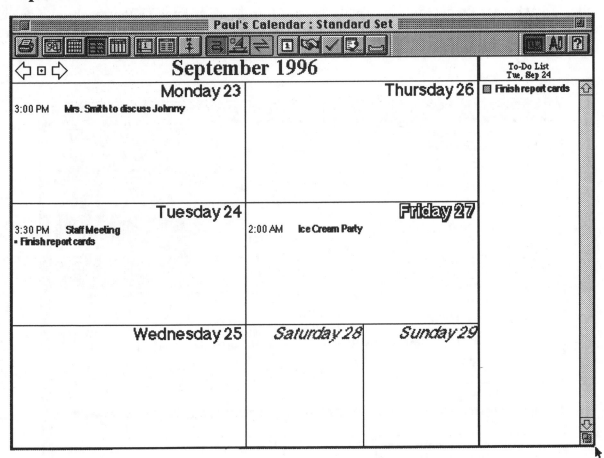

(Now Up To Date, Now Software)

TEACHER TECH TOOLS *(cont.)*

PORTFOLIO AND ANECDOTAL RECORD TOOLS

Teacher Task: creating different types of portfolios for each student, showing student progress over time, designing methods of storing student work, presentation of final product for teacher, student, parent and school officials

Learning Curve: Moderate to high

Suggested Software: *Scholastic Electronic Portfolio* (Scholastic), *Grady Profile* (Aurbach & Assoc.), *HyperStudio* (Roger Wagner Publishing), *Learner Profile* (Sunburst)

Advantages: Portfolios are a compelling and concrete way to display student progress over time. Portfolios are rapidly becoming an integral part of the classroom. When students participate in the creation of their own portfolio, they are motivated and develop a sense of pride and responsibility. One of the main drawbacks to paper-based portfolio management, however, is storage and the fragility of the actual file (or box). Electronic portfolios are powerful tools which transform the traditional paper portfolio into exciting multimedia presentations while solving the storage problem at the same time. Movies can be copied from a video cassette onto an electronic portfolio, artwork can be scanned and the images imported, students recording themselves narrating text are all ideas for an electronic portfolio. *The Learner Profile* (Sunburst) and *Newton Message Pad* (Apple) allow teachers to quickly make notes, collect data then "send" the data to a Mac or Windows based portfolio. One small box could hold all the portfolios for your entire class (on disk or CD-ROM).

Example:

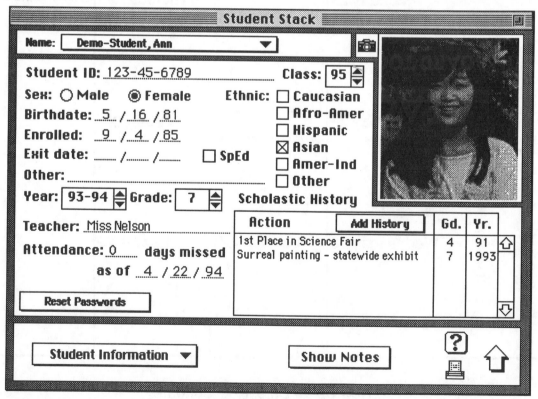

Grady Profile (Aurbach and Assoc.)

TEACHER TECH TOOLS *(cont.)*

BULLETIN BOARD TOOLS

Teacher Task: creating a variety of bulletin board displays

Learning Curve: Flat

Suggested Software: *Print Shop Deluxe* (Broderbund)

Advantages: For many teachers the job of tearing down and putting up a new bulletin board is not a favorite one. Not only is this task time consuming but all the decorative borders and clip art are expensive products usually paid for as out-of-pocket expenses by the teacher. Unfortunately, there hasn't been a computer invented yet that can tear down and put up new bulletin boards for you. However, the computer can save you a lot of money as well as give you more creative freedom and options where bulletin board displays are concerned. Graphics programs (like *Print Shop Deluxe*) contain hundreds of graphic clips and designs. These graphics cover many different themes like holidays, environment, school subjects, and sports. If you desire more extensive designs around a particular theme *Print Shop Deluxe* comes in theme specific packages ("Food and Dining," "Cats and Dogs," "People at Work" etc.) To make decorative-theme related art, choose a graphic and use the paint/draw tools to stretch it to the desired size. Print it on a color printer, or better yet, print it black and white and ask a child to color the design. Use the same strategy to make bulletin board borders. For the border you can choose from one of the standard borders included or design your own. Always keep in mind that students can do a great deal of this work too!

Example:

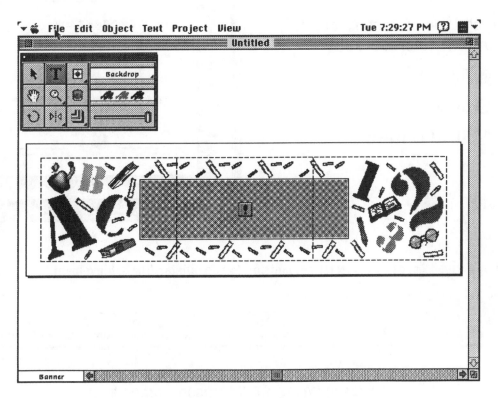

Print Shop Deluxe (Broderbund)

TEACHER TECH TOOLS *(cont.)*

INCENTIVE TOOLS

Teacher Task: creating certificates and awards for special and unique activities and situations

Learning Curve: Flat

Suggested Software: *Award Maker Plus* (Baudville), *Print Shop Deluxe* (Broderbund), any word processing or desktop publishing program

Advantages: It is a well known fact that educators spend much of their personal income on out-of-pocket expenses for their classrooms. One type of expense is in the area of rewards and incentives for students. Not only are commercial certificates and awards expensive, but they often do not address the specific behavior or activity you wish to acknowledge. There are many software programs available which give you the freedom and creativity to design your own incentives. Use a color printer to really dress up a certificate. If you don't have access to a color printer, use colored paper and add a sticker. Put your Tech Buddy to work in creating certificates for you, too.

Example:

Microsoft Works 4.0 (Microsoft Corporation)

TEACHER TECH TOOLS *(cont.)*

LESSON PLANS

Teacher Task: writing routine lesson plans, writing lesson plans for substitute teachers, writing repeat weekly and daily lesson activities in the plans

Learning Curve: Moderate

Suggested Software: Any word processing program (See Word Processing on page 159 and the bibliography of suggested software.)

Advantages: Writing lesson plans is one of many time consuming tasks required of teachers. Writing special plans for a substitute teacher requires extra time and consideration too. And there are often many repetitious activities each week or day that need to be handwritten into the schedule. Using a word processing software program can greatly save time and energy where lesson plans are concerned. Design computer-generated lesson plans by creating a template (standard blank form that will be used again) and input lesson instructions. A template can be easily created by using the "draw" or "paint" component of your word processing software. With this standard template, the automatic and routine activities (roll, calendar, silent reading, breaks, etc.) can be prewritten to eliminate the need of duplicate writing each week. Often there isn't enough room (or too much room) in the boxes in the printed lesson plan books. With a computer-generated template you can easily adjust the boxes to any size to fit the length of your written instructions. For substitute plans, invest some time and create two or three lesson plans for those last-minute situations. For those teachers who like to keep their lesson plan books of prior years for reference, computer lesson management is a much more efficient way. Depending on how you organize your files, lesson plans can easily be retrieved by date and several years of lesson plans can fit onto one disk. And typewritten lesson plans are neat and easier to read too!

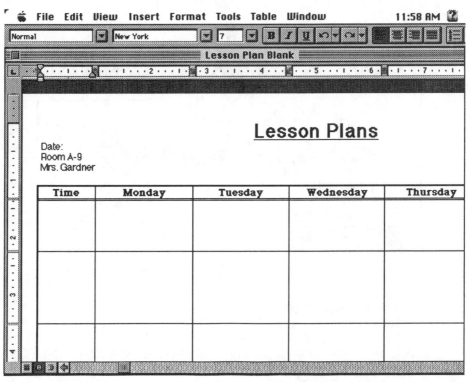

TEACHER TECH TOOLS *(cont.)*

SEATING CHART TOOLS

Teacher Task: seating charts for general use and substitutes, fairness in selecting students to answer questions and offer input

Learning Curve: Flat

Suggested Software: *Quick Seat* (HI-TECH of Santa Cruz)

Advantages: While primary level teachers may not have as much use for seating charts as do upper grade teachers there are some advantages to using this kind of computer program. Seating charts are also very beneficial substitutes or parent helpers however. With the continual rearranging of groups at the primary level it's helpful to have a graphic organizer of the classroom set-up. The computer program can design several different plans for tables and desks which you can use when creating student work groups. These plans are also handy when pondering what is the best way to set up your classroom. You can try a variety of configurations without having to actually move the furniture. These blank seating plans can also be used for interesting activities for students. Create a plan with just a few table symbols and use during center time as a record sheet for students when they rotate through centers. Make a blank form of the classroom set-up and students can use it for a map activity. *Quick Seat* has a feature which can print attendance sheets and class lists (by birthdays, last names, parent's name, etc.) and a student "random picker." When conducting a class simulation or other group activity the computer keeps track of who was called on last and randomly chooses names for equity.

Example:

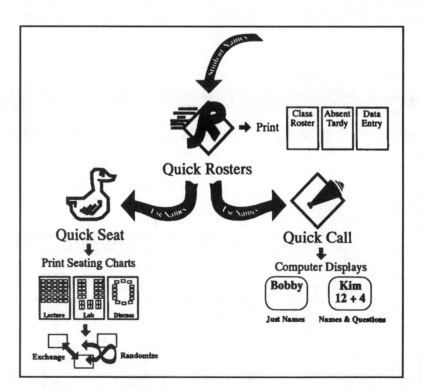

Quick Seat (Screen shot printed with permission from HI-TECH)

TEACHER TECH TOOLS *(cont.)*

SIMULATION TOOLS

Teacher Task: facilitating a simulation for the entire class

Learning Curve: Flat to Moderate

Suggested Software: *The Great Ocean Rescue, Choices! Choices*! (Tom Snyder Productions), *Science Sleuths* (Videodiscovery)

Advantages: Simulations are a terrific way of providing authentic learning experiences for children. Simulations require that kids work together and collaborate as teams. By working in cooperative learning groups, students not only learn valuable content, but critical thinking and social skills are reinforced too. Due to the rising popularity of simulations, there are many software-driven simulations available. There are several advantages to using a technology-driven simulation over a strictly paper-printed one. The computer can keep track of various management tasks like points, questions and answers, and random student picking. Some simulations use laserdisc technology (with barcodes) which allows for vast amounts of information, photos, movies, graphs, and other related data to be used. Without the aid of technology, the teacher would need to research, locate, and store all of the necessary materials him/herself. Technology-driven simulations take all of the work and administrative tasks away so the teacher can focus on facilitating and enjoying the activity.

Example:

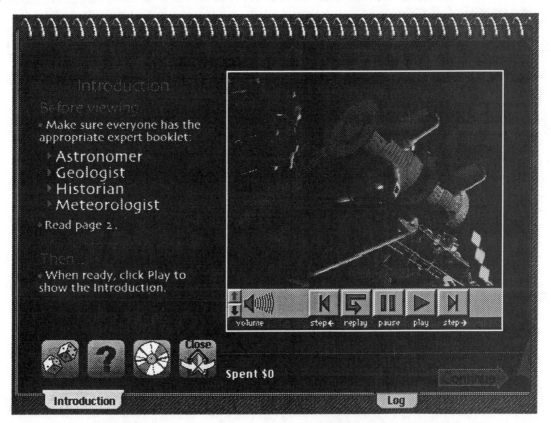

The Great Ocean Rescue (Tom Snyder Productions)

TEACHER TECH TOOLS *(cont.)*

CUSTOMIZED HANDOUT TOOLS

Teacher Task: creating tests, quizzes, puzzles, flash cards and other student response sheets

Learning Curve: Flat

Suggested Software: *Make a Flash #* (Teacher Support Software), *Teacher's Tool Kit* (HI-TECH of Santa Cruz, set includes *Word Search, Word Scramble, Word Match, Multiple Choice*), *Word Bingo* (HiTECH of Santa Cruz)

Advantages: Whether you are a primary or upper grade teacher there is always a time when some kind of standardized form is used. This form could be for assessment, a center activity, free exploration or group activity. Over the course of a year, teachers spend many hours creating and designing these forms by hand. Put the computer to work for you and cut your work time in half by using this kind of teacher utility software program. Imagine no more painstakingly written in letters in little boxes for cross word puzzles and word searches. Bingo cards can be created in just minutes. No more index cards and messy magic markers when making flashcards. Most of these programs are easy enough for an older student (Tech Buddy) to create many of these forms for you.

Example:

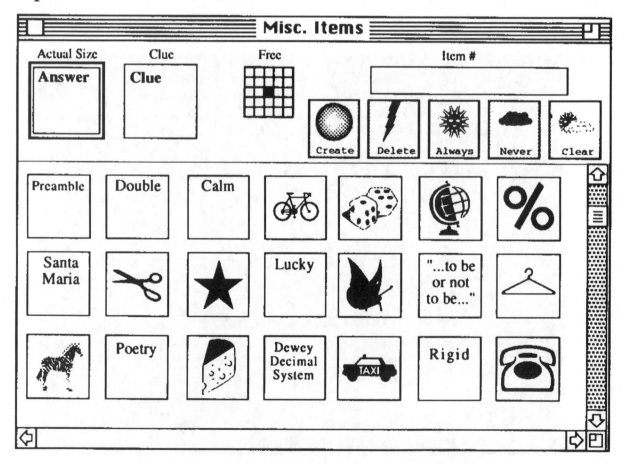

Word Bingo (Reprinted with permission from HI-TECH)

TEACHER TECH TOOLS *(cont.)*

WORD PROCESSING TOOLS

Teacher Task: letters to parents, summaries for student files, lesson plans, text to input in newsletters and multimedia projects, and any time typewritten text is used.

Learning Curve: Moderate

Suggested Software: *Microsoft Works* (Microsoft), *Microsoft Word*, (Microsoft) *Claris Works* (Claris), *WordPerfect* (WordPerfect)

Advantages: Word processing is a wonderful invention! It is a software application which is similar to typing on your old typewriter but it gives you much more power and freedom and takes away the pain of making corrections. By using a word processing program as opposed to a typewriter, you can choose the style, font, and size of your type easily. If, after typing a document, you decide you want a sentence or paragraph revised or moved, spot word processing allows you to quickly and easily "cut and paste" text. By using a word processor instead of a typewriter, you are able to save your document (either onto the computer or a disk) for later use; no more typing all of the text over. Many word processing programs also provide other helpful tools like databases, calendars, built in stationery (for educators and business), graphics and drawing tools. Aside from the ease of use, by using word processing your documents will have a professional and polished look. Typing is now actually fun!

Example:

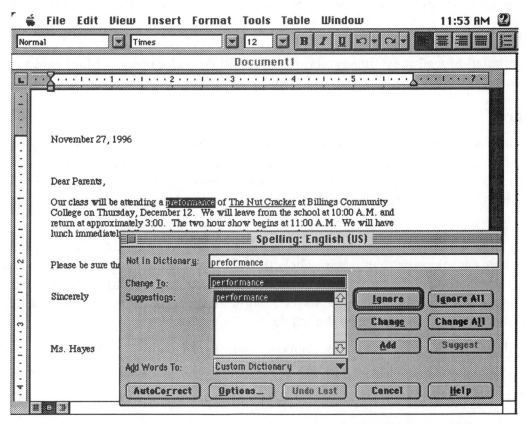

Microsoft Word © (Screen shot printed with permission from Microsoft Corporation)

THE GREAT ELECTRONIC ENCYCLOPEDIA

Grade Level: 5–8

Content Area: Study Skills

Skills and Concepts: Using an encyclopedia on CD-ROM, problem solving strategies, study skills

Hardware:

Mac or IBM multimedia computer with CD-ROM

Software:

Any multimedia encyclopedia (See suggested software page 32)

Other Materials:

- One Electronic Scavenger Hunt handout for each pair of students (page 162)
- The volume of a standard set of encyclopedias that includes space exploration

Summary:

This lesson is meant to introduce students to the use of electronic research tools. Students will use several strategies to search for information using the computer and an encyclopedia on CD-ROM.

Before the Lesson:

The teacher should spend some time exploring the CD-ROM encyclopedia. Make sure you know how to search using keyword, title, timeline, and media search tools.

Procedure:

1. Display the volume of the encyclopedia mentioned above and ask the class if they know what it is and what kind of information can be found in it. Talk about how one searches for information in it. Pick the subject of space exploration and have one of the students see how quickly they can find the information. Have him/her tell the class how much information (text, pictures) there is on the subject.

2. Using large screen projection options on page 23 or with groups on the computers, introduce the electronic encyclopedia to the class. Show them how to use the title, keyword, timeline, and media search tools. Use the title search tool to search for space exploration. Tell the class how many pages of text there are on the subject. Show all the media (e.g. photographs, sounds, video clips, animation) that is linked to the article.

3. Distribute The Great Electronic Encyclopedia Scavenger Hunt (page 162) to each student.

THE GREAT ELECTRONIC ENCYCLOPEDIA *(cont.)*

Management:

One–Computer Classroom:

Large Group Option: Using the large screen projection options on page 23, display the encyclopedia's menu of search options. Read the first direction on the handout. Tell the students that for each step in finding the information, you will move the selector over different parts of the screen. Tell them to give thumbs down if the selector is in the wrong position and thumbs up when it passes over the correct position. Move the mouse so that the selector passes over the search tools. When the class agrees that you are over the correct tool, click that tool. Repeat the steps until the information needed is found. Have the class write down their responses. Repeat for all the items on the hand-out. If you wish, have students lead the activity while you walk around and monitor understanding.

Rotation Option: Place the computer at the back of the classroom so as not to disturb the class. Rotate pairs of students through the computer to complete the activity. See the rotational station method on page 117.

Pod of Computers:

Determine how many students your pod of computers can support at one time. Then divide the class into equal groups of that size. Example: If your pod has five computers and each computer has room for two students to work together, it will support ten students. If you have 30 students in your class, you can divide the class into three groups of ten. Have the students rotate through centers during the class period. This allows the teacher to work with a small group while the computer group works independently. Possible companion centers include:

Writing: Have the students write a set of directions for finding information on an electronic encyclopedia. Later have the students read the directions as you follow them with the computer. This is a good demonstration of how to be complete when writing directions. It can also be very comical if you are quite literal when following the students' directions.

Research Center: Use a standard set of encyclopedias to find information on the same topics as in the scavenger hunt. Have the students compare the two mediums.

Computer Lab:

Utilize the lab at your school to complete the activity. This will give most of your students full access to the tools.

Extension Activities:

- Customize the scavenger hunt worksheet to involve topics that are being studied in class.
- Have the students explore the electronic encyclopedia and develop their own electronic scavenger hunt forms. They, in turn, challenge others to find the information.
- Develop custom scavenger hunts on other electronic resources such as atlases, dictionaries, almanacs or content area programs.

Tech Tip: Most multimedia computers have headphone jacks. Utilize headphones whenever students are working with media that includes sound. This will reduce distraction in class.

THE GREAT ELECTRONIC ENCYCLOPEDIA *(cont.)*

Scavenger Hunt

Name(s)_____ Date: _____

Use the search tools included in the CD-ROM encyclopedia to locate these items.

1. Browse the title index and find the article on kangaroos. Write the first sentence of the article below.

   _____

   _____

2. Use the keyword search to find "space." How many articles contain the word "space"?

   _____

   _____

   What article has the most occurrences of the word "space"?

   _____

   _____

3. Use the sound search tool to find a speech clip by an American president.

   What is the name of the president you chose?

   _____

   _____

   Write the first sentence in the speech clip below.

   _____

   _____

4. Use the video search tool to locate a video of an animal. Describe what the animal does in the movie.

   _____

   _____

5. Find an animation of a machine at work. What did the animation show?

   _____

   _____

6. Find a map of an African country. Tell the steps you used to find it.

   _____

U.S. HISTORY TIME LINE

Grade Level: 8

Content Area: History/Social Studies

Skills or Concepts: Vocabulary, teamwork, research, organizational skills, using reference materials on CD-ROM

Hardware:

Any IBM Compatible or Macintosh multimedia computer with CD-ROM

Software:

Any CD-ROM almanac, atlas or encyclopedia (See Suggested Software page 266)

TCM Resource Book: *Cooperative Learning Activities for Social Studies* (TCM 654)

Other Materials:

- One piece of butcher paper per team
- A set of felt tipped markers, crayons, or colored pencils for each team
- Glue or tape for each team

Summary:

Teams will create a time line highlighting significant events in U.S. history.

Before the Lesson:

Teach the students to use search tools included in CD-ROM reference materials.

Procedure:

1. Hand each group a copy of pages 165 and 166 (one epoch per team should be highlighted.)

2. Team members are to then use CD-ROM reference materials to research important events that happened during that epoch. If computer resources are limited, have other research materials available.

3. Team members then discuss and agree on five or six significant events that will be added to the class time line.

4. Team members must then work together to develop their section of the class time line. Printed images from the CD-ROM and drawings can be added to decorate the time line.

5. A spokesperson from each team can be chosen to present the time line to the rest of the class.

U.S. HISTORY TIME LINE *(cont.)*

Managment:

One-Computer Classroom:

If only one computer is available for this activity, use both electronic materials and standard print materials to complete the project. Give each group 15–20 minutes to find and print resources from the computer. These resources can be taken back and used along with other printed materials to complete the project.

Pod of Computers:

Centers Option: The pod of computers can act as a station in which each of the members of the group uses a different source such as an encyclopedia, atlas, almanac, or content CD-ROM to research the epoch.

Expert Option: In this option, a member or members is given the job of computer expert. While the others in the group design the timeline using printed media, the computer expert gathers electronic research and brings it back to the group.

Computer Lab:

The computer lab can be utilized so that all students have access to the research tools.

Extension Activities:

Instead of creating the time line conventionally have the students use the program *Timeliner* by Tom Snyder Productions. This program generates scaled time lines based upon the user's specifications. The program then prints the timeline with the specified information to whatever scale is requested.

Create an interactive time line using photocopied barcodes glued, taped, or laminated to the class time line. These bar codes can operate a laserdisc that displays images of the events. *GTV* by National Geographic or *Visual Almanac* by Voyager are great resources for this activity.

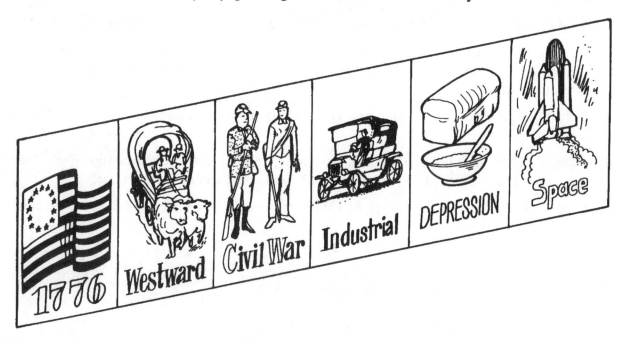

U.S. HISTORY TIME LINE *(cont.)*

U.S. TIME LINE

Directions: Your team has been given an epoch in U.S. history to research. An epoch is an interval of time or a period in the onward course of history. History is a record of our past.

An interesting way of looking at the events of our nation's past is through a time line. When your epoch is ready, it will be added to a time line which the whole class is making. One of the following epochs should be highlighted for your team.

U.S. History

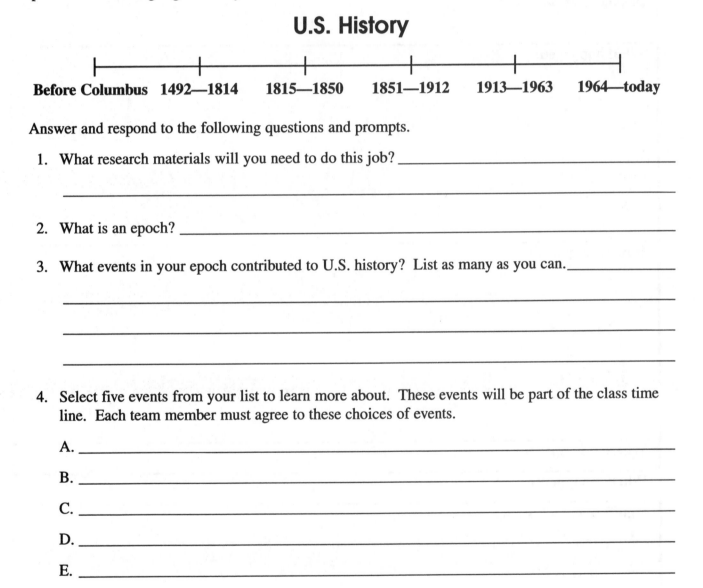

Before Columbus   1492—1814   1815—1850   1851—1912   1913—1963   1964—today

Answer and respond to the following questions and prompts.

1. What research materials will you need to do this job? _____

   _____

2. What is an epoch? _____

3. What events in your epoch contributed to U.S. history? List as many as you can._____

   _____

   _____

   _____

4. Select five events from your list to learn more about. These events will be part of the class time line. Each team member must agree to these choices of events.

   A. _____

   B. _____

   C. _____

   D. _____

   E. _____

U.S. HISTORY TIME LINE *(cont.)*

U.S. TIME LINE *(cont.)*

5. Complete the chart below for each event. You may wish to work together on a chart for each event, or you may assign team members different charts to complete. Each team should complete one chart for each of the five events chosen.

Title of event:
People involved:
What happened:
How it happened:
Where it happened:
When it happened:
Significance to history:
References used for this information:

SCALING THE SPACE SHUTTLE

Grade Level: 6–8

Content Area: Math/Science

Skills and Concepts: Size of the space shuttle, using interactive CD-ROM, observation, scale

Hardware:

- Any multimedia-capable IBM or Macintosh computer with CD-ROM, check software for minimum RAM required
- Large screen projection device (optional).

Software:

Space Shuttle CD-ROM (The Software Toolworks) or any CD-ROM encyclopedia

TCM Resource Book: *Space* (TCM 639)

Other Materials:

- Scaling the Space Shuttle handout
- At least 250 feet (228 m) of string per group
- One yard or meter stick per group
- One pair of scissors per group

Summary:

Students use the computer to gather size information about the space shuttle. They will then lay out the dimensions of the space shuttle with string, in order to visualize its size and name its components. Finally the groups will cut the string in order to gain a more concrete concept of scale.

Before the Lesson:

Experiment with *The Space Shuttle* CD-ROM or the multimedia encyclopedia article on the space shuttle. Locate cross sections, interior photos, interior and exterior photos, movies, and diagrams.

Procedure:

1. Divide the class into groups of three or four.
2. Distribute the Scaling of the Space Shuttle handout and tell the class that it is a scale drawing. This means that the drawing is proportional to the actual size of the space shuttle. Every dimension has been reduced in the same proportion. "It's smaller, but it looks the same." The length of the actual shuttle is to the length of the scale drawing as the width of the actual shuttle is to the width of the scale drawing.

SCALING THE SPACE SHUTTLE *(cont.)*

3. Have students use the CD-ROM to gather information about the shuttle orbitor, then complete the Scaling the Shuttle worksheet. Make sure that students have time to view photos and video clips in order to get an understanding of the size of the shuttle. (See hardware configurations below for management ideas.) This can be done prior to the lesson if computer resources are scarce.

4. Discuss the difference between the photo/diagram size and the actual size. Discuss the concept of scale, and that it is sometimes hard to visualize the actual size of something from a scale drawing.

5. Distribute the string, scissors, and yard sticks and move to the playground.

6. Have the students cut the string to the length and width of the shuttle. Then lay them on the ground in a "T" shape. It is easier to visualize if students stand at the ends of the strings.

7. Have the students cut two strings the length and width of the scale drawing. Have them determine how many of the smaller lengths will go into the corresponding longer lengths. Some students will pass the string end over end, others divide the larger measure by the smaller. They should then use the information to fill in the scale at the bottom of the drawing.

Management:

One–Computer Classroom:

Whole Class: Use large screen projection options to show the media and information about the shuttle. (See page 23.)

Pod of Computers:

Make your pod of computers one of three stations that the students will experience. In this station the group uses the CD-ROM to learn about the different parts of the space shuttle. The other two stations would include the size layout using string and the diagramming handout.

Computer Lab:

Have the students each experience the CD-ROM prior to or immediately following the other two activities. This will allow the students to have more access to the technology.

Extension Activities:

Write reports on the shuttle using the CD-ROM resources. Some of the topics covered by the CD-ROM are: Shuttle Missions, Mission Control, Training, Living in Space, and the Future of the Shuttle.

SCALING THE SPACE SHUTTLE *(cont.)*

Directions: Fill in the length and wing span of the shuttle in the blanks. Do NOT fill in the scale until after the activity.

Length: _____

Wing Span: _____

Scale: _____

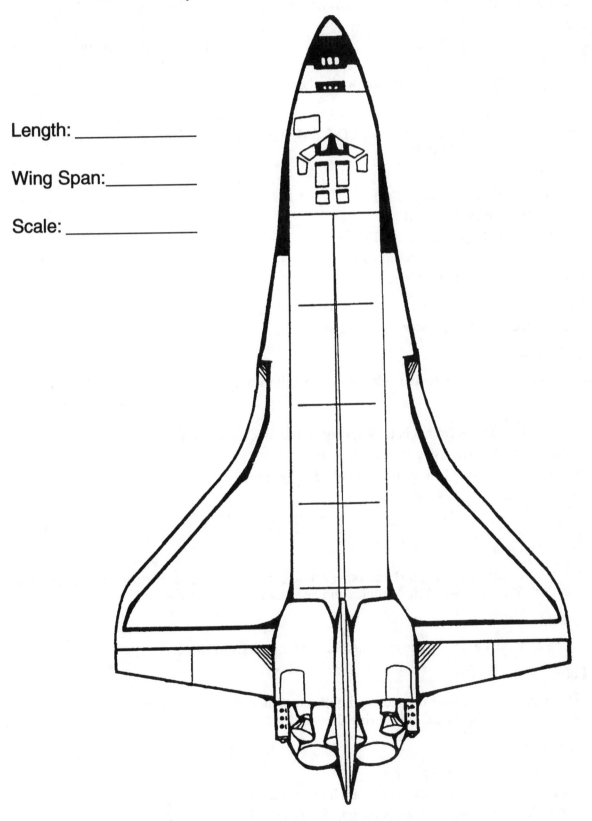

Greek Oratory

Grade Level: 5–8

Skills and Concepts: Ancient Greece, effective writing, public speaking, teamwork

Hardware:

- Computer with CD-ROM
- Any Electronic learning material relevant to the theme

Software:

Encyclopedia; *Ancient Greece*, Clearvue, CD-ROM, *Ancient Civilizations*, Entrex, CD-ROM, *Heroic Tales*, Westwind, CD-ROM

Materials:

- one story Frame per student (page 171)
- one set Oratory Topic cards (page173)
- one Prewriting Activity per pair (page 174)
- one Daily Writing Activity per student (page 172)
- several reference books on the subject

Summary:

Students will write and present an oratory to the class

Before the Lesson:

Teach students to use CD-ROM materials relevant to the unit to find information about their topics

Procedure:

1. Have students draw topics from a hat. Students with duplicate topics will be partners.
2. Have partners discuss roles using Prewriting Activity.
3. Do computer research based on decisions made during prewriting activity.
4. Write oratory using Student Writing Sample.

Management:

One-Computer Classroom:

Have students begin research by using text and other reference books. Excuse partners that are on-task to use the computer. Students should find articles and print them within a time limit.

Pod of Computers:

Same as one computer, only excuse more students for longer periods of time.

Computer Lab:

Have the student partners do all their research using the computer. Print out any articles that might be used for research and media for visual aids during the oratory.

Extension Activities:

- Use a word processor to write oratories.
- Use a hypermedia program to develop visual aides for the oratory.
- Do the oratory as a modern TV news editorial. Record it using a video camera.

GREEK ORATORY *(cont.)*

STORY FRAME

Name _____Date _____

Athens was the first_____. We have acquired many of our ideas about government from

the people of Athens, although there are many differences. Because they would grow up to vote, all of

the boys of Athens who would become citizens were educated. All of the_____of Athens

could vote in the_____.

Hovever, many of the people such as women, resident aliens, and_____were not

considered citizens. In fact, Greek citizenship had a very special status. The Greeks considered most

outsiders, especially those who spoke other languages, to be_____.

Athens was also famous for its arts and sciences. Its_____wrote plays that are still being

performed today; its_____delivered powerful speeches; and the work of

its_____are still read. A great thinker or_____was an important person.

Three of the most famous Greek philosphers are_____,_____,

and_____.

Athens also represents the highest achievements of Greek architects. They built many temples on

the_____, a fortified hill near the center of Athens. The most famous of these temples is

the_____, built in 447 B.C. in honor of Athena, the patron goddess of the city.

GREEK ORATORY *(cont.)*

DAILY WRITING ACTIVITIES

Use the activities as appropriate to your studies.

Myth

1. Do you think Prometheus did the right thing? Explain your answer.

2. If you had the skill of Daedalus and could make any machine that you wished, what would you make? Tell why.

3. How does this story explain the seasons of the earth? Try to make up another story that would explain why there are different seasons on the earth?

4. Explain how magic helps tell the story of *Jason and the Argonauts*. If you could have a magical power, which one would you choose?

5. Do you think the Greeks were justified in attacking the Trojans for the reasons given in the *The Iliad?* Why or why not?

6. Do you think this story makes war seem like a good thing to do? Why or why not? Do you know anyone who was involved in a war? What does he/she say about it?

7. Odysseus certainly had a great adventure. Imagine you went to a land where strange creatures lived and bizarre things happened. Describe your trip.

8. Both Odysseus and Penelope showed a lot of courage and determination in this story. Do you think one of them showed more or do you think they showed the same amount? Why or why not?

History

1. Imagine a whole new civilization were discovered tomorrow. What would you want to know about it?

2. Would you rather live in Athens or Sparta? Justify your answer.

3. What sport do you think demands the most strength and grace? Defend your answer.

4. In Greek, the word philosophy means "love of wisdom." Describe a person who you think is wise. Why is that person wise?

5. What do you think of women's lives in Greece? What parts of it were unfair?

6. Before people had money with which to buy things, they used a system called barter where people traded what they grew or made for what they needed. Would such a system work today in our culture? Why or why not?

7. Do you think the life of children in ancient times was easier or harder than it is today? Defend your answer.

GREEK ORATORY *(cont.)*

ORATORY TOPICS

	Athens		**Athens**
	Sparta		**Sparta**
	Plato, Socrates, and Aristotle		**Plato, Socrates, and Aristotle**
	Parthenon		**Parthenon**
	Oracle of Delphi		**Oracle of Delphi**
	Olympic Games		**Olympic Games**
	Minotaur/Crete		**Minotaur/Crete**
	Greek Gods		**Greek Gods**
	Trojan War		**Trojan War**
	Alexander the Great		**Alexander the Great**

GREEK ORATORY *(cont.)*

GREEK ORATORY
Pre-Writing

Name_____Date_____

Directions

- Draw a topic slip with the name of your topic on it.
- Find the classmate who drew a duplicate slip. He or she will be your partner.
- Start preparing for your speech by completing the activities on this page.

Activities

1. Start by discussing the topic with your partner. Use the questions below to guide your discussion. What will you need to research? How will you divide the work?_____

_____

_____

_____

How will you divide the speech? Who will do which part? _____

_____

_____

_____

2. Do your research and meet to write your speech. The teacher will tell you how much time you have.

ELECTRONIC RESEARCH

Grade Level: 4–8

Skills and Concepts: Research, interpreting and applying information

Content Area: All

Hardware:

Computer with CD-ROM

Software:

Any Electronic Learning Material

Other Materials:

One to three Electronic Research Recording Sheets per student or group of students

Summary:

The student will conduct research on a given topic and record sources.

Before the Lesson:

Teach students to use CD-ROM materials. Select writing topic(s) and outline subtopics.

Procedure:

1. Set the stage for the activity by telling the students that they will be researching their topics using the computer. Remind the students that the text or media they are selecting must relate to the topic.

2. Distribute Research Recording sheet. Go over directions.

3. Allow students to explore computer resources that apply to the topic, filling out the Recording sheet as they go.

Extension Activities:

- Use a word processor or desktop publisher to capture text or media.

- Use a hypermedia program to develop an interactive project. (See Creativity and Presentation Lessons on pages 202–221.)

- Use the Internet search tools to locate information and media needed. (See Telecommunications Tools on pages 88–109.)

ELECTRONIC RESEARCH *(cont.)*

ELECTRONIC RESEARCH RECORDING SHEET

Name: _____ Date: _____

1. Title or Description:_____
   _____

   Type of Media:_____ Source: _____

   How does this relate to your topic?_____

   _____

   _____

   How will it add to the overall effectiveness of your project? _____

   _____

   _____

2. Title or Description:_____
   _____

   Type of Media:_____ Source: _____

   How does this relate to your topic?_____

   _____

   _____

   How will it add to the overall effectiveness of your project? _____

   _____

   _____

3. Title or Description:_____
   _____

   Type of Media:_____ Source: _____

   How does this relate to your topic?_____

   _____

   _____

   How will it add to the overall effectiveness of your project? _____

   _____

   _____

IN TIMES OF CRISIS

Grade Level: 7–8

Content Area: Social Studies

Skills and Concepts: Identifying and defining crisis, researching, note taking

Hardware:

- IBM or Macintosh compatible computer
- Printer

Software:

Any U.S. History content CD-ROM, such as *Point of View: An Overview of U.S. History* (Scholastic Software), *Time Almanac* (TimeWarner)

Other Materials:

In Times of Crisis handout (page 179)

Summary:

In this lesson, students identify a president and at least one crisis that took place while he was in office.

Before the Lesson:

Spend time familiarizing yourself with the program that will be used. Teach the students to use the search devices included in the software.

Procedure:

1. Students should select a president and read the article about him. It is best if students are required to pick different presidents.

2. Students should select at least one major crisis that the president faced.

3. Using the In Times of Crisis handout, students print out or take notes on information central to the president and the crisis.

4. Have each student review the information he/she found with the class. Some questions might include the following: What presidents were faced with a similar crisis? How did each react? Which presidents were more proactive? Reactive? Which were better in times of crisis? Does history view their efforts differently than the people did at the time?

IN TIMES OF CRISIS *(cont.)*

Management:

One-Computer Classroom

Students can be assigned this activity several days before the in-class discussion so that it can be completed in a rotational schedule.

Pod of Computers:

The pod of computers can serve as a rotational station as described on page 119.

Computer Lab:

Instead of using the worksheet, have each student fill in his/her notes on a word processor. They can also copy and paste important quotes that support their comments from the reference program to their documents.

Extension Activities:

- Use a word processor to write a report about the crisis. Insert pictures taken from the software to add meaning to the report.

- Have the students make several Venn diagrams that compare the events and the leaders. Draw programs can be utilized to make these, then the image can be placed in reports.

Cuba Missile Crisis

IN TIMES OF CRISIS *(cont.)*

Name(s): _____ Date: _____

Name of President: _____

In office from: _____ until _____

Describe the crisis which was faced:

_____

_____

_____

_____

How did the president deal with the crisis?

_____

_____

_____

_____

How does history judge his handling of the crisis?

_____

_____

_____

_____

How would you have handled the crisis?

_____

_____

_____

_____

TAMING THE THESAURUS REX

Grade Level: 4–8

Content Area: Language Arts

Skills and Concepts: Using the thesaurus, identifying adjectives and adverbs, identifying or using descriptive language, following written directions.

Hardware:

Any IBM or Macintosh compatible computer

Software:

Any word processor with a thesaurus, such as *Microsoft Works* (Microsoft), *Microsoft Word* (Microsoft), *Claris Works* (Claris), *The Student Writing Center* (The Learning Company)

Other Materials:

Paper and pencils

Summary:

This activity is meant as an introduction to using the thesaurus on a computer. The students will compare an original paragraph to one with more descriptive language.

Before the Lesson:

Become familiar with the thesaurus program. If it is built into a word processor, practice checking and replacing words in a paragraph. Teach the students how to launch the program, search for a word, and replace words with the thesaurus.

Procedure:

1. Have each student write an original paragraph describing a family member. It will be nearly impossible to write a description without using adjectives and adverbs. (This can be done away from the computer if resources are minimal.)

2. Go over the directions on the task card carefully with the class. If you have a large screen projection device, model the task for everyone to see.

3. Give the students copies of the task sheet on page 182 to use at the computer.

4. After completing this exercise, have the students read both paragraphs to the class to determine which is better.

TAMING THE THESAURUS REX *(cont.)*

Management:

One-Computer Classroom:

Because of the time that it takes students to input text, it will be impossible for everyone to do this activity on one computer. Assign some students to do this on the computer with others working with printed thesauruses. This activity can be done several times during the course of the year using a different writing subject each time. In this way students will each get to use the computer and everyone willbenefit from the increase in vocabulary.

Pod of Computers:

Managed the same way as the one-computer classroom, but with more students using the computers.

Computer Lab:

Doing this activity in a lab setting will mean that each student should be able to finish in one class period.

Extension Activities:

- Have students use the thesaurus to enhance their creative writing.
- Use the thesaurus to define vocabulary words.

TAMING THE THESAURUS REX *(cont.)*

Task Sheet

1. Start a new document in a word processing program.

2. Type your paragraph at the top of the page. Be sure to use correct spelling and punctuation.

3. When you finish your paragraph, you will need to make a second copy below the first. One will be left as it is, the other will be edited using a thesaurus. To do this you must do the following:

   - Highlight the paragraph by going to the Edit menu and select "Select All"

   - Return to the Edit menu and select "Copy"

   - Move the cursor below your original paragraph. If there are no empty lines between your original paragraph and the cursor, press the return or enter key 23 times to make spaces.

   - Return to the Edit menu again and select "Paste".

   - You should have a second copy of the paragraph below the first

4. Find the first adjective in your paragraph and highlight it by using the mouse to double-click the word.

5. Find the thesaurus in one of the menus at the top of the screen and choose it from the list. (It is in different menus depending on the program you use.)

   The thesaurus is under the _____ menu in my program.

6. The thesaurus will give you several synonyms (words with the same meaning) for the word you have highlighted. If one is better than the adjective that you wrote click "Replace". If none are better click "Ignore" or "Cancel."

7. Repeat steps 4-6 for all the adjectives and adverbs in your paragraph.

8. When you finish, save your writing and print out your page.

AUTOBIOGRAPHICAL POEM

Grade Level: 4–8

Content Area: Language Arts

Skills and Concepts: To introduce, inform, and analyze poetry

Hardware:

Any IBM or Macintosh compatible computer

Software:

- Any word processor, such as *Microsoft Works*, *Word* (Microsoft), *Claris Works* (Claris), *The Student Writing Center* (The Learning Company), etc.

- An electronic clip art collection

Other Materials:

- Clustering Worksheet (page 185)
- AutoBio Poem Worksheet (page 186)

Summary:

Students analyze themselves to provide an introduction to the rest of the class. He/she will use a word processor to add pictures to a poem that describes themselves.

Before the Lesson:

Practice inserting pictures from a clip art collection. Class time can be saved if you provide students with a printed copy of a clip art collection that can be used to make selections. Clip art collections are fairly inexpensive and can be found at most software retailers.

Procedure:

1. Teacher should model the process of clustering using the attached Clustering worksheet.

2. Have the class do the cluster worksheet about themselves.

3. Using the clustering worksheet, the teacher should model the writing of a ten-line autobiographical poem with the class. Here is an example:

Line 1:	Your first name:	Mary
Line 2:	Four descriptive traits:	Honest, caring, curious, energetic
Line 3:	Sibling of...	Sister of Mark
Line 4:	Lover of.....	Laughter, sports, challenge
Line 5:	Who feels...	Happy when boating
Line 6:	Who needs...	Friendship
Line 7:	Who gives...	Encouragement
Line 8:	Who fears...	Pain and sorrow
Line 9:	Who would like to see...	The end of hunger in the world
Line 10:	Your last name	Jones

AUTOBIOGRAPHICAL POEM *(cont.)*

4. Have the class write their own poems using the AutoBio Poem worksheet.

5. Students will then type the poems into a word processor and insert pictures that relate to their descriptions next to the lines that they correspond to.

Management:

One-Computer Classroom:

Once the poems are finished, use the traditional rotation method to finish the publishing of the poems. (See page 113.) If a printed book of the electronic clip art images is available, have the students insert the index number near the picture line which they want it. This will decrease the time they will spend at the computer.

Pod of Computer:

This activity works very well as a station-type activity. (See page 119.)

Computer Lab:

Use a draw or paint program to customize the clip art before placing it in the document. This is done by placing the clip art image in a paint program and using the assorted tools they offer to change the original. Make sure the students use the "Save As" command to save their new clip art image as a different name. Otherwise the original will be changed to their modified version. This can be avoided by locking the original. See software documentation to find out how to lock originals.

Extension Activities:

Have the students make their own collection of clip art by using a screen capture program to collect pictures from other programs. For example, if a program has a drawing or photo you like, you can use a screen capture program to make a copy of it. These can then be used to insert into documents. These programs are available free or for a low cost through online services and the Internet. Software retailers also carry several different types of these programs.

AUTOBIOGRAPHICAL POEM *(cont.)*

CLUSTERING ACTIVITY SHEET

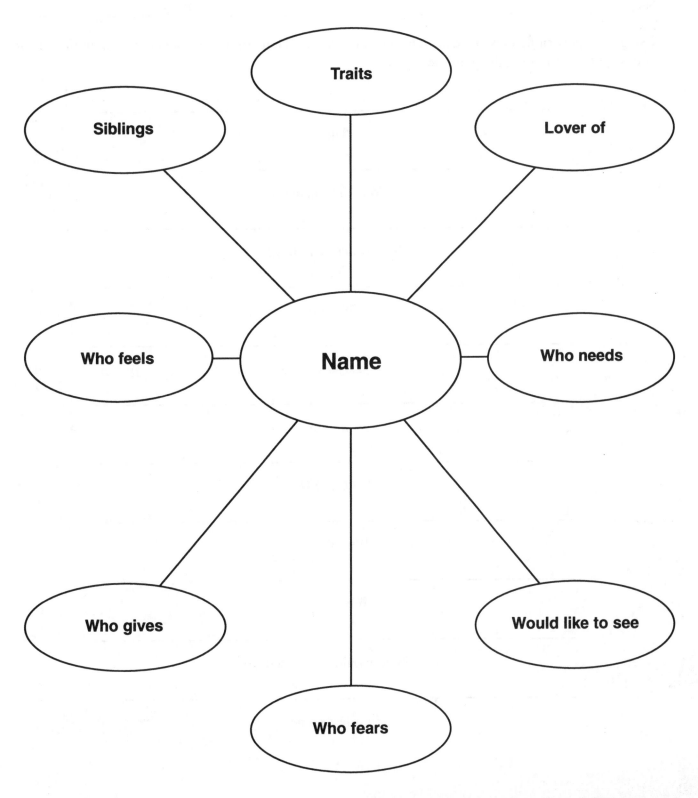

AUTOBIOGRAPHICAL POEM *(cont.)*

AUTOBIO POEM

Name: _____ Date: _____

Using your prewriting cluster, write your poem below. In the margin, make any notes about the clip art you would like to use in the published copy.

_____

Title

_____

Your first name

_____ _____ _____ _____

Four descriptive traits

_____

Sibling of

_____

Lover of

_____

Who feels

_____

Who needs

_____

Who gives

_____

Who fears

_____

Who would like to see

_____

Your last name

FORM LETTER TEMPLATES

Grade Level: 4–8

Skills and Concepts: Writing a business letter, making a word processing template

Hardware:

- Any computer that supports word processing capabilities
- Printer

Software:

Any word processor, such as *Microsoft Works*, *Word* (Microsoft), *Claris Works* (Claris), *The Student Writing Center* (The Learning Company), etc.

Other Materials:

Business Letter Template handout (Page 189.)

Summary:

Consumers get form letters all the time. Now your students can use the same technology that the marketing companies use to send out large mailings. The students will develop a template of a business letter, omitting certain pieces of information that will become specific for each form letter. They will then use the computer to generate several letters to different companies whose products they enjoy. Many companies have promotional products they send out to students who write them. Have the students bring in several packages of products they enjoy.

Before the Lesson:

Be sure to understand the "Save As" command in a word processor. This command allows the user to save an existing letter document by another name. In order to keep the original form letter intact, the students will need to save their changes as another name.

Have students collect addresses of companies whose products they like or even dislike from labels and packages.

Procedure:

1. Introduce the skill of business letter writing.

2. Tell the students that they will be writing a form letter to a number of companies whose products they enjoy.

3. Pass out Business Letter Template instructions and go over together.

4. Based upon the amount of computer resources, assign students to the computers with instruction sheet and addresses of companies.

FORM LETTER TEMPLATES *(cont.)*

Management:

One–Computer Classroom:

To save computer time, put together a template on the word processor that has the placement of return address, receiver's address, date, greeting, body, and salutation. The student will then input the information and use the Save As command to make his/her template.

Computer Pod:

Make the pod a center where the form letters are produced. Companion centers might include studying about the role of advertising in business, developing a product description, putting together an advertising campaign for a product.

Computer Lab:

Have letters written by hand before going to the lab. This will speed up the process and allow the students to create more letters.

Extension Activities:

- Have students send form letters to lawmakers expressing views on issues.

- Have students send letters to professional or college sports teams. Sports almanacs list addresses of college and professional teams.

- Have students design their own personalized letterhead as a template activity.

- Have students write invitation letters to parents for parent night activities.

- Put together a database of the addresses companies, sports teams, lawmakers, parents, etc. (See Data Analysis lesson plans page 78.) Use mail merge to automatically address the form letters.

FORM LETTER TEMPLATES *(cont.)*

Name: _____ Date: _____

BUSINESS LETTER TEMPLATES

Many times businesses make letter templates so that they can send many copies of the same letter to different people. A template is a document that is set up beforehand with things like a heading, body, and closing that are the same. All you have to do each time is type in the information that is different for each letter. With the aid of the computer you can now make letter templates.

Instructions:

1. Start the word processor and get a blank document.

2. Type the information in the heading, greeting, body, and closing that will be the same in every letter. Use the correct form of a business letter. Leave blanks where information will be different.

3. Save the letter, giving it a name like "Business Template." This template will always be the same if you don't save any changes with the same file name.

4. Now reopen the "Business Template" and type the specific information for the business that you are writing.

5. If you want to save this letter, choose the **Save As** command and give the letter another name, possibly the name of the company you are sending it to. Now you have two files: one is the Business Template, and the other is the company letter.

6. If you want to do another letter open the Business Template again. All the spaces for specific information should be empty.

7. Repeat the steps as many times as you need letters.

8. Print the letters.

AN ECOLOGICAL NEWSPAPER

Grade Levels: 6–8

Content Area: Science, Language Arts

Skills and Concepts: Newspaper writing, research, editing, cooperating

Hardware:

- Any computer that supports word processing with columns
- Printer
- Scanner (Optional)
- Digital Camera (Optional)

Software:

Any word processor, such as *Microsoft Works, Word* (Microsoft), *Claris Works* (Claris), *The Student Writing Center* (The Learning Company), etc.

Other Materials:

- Proofreading Symbols handout, one per student (page 192)
- News Story Outline handout, one per student (page 193)

Summary:

This is a cooperative learning activity in which students create a newspaper about ecological issues. Each student in the group takes on the role of a different type of newspaper writer. The computer is used to publish the finished project.

Before the Lesson:

Learn to make a column-type newspaper/newsletter layout in your word processor or desktop publishing program. You will need to teach one person from each group how to do this. This student will take on the role of editor, deciding what stories go where and completing the layout.

Spend a period having students explore a real newspaper to find out how it is organized. Teacher Created Materials publishes an excellent series of resource books called *Using the Newspaper*. These have several good lead-up activities to producing your own newspaper.

AN ECOLOGICAL NEWSPAPER *(cont.)*

Procedure:

Use a publishing program to arrange all the articles into a newspaper by cutting and pasting each into a template. This can be done by students or the teacher. If your school has a wide carriage printer, this can be done in the same size as a newspaper.

Management:

One-Computer Classroom

Have the editors in each group type and layout the group's newspaper on the computer. This activity can be adapted to other units throughout the year allowing the students to produce different editions. The editor's job can be rotated so that everyone has a chance to layout the newspaper. In subsequent editions, the first editor can help train the new editors.

Pod of Computers:

A. Have all the editors work on the computers to complete the project at one time.

B. Have each team use the computers to type and edit their stories. Then transfer all the story documents to one computer with a disk so that the editor can copy and paste the stories into one layout.

Computer Lab:

Same as Pod option B.

Extension Activities:

Go on a field trip to an area that has ecology issues related to it. (Ex: a landfill, building area, national park, industrial area). Take pictures with a digital camera (or with a regular camera and have them digitally developed) for use in newspaper.

Write form letters (see form letter activity) to lawmakers asking for their views on certain ecological issues.

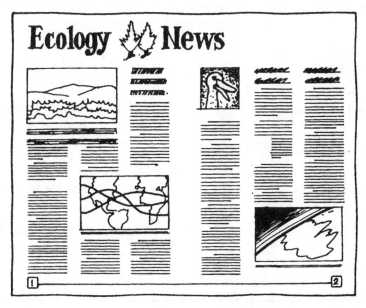

AN ECOLOGICAL NEWSPAPER *(cont.)*

PROOFREADING SYMBOLS

Proofreading is a necessary and important aspect to newspaper writing because information published should be as accurate and neat as possible. Some symbols have been devised to indicate what changes must be made.

When you proofread you should first determine which words or changes need to be made. Next, circle the word or area. Then, write the proper proofing mark.

A sample paragraph has been proofed below, and at the bottom of the page is a proofreading chart for you to keep handy when proofing anything you write.

There are over 1,000 endangered animals in the united states alone. dolphins beavers brown bears, and the bald eagle are just a few of the species that may become extinct if steps are not taken to protect them Other animals that are on the endangered list include the gorilla, Siberian Tiger, elephant, cheetah, giant panda, and the chimpanzee.

You can help save these animals by following the 3 helpful guidelines below.

- Buy tuna from companies who do do not catch or process dolphins.
- Learn about endangered species in your locale. Write to your Congresman and enlist their help.
- Do not buy any thing made out ivory, tortoise shell, or reptile skins.

Cut out:

Proofreading Chart

◡	tighten up spaces	spell	spell out the word
¶	start a new paragraph	^	insert (a letter, word, comma, hyphen, apostrophe)
no	should not begin a new paragraph	℘	delete (letter or word)
( )	use parenthesis	lc	use lower case letters
#	add more space	≡	use a capital letter
-	use a hyphen	⊙	use a period

AN ECOLOGICAL NEWSPAPER *(cont.)*

NEWS STORY OUTLINE

News stories are built around the five W's (WHO, WHAT, WHERE, WHEN, WHY) and HOW. A good news reporter uses these key words to make sure that all the important information is included in a story. In addition, the words help to organize facts and serve as an outline for taking notes.

The following outline will help you organize your notes for your story.

Date:

WHO:

WHAT:

WHEN:

WHERE:

WHY:

HOW:

Other Details:

HISTORIC PAMPHLETS

Grade Level: 6–8

Content Area: Social Studies, Language Arts

Skills and Concepts: History content, writing skills, mapping skills

Hardware:

- Any IBM or Macintosh compatible computer with a word processor
- Printer
- Scanner (optional)

Software:

- Any word processor, such as *Microsoft Works*, Word (Microsoft), *Claris Works* (Claris), *The Student Writing Center* (The Learning Company), etc.
- An electronic atlas on disk or CD-ROM (optional)
- A multimedia encyclopedia (optional)

Other Materials:

- Pamphlet Layout Worksheet (pages 196 and 197)
- Several different informational travel pamphlets (optional)

Summary:

This lesson is meant as a culminating activity for any history or geography unit on a specific country, state, or other geographic region. Students will develop an informational pamphlet on the area that they have studied.

Before the Lesson:

You and your students should learn how to change the page layout in your word processor to landscape. This mode lays out the paper in a horizontal fashion. Since this is a trifold pamphlet, you should also be able to create three equal columns with enough space in between to fold the paper without losing words. To save time, make a template of the layout for the students to use.

If you have an older word processor that does not support columns, make each column a separate page of a document and set the margins the same width as one column. After the document is printed, just cut it apart and glue it into a pamphlet. To save time, make a template of the layout for the students to use.

HISTORIC PAMPHLETS *(cont.)*

Procedure:

1. Tell the students that they will be creating informational pamphlets for the area that they have been studying. Have the students look at several different pamphlets from historic monuments, other states or countries, amusement parks, etc. Then brainstorm a list of attributes that effective pamphlets have. (e.g., Colorful title column, Ten Reasons to Go There, Sights and Sounds, Map column, The People, etc.)

2. Have each student or group of students decide on six attributes. One should be the title.

3. Have the students fold the Pamphlet Planning work sheet on pages 196 and 197 as shown below and use it to plan the layout of their pamphlet. Title each section, draw squares where pictures will go and label them, and draw lines where text will go.

4. Have students write the text for all the parts. Make sure to tell the students that they should be as brief but as descriptive as possible in each section.

5. Have the students collect pictures for their pamphlets. (See the software section page 54 for ways of collecting digital pictures). Atlas and encyclopedia programs are good sources for the media.

6. Put together the final pamphlet on the computer.

Management:

One-Computer Classroom:

Use cooperative learning groups of 36 members to complete the project. Have each student take one or two different sections of the pamphlet. The teacher should set up a template for each group to work from.

Pod of Computers:

If each student is completing a project individually, use the Rotational Station Method on page 119. If you have chosen the cooperative group method, make as many groups as you have computers. On publishing day, divide up each group so that the project group works on one computer to complete the project.

Computer Lab:

Students should work individually or in pairs to complete the project. Students should complete the layout and write the sections prior to going to the lab.

HISTORIC PAMPHLETS *(cont.)*

PAMPHLET LAYOUT WORKSHEET

Directions: Draw squares where pictures should be placed. Make notes in the squares about what type of picture needs to be there. Place the pictures where they belong.

Title Panel

Back Panel

Inside Fold

HISTORIC PAMPHLETS *(cont.)*

PAMPHLET LAYOUT WORKSHEET

Open Inside Right Panel

Open Inside Center Panel

Open Inside Left Panel

SPELL CHECKER SPELLING

Grade Level: 4–8

Content Area: Students with special needs in Language Arts

Skills and Concepts: Spelling, using a spell checker

Hardware:

- Any IBM or Macintosh compatible computer with a word processor
- Printer

Software:

Any word processor with a spell checker, such as *Microsoft Works*, *Word* (Microsoft), *Claris Works* (Claris), *The Student Writing Center* (The Learning Company), etc.

Other Materials:

List of Spelling Words

Summary:

Students with spelling difficulties can be trained to use the spell checker to overcome weaknesses and strengthen skills while learning to use the spell checker. The student will type a list of words and then use the spell checker to identify the appropriate spelling.

Before the Lesson:

Understand how to use the spell checker.

Procedure:

1. Have one student dictate spelling words to another who types them into the word processor.

2. After each word, have the student use the spell checker to identify the correct spelling. If the spelling is incorrect, the spell checker will display a list of words that are close in spelling to the attempt. If the student can identify the correct spelling in the list, he/she chooses that spelling and moves on. If the word is not in the list, the student must try different spellings until the word can be found. This strengthens the word identification skill of spelling. Note: Many proper nouns are not in spell checkers. If your list includes words that are not in the spell checker, they can be added to it using the custom dictionary option.

Management:

One-Computer Classroom:

Have pairs of students work on this while others in the class work on other spelling assignments.

Pod of Computers:

Have one student give the words to a larger group of students.

Computer Lab:

Teacher gives the words to the all of the students who practice the skill.

Extensions:

Once the skill has been mastered, use the spell checker on writing and other assignments.

WANTED POSTERS

Grade Level: 4–8

Content Area: Language Arts, Literature

Skills and Concepts: Reading comprehension, character analysis, descriptive language

Hardware:

- Any IBM or Macintosh compatible computer
- Printer
- 35mm camera

Software:

Any word processor that has a draw program, such as *Microsoft Works, Word* (Microsoft), *Claris Works* (Claris), *Story Book Weaver* or a separate draw program like *Kid Pix* (Broderbund) or *Flying Colors* (Davidson)

Other Materials:

Character Analysis worksheet page 201

Summary:

The students will make wanted posters of characters in pieces of literature using pictures of themselves that they modify to look like the character.

Before the Lesson:

Take pictures of all the students in class and have them digitally developed (See Capturing Pictures page 54.) It is a good idea to do this 2–3 times throughout the year so that updated photos can be used in projects and teacher-made awards. Learn to use the draw program included in most word processors. Open a photograph in the draw program and change it with the draw tools. Save the photo and insert it into a word processing document. Make a template of the wanted poster to save computer time.

Procedure:

1. Have the students use the Character Analysis worksheet to brainstorm words and phrases that describe the character traits of one of the main characters in the story.

2. At the computer, have the students open their photo in a draw program. Tell them to use the draw tools to make their pictures look like the character.

3. Have them save the new pictures as a different file name to avoid replacing their original picture with the modified one.

WANTED POSTERS *(cont.)*

4. Have them insert the picture that they modified into a wanted poster template that you made prior to the class.

5. Have students type their character descriptions below the picture.

6. Print and display these around the room. They are quite an incentive for learning about characters in a piece of literature.

Management:

One Computer Classroom:

Use the pass-it-on-method (page 132) for teaching students how to create their posters.

Pod of Computers:

Use the Rotational Station Method (page 119) to manage the completion of these projects.

Computer Lab:

Make several copies of the disk with student's pictures on them. This will keep students from being off task while waiting to work on their pictures.

Extensions:

Student pictures can be used for several different projects including:

- student awards
- portfolios
- autobiographies
- newsletters

Have a wanted poster contest. Awards can be given for best physical description, best character description, best art work, and best overall design.

WANTED POSTERS *(cont.)*

Name: _____ Date: _____

WHAT A CHARACTER!

Directions: Choose your favorite character from a piece of literature and answer the following questions.

Character's Name: _____

What does the character look like?

_____

_____

_____

_____

Find as many words as you can from the book that describe what the character looks like.

_____

_____

_____

Describe what type of person the character is. Find words from the book that describes his personality.

_____

_____

_____

What does the character do that leads you to believe that he/she is how you describe him/her?

_____

_____

_____

_____

FIELD TRIP SLIDE SHOW

Grade Level: 4–8

Content Area: Any

Skills and Concepts: Planning, cooperation, effective presentations, using a slide show program

Hardware:

- An IBM or Macintosh compatible computer with multimedia capability
- One of the following:
- A digital camera, regular 35mm camera, or scanner

Software:

Any presentation program such as *Kid Pix Studio* (Broderbund), *HyperStudio* (Roger Wagner Publishing), *Digital Chisel* (Perian Springs). Newer versions of integrated word processing (Works) programs, such as *Claris Works* (Claris) and *Microsoft Works* (Microsoft) have built-in presentation components.

Other Materials:

- Slide Show Storyboard (page 204)
- Slide Detail Worksheet (page 205)

Summary:

Following a field trip, students will work in cooperative groups to make a digital slide show that presents what they saw as well as what they learned. Although this lesson is centered around a field trip, any in or out of class activity can be used.

Before the Lesson:

If your school has a portable digital camera, take pictures of important activities during a field trip. (See page 27.) Use the camera's software to transfer the pictures to the computers that students will be using to do this activity. If your school does not have a digital camera, use a 35mm and either have the film digitally processed or scan the pictures with a scanner (See page 54.) Spend time learning how to make a slide show with whatever presentation program you have available. Put together a short slide presentation to use as an example during class.

Procedure:

1. Divide the class into groups of four and assign the following roles to members of each group:

    Graphic Artist: Does the art and layout of the project

    Engineer: Puts the project together on the computer

    Writer: Writes the descriptions that go into the project

    Director: Is responsible for making sure that the entire project comes together based on the group's vision for it. Also helps resolve conflict between the members of the group.

FIELD TRIP SLIDE SHOW *(cont.)*

2. Tell the students that they will be working together to create a digital slide show of sights and/or activities that they have experienced during their field trip. Show a slide presentation that you put together.

3. Have them brainstorm major activities and/or sights.

4. Have the students settle on a set number of slides. Five to ten is usually good for the first slide show.

5. Have the groups plan their shows using the Slide Show Storyboard Worksheet. Groups will need one worksheet for every six slides in their show. The show should tell the story of the trip.

6. Groups should complete one Slide Detail Sheet for every slide in their show.

7. The Engineer uses the Slide Detail Sheets to create the slideshow.

8. If a large screen projection device is available, groups should present the slide show to the class or others. (See page 23.)

Management:

One-Computer Classroom:

Plan the show as an entire class, then have groups develop sections of the slideshow. The culmination of their efforts will be a single slide show.

Pod of Computers:

Have Engineers use the computers to start laying out the slide show after the group finishes the storyboard. As the groups finish the detailed sections, they are given to the engineer for completion. Make sure that other activities are available for down time.

Computer Lab:

Have the groups complete the preliminary planning prior to going to the lab. Have them divide up the slides so that everyone puts one together on the computer. The engineer then puts all the slides together into a slide show.

Extension Activities:

Video tape the slide show to take home. (See page 202.)

Have the slide show run in a continuous loop during parent nights or other school activities.

FIELD TRIP SLIDE SHOW *(cont.)*

SLIDE SHOW STORYBOARD

Name(s): _____ Project Name: _____ Date Due: _____

Directions: Lay out the story of your slide show here. Make notes and sketches that summarize what each slide will contain.

Slide 1

Notes

Slide 2

Notes

Slide 3

Notes

Slide 4

Notes

Slide 5

Notes

Slide 6

Notes

FIELD TRIP SLIDE SHOW *(cont.)*

SLIDE DETAIL WORKSHEET

Name(s) _____ Project: _____ Date: _____

Directions: Sketch what you want the slide to look like in the box. Be sure to include titles and where any text will be located. Write the text in the space provided below.

\
\
\
\
\
\
\
\
\
\
\

_____

_____

_____

_____

What transition effects will be used?

_____

Will there be a sound or recording?   Yes   No

If so, describe the sound or recording that will be used.

_____

OCEAN COMMUNITIES HYPERMEDIA REPORT

Grade Level: 5–8

Content Area: Science and language arts

Skills and Concepts: Ocean animal communities, writing an informational report, using a hypermedia program to develop a presentation

Hardware:

An IBM or Macintosh compatible computer that supports multimedia

Software:

- A Hypermedia program like *HyperStudio* (Roger Wagner Publishing) or *Linkway* (IBM Eduquest)
- Optional media sources
- *The Great Ocean Rescue* CD-ROM (Tom Snyder Productions)
- A multimedia encyclopedia, such as *Grolier* or *Compton's*
- *The Sea World Homepage* http://www.seaworld.com

Other Materials:

- Hypermedia Planning Sheet (page 208)
- Ocean Communities Storyboard (page 209)

Summary:

This is meant to be a culminating project in which students display their knowledge of ocean animal communities. The entire learning process will take several days of work. The students will, individually or in groups, create a menu-driven hypermedia report about ocean animal communities.

Before the Lesson:

The students should have a good working knowledge of their hypermedia authoring program. They will need to be able to create screens, add photographs, construct buttons and add movies (optional). See page 65 for a detailed explanation of what these hypermedia programs are.

Procedure:

(Week one or during the unit)

1. Students should research and write detailed reports on the three ocean animal communities. Their writing will become the core of the hypermedia report. Tom Snyder Productions' *The Great Ocean Rescue* is a great resource for teaching this topic as well as all the ocean sciences. It is designed to be an entire teaching unit with four different class simulations. Text books and other reference materials can also be used. The three communities include:

   - polar communities
   - temperate communities
   - tropical communities

OCEAN COMMUNITIES HYPERMEDIA REPORT *(cont.)*

(Week Two)

2. After the report is finished, students should explore different computer resources in search of media (photos, diagrams, sound clips, video clips) that will support and enhance their writing. Sources might include those listed in the optional media section above. See Electronic Research on pages 175 and 176, and capturing pictures on page 54.

3. A story board detailing the project should then be done to give the students a conceptual basis for the project. See Ocean Communities Storyboard.

4. Using their storyboard as a guide, students need to plan the detail for each screen of the project. See Hypermedia Planning Sheet.

(Week 3)

5. The students then create the computer project using their planning sheets and storyboard as guides.

6. Finally, the projects should be displayed or presented to the class. They can also be videotaped for viewing at home (See pages 24 and 25.)

Management:

One-Computer Classroom:

Because of the amount of time it takes to put this type of project together, usually a week of 40-minute periods for the computer portion, it is unlikely that an entire class would be able to complete this project on a single computer. Divide the project up among teams so that each has a part of the total project.

Pod of Computers:

This type of setting is perfect for this project. Have students work in pairs and rotate into the computers in the Rotational Station Method discussed on page 114. Other stations can include the reading of a literature book with an ocean theme and doing science experiments and activities.

Computer Lab:

The extra resources of the computer lab make it very suited for this activity. Make sure that all the preliminary activities, such as Storyboarding and Planning Details, are finished prior to starting the lab.

OCEAN COMMUNITIES HYPERMEDIA REPORT *(cont.)*

COMPUTER HYPERMEDIA PLANNING SHEET

Name(s): _____   Date: _____

Topic: _____   Screen Number: _____

Directions: Complete one of these sheets for every screen in your multimedia report. Draw the screen as you want it to look. Indicate the placement of graphics, drawings, buttons. Answer the questions below.

Notes	File Edit Move Tools Objects Colors

1. Describe the background of the screen. What, if any graphics or drawings will you use? What source(s) will you use for the graphics (clip art libraries, paint tools, scanner)? _____
   _____

2. Describe the use of text on this screen. Will the text be in a text block? Where will the text be located? _____
   _____

3. Describe any buttons on this screen. What actions will the buttons carry out? (i.e., play digital movies, animation or sounds, link to other screens, etc.) _____
   _____

OCEAN COMMUNITIES HYPERMEDIA REPORT *(cont.)*

OCEAN COMMUNITIES HYPERMEDIA STORYBOARD

Name(s): _____ Date: _____

Directions: Roughly sketch what the screens will look like. Be sure you indicate buttons, text, pictures, and movies.

WHAT'S IN A CIRCLE?

Grade Level: 7–8

Content Area: Math

Skills and Concepts: Visualization of math concepts, the area of a circle, using a paint program.

Hardware:

An IBM or Macintosh compatible computer with multimedia capability

Software:

- A paint and draw program, such as *Kid Pix* (Broderbund), *Flying Colors* (Davidson), or any integrated word processing program that includes a draw component
- Large screen projection device (optional)

Note: There are math paint and draw programs available, such as *Geometry Concepts* by Ventura. This program has tools specific to math and is fantastic for visualization of math concepts.

Other Materials

"What's in a Circle?" handout (one per student, page 212)

Summary:

The students will use a paint program to cut apart a circle in order to estimate its area.

Before the Lesson:

Become familiar with a paint and draw program. Make sure that you are able to use the selector tool to "cut out" portions of the circle. This lesson assumes that the area of regular polygons has been covered and students have a good knowledge of the concept.

Procedure:

1. Discuss with the class that circles, like other polygons, have area. This area is expressed in the amount of square units.

2. Pass out the "What's in a Circle?" handout and go over the directions.

3. Depending on the amount of computer resources available, complete the exercise as individuals, groups, or as a demonstration using a large screen projection device.

WHAT'S IN A CIRCLE? *(cont.)*

Management:

One-Computer Classroom:

This activity is best done as a presentation using some type of large screen projection strategy. (See page 23.)

Pod of Computers:

Have students work in pairs to complete the activity. Other stations can include the more abstract calculations using pi.

Computer Lab:

This is the best environment for this particular lesson. Students can learn to use the paint program and learn the concept at the same time.

Extension Activities:

- Cut and paste the picture into a word processor and write an analysis of the activity.

- Do the same activity with other polygons.

- Introduce the concept of pi and use Geometer's Sketch Pad to show how it was discovered.

WHAT'S IN A CIRCLE? *(cont.)*

Name: _____ Date:_____

The area of a circle is expressed in square units. This is sometimes hard to see because squares don't fit inside circles evenly. A computer paint program can help you estimate the area of a circle. Follow the directions below to estimate the area of the circle above.

1. On the computer screen, draw a perfect circle with the radius of 1.5 inches (3.75 cm). If your paint program does not have measuring rulers, hold this paper up to the screen so that the background glows through it. Draw the circle using the one above as a guide. **Note:** Most paint programs require you to hold down the "shift" key while using the oval tool in order to make a perfect circle.

A   1.5 inch   B
         (3.75 cm)

1 inch (2.5cm)

1 inch (2.5 cm)

2. Using the square tool, draw several one inch squares on the bottom of the screen. **Note:** Most paint programs require you to hold down the "shift" key while using the rectangle tool in order to make a perfect square. Fill in the square with a color different from the outline of the circle.

3. Estimate the amount of one inch squares that could be placed on the circle._____

4. With the cut tool, place the squares into the circle. Cut off pieces of squares to fit irregular areas. Keep track of how many whole squares and fractions fit into the circle.

5. About how many squares fit into the circle? _____

6. Was your estimate high or low? _____

7. Is a circle an efficient use of space? Why or why not?

_____

_____

_____

INTERACTIVE LIMERICK

Grade Level: 5–8

Content Area: Language Arts

Skills and Concepts: Writing poetry, using a hypermedia program

Hardware:

- An IBM or Macintosh compatible computer with multimedia capability
- A microphone (built in to many multimedia computers)

Software:

A hypermedia program, such as *HyperStudio* (Roger Wagner Publishing), *Hypercard* (Apple), *Digital Chisel* (Perian Springs), *Multimedia Studio* (Davidson)

Other Materials:

- "Limerick" handout (page 215)
- A poetry book with several examples of limericks
- An interactive book like *Broderbund's Living Book series* (optional)

Summary:

The students will create an interactive poem much like *Interactive Children's books* that are so popular on CD-Rom.

Before the Lesson:

Spend some time familiarizing yourself with your hypermedia program. At minimum, students will have to know how to use the text tool and create a button that activates a recorded sound.

Procedure:

1. Read several limericks to the class so that they learn the rhythm. Show the class an interactive book like *New Kid on the Block* by Jack Prelutsky (Broderbund).

2. Teach the students the poetic form of a limerick.

3. Pass out the *"Limerick"* handout and complete the practice section.

4. Have the students write a humorous original limerick.

INTERACTIVE LIMERICK *(cont.)*

5. Have the students type the limerick on a single screen of a hypermedia program.

6. Place buttons that activate sounds over any words that rhyme. Record funny sounds that are associated with the rhyming words. When the user activates the button, the sound will play.

Example:

I once knew a man who went to the Sun. When the "Sun" button is clicked with the mouse, a student recorded sound says, "Whew, it's hot!"

Management:

One-Computer Classroom:

Use the Pass It on Method to teach students how to put together this project. If students work as partners, they will be able to help each other with the program. (See page 132.)

Pod of Computers:

This activity runs very smoothly using the Rotational Station Method of management. (See page 119.)

Computer Lab:

Because of all the recording, this activity can be relatively loud. You may want to reinforce that others are recording around them and low volume levels are needed.

Extension Activities:

- Make interactive children's books and share them with an elementary school "buddy" class. Note: Broderbund's interactive stories are great examples of interactive books.
- Make hypermedia poetry books that have many different styles of poetry included.
- Use animation and other special effects included in many hypermedia programs to create other unexpected twists in the interactive poem.

INTERACTIVE LIMERICK *(cont.)*

LIMERICK

A Limerick is a five-lined poem with a rhyme scheme of a-a-b-b-a. Lines 1, 2, and 5 are longer than lines 3 and 4. Here is an examle.

> There once was a teacher named Gray
>
> Who said to his students one day,
>
> "Now, you have until one,
>
> Get a Limerick done."
>
> The class groaned the hour away!

Fill in the blanks in the Limerick below. Use the words from this list that follow the rhyme scheme and make sense.

silly	right	McCorn	tear is	embarrass
trance	horn	around	fight	dynamite
Darris	up	dance	chilly	enhance
rip	Yance	trip	ground	hilly
McBright	pup	Willy	born	sight

There once was a young boy named _____ a

For whom nothing could ever be_____ a

'Til at lunch he did _____ b

And we all heard a _____ b

But I won't tell you where the _____ ! a

Make up your own Limerick. You may use any rhyming words from the list above or some rhymes of your own. Make it funny!

_____ a

_____ a

_____ b

_____ b

_____ a

AN INTERACTIVE BOOK REPORT

Grade Level: 4–8

Content Area: Literature, language arts

Skills and Concepts: Reading comprehension, parts of a plot, evaluation

Hardware:

an IBM or Macintosh compatible computer with multimedia capabilities

Software:

A hypermedia program, such as *HyperStudio* (Roger Wagner Publishing), *Digital Chisel* (Perian Springs), or *Linkway* (IBM)

Other Materials:

- Interactive Book Report worksheet (pages 218 and 219)
- Hypermedia Planning Sheet (page 208)

Summary:

The students will use a hypermedia program to make an interactive book report. The information that the students must report is very specific, but how it is presented is very open-ended and creative.

Before the Lesson:

The teacher should spend time learning how to use different media and objects (like buttons) on the screen prior to teaching the use of the program. This lesson assumes that students have working knowledge of the program. See The Creativity and Presentation section for tips on the teaching of these types of programs. Students should complete the writing and planning portion of the project prior to using the computer.

Procedure:

1. Students should fill out the Interactive Book Report worksheet on a book that they have finished reading.

2. Using Hypermedia planning sheets, students will use the information to design screens that illustrate the parts of the story. They will need one sheet for each of the following:

   -characters

   -setting

   -plot

   -introduction, problem, steps to solving the problem, resolution

   -conclusion

   -review evaluation

AN INTERACTIVE BOOK REPORT *(cont.)*

3. Students should be allowed to use any media that enhances the telling of the story. They should also have a plan as to how the screens will be linked.

4. After the planning sheets have been approved, students can use them to create their book reports on the computer. Make sure that they stick to their original plan or they will not finish in a timely fashion.

Management:

One-Computer Classroom:

Use this project as a reward for completing- a predetermined amount of books. This becomes an incentive and can be done during silent reading periods.

Pod of Computers:

Have a third of the class work on these projects for a week while others read and/or plan their projects. The students then rotate in week-long time periods.

Computer Lab:

Students should complete planning sheets prior to going to the lab.

Extension Activities:

HyperStudio allows you to link the projects to a menu or index. Create a link for a classroom book review. Students can use this index when deciding on a book. If the school library has a computer, *HyperStudio* can be used by the entire student body.

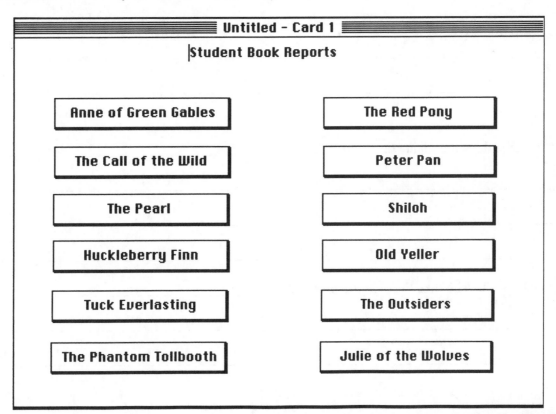

Untitled – Card 1

|Student Book Reports

Anne of Green Gables	The Red Pony
The Call of the Wild	Peter Pan
The Pearl	Shiloh
Huckleberry Finn	Old Yeller
Tuck Everlasting	The Outsiders
The Phantom Tollbooth	Julie of the Wolves

AN INTERACTIVE BOOK REPORT *(cont.)*

INTERACTIVE BOOK REPORT

Name: _____ Date: _____

Book Title _____

Author: _____

Publisher: _____

Main Characters:

Name and description of the main characters.

Character Name: _____

Description: _____

Character Name: _____

Description: _____

Setting:

Describe the setting (time and place) of the book. _____

_____

_____

_____

Plot:

What problems does the main character(s) face? _____

_____

_____

_____

What steps does he/she take to solve the problem? _____

_____

_____

AN INTERACTIVE BOOK REPORT *(cont.)*

HOW DOES THE BOOK END?

Evaluation:

Did you enjoy the book? Why or why not?

_____

_____

_____

_____

_____

_____

_____

_____

If you were selling this book to someone, what would you say to them in order to get them to buy it?

_____

_____

_____

_____

_____

_____

_____

_____

_____

MULTIMEDIA MATH MAGIC

Grade Level: 4–8

Content Area Math

Skills and Concepts: problem solving, analyzing a problem

Hardware:

- An IBM or Macintosh compatible computer with multimedia capabilities
- Large screen projection device (page 23)

Software:

A hypermedia or slide show presentation program such as *HyperStudio* (Roger Wagner Publishing), *Kid Pix Studio* (Broderbund), *Digital Chisel* (Perian Springs), *Claris Works 2.0* or higher (Claris)

Other Materials:

Paper and pencil

Summary:

The students will create a slide show that illustrates the steps to solving a math problem. They will then become guest speakers teaching the class how to do the computations.

Before the Lesson:

Students should be assigned different types of computational or problem solving exercises. Each receives different types of problems with several examples. This can be as simple as assigning them a skill in a math text book. Students need to master the skill and then use one problem as an example to write an analysis of the steps used in solving it, with visual aides.

Procedure:

1. Tell the students that they each will be teaching a math lesson over the next few weeks. They will be using the computer as an aid to do this.

2. Day one: Assign each student a different skill that they must master. This can be as simple as using a math text book to divide up the skills. Tell them that they need to learn how to solve one problem and then write an analysis of how they solved it.

Example: Adding decimals to other decimals 367.92 + 1238.205

> **Step 1:** Write the two decimals over each other so that the decimal points line up.

MULTIMEDIA MATH MAGIC *(cont.)*

Step 2: Bring the decimal straight down under the sum line.

Step 3: Add the numbers making sure the sums are directly below the add ends and carry where necessary.

3. Day Two: Have the students make a slide show that shows the steps of solving the problem. (Use one slide per step.) More advanced computer students can even use animation to illustrate the skills.

4. Subsequent Days: Using a large screen projection device connected to the computer, have the students introduce the new skills to the class by showing their slide show and explaining the steps.

Management:

One-Computer Classroom:

Have student partners make the slide shows for lessons that will be presented 2–3 weeks later. Rotate the class through the computer station one team per day.

Pod of Computers:

Have several students work on their presentations each day. Depending on the amount of computers and the sophistication of the problems, you should be able to finish a class rotation in a week. This means several lessons and lesson plans are finished for a month.

Computer Lab:

If the planning is done ahead of time and the students are familiar with the program, students should be able to complete this assignment in one to two periods.

Extension Activities:

- Use the slide show lessons to help students catch up when they have missed school. A returning student can view the lessons that he/she missed at the computer.

- Create slide shows of more complex problem solving and logic exercises. Geometric concepts are easily introduced using the drawing tools in these programs.

HOW'S THE WEATHER?

Grade Level: 4–8

Content Area: Science, language arts

Skills and Concepts: Observation, making a hypothesis, analyzing, descriptive writing

Hardware:

An IBM or Macintosh compatible computer with an Internet connection

Software:

Either a Web browsing program, such as Netscape or Mosaic, or a commercial online account that supports the World Wide Web

Other Materials:

- How's the Weather? Map Task Sheet (page 224)
- How's the Weather? Worksheet (page 225)
- blue, green, and red crayons

Summary:

The students will look at a series of weather satellite images in order to make a hypothesis about the direction that weather patterns move in the United States.

Before the Lesson:

Using a web browsing program, open the URL for The Space Science and Engineering Center (SSEC) at http://www.ssec.wisc.edu/data/index.html#sst and use the task card to duplicate what the students will be doing. These sites change periodically, so you may have to update the task card. There are satellite images of the United States in 12 hour intervals. Open each by clicking the corresponding hotlinks (colored words that act like buttons). Make a bookmark for the site so that students can easily navigate there. In most web browsers this is done by going to the Bookmark menu and choosing "Add a Bookmark." The bookmark now appears in the bookmark menu.

Procedure:

1. Team the students in pairs to complete the lesson.

2. Tell the students that they will be looking at pictures of the United States taken from a weather satellite and will be making a guess or hypothesis about the patterns of weather in the United States. Which way do storms usually move? Can we predict where a storm is going?

3. Tell the students that they need to follow the directions on the task card very carefully.

HOW'S THE WEATHER? *(cont.)*

4. Pass out the task cards and maps to the class. Have students go to the computer and complete the assignment.

Management:

One-Computer Classroom:

This project can be done over several days. The data will be different, but the student's hypothesis about the movement of storms should be similar. If being on the network is costly, print one set of the pictures for students to look at without signing on to the Internet. This can also be done as a whole class activity using a large screen projection device.

Pod of Computers:

Use the rotational station activities to allow students to use this Internet tool. Other stations can include various weather patterning exercises and experiments.

Computer Lab:

If the lab has the ability of multiple simultaneous connections, have each student or pairs of students complete the exercise.

Extension Activities:

- Check the satellite images over several days to track storms as they move.

- Have students do a videotaped weather forecast. Bring up the images on the computer screen or large screen projection device and position the video camera so that both the screen and the student can be seen. Have the student explain the weather patterns.

- Make a slide show of several images. The images can be copied and inserted into a slide show. The pictures can then be run in a loop so that they appear animated.

HOW'S THE WEATHER? *(cont.)*

HOW'S THE WEATHER? TASK SHEET

Name(s) _____ Date _____

1. Make an Internet connection and start the web browsing program.

2. With the mouse, go to the Bookmark menu and choose The Space Science and Engineering Center (SSEC) bookmark. The connection may take a few minutes to complete.

3. Click on the hotlink (colored word) for a 36 hour satellite image. This is a picture of the United States from a satellite within the last 36-hours.

4. With a blue crayon, copy the outline of the cloud pattern shown on the screen to your map. Use the states as a guide and be as accurate as you can.

5. Click the Back button at the top of the screen. This will take you back to the last screen.

6. Click the hotlink for a 24 hour satellite image. This is a satellite picture of the United States 12 hours after the first picture.

7. With a green crayon repeat step 4 using the 24 hour image as a guide. Use your pencil to draw arrows in the direction the clouds seem to be moving.

8. Click the Back button at the top of the screen. This will take you back to the last screen.

9. Click the hotlink for a 12-hour satellite image. This is a satellite picture of the United States 12 hours after the second picture.

10. With a blue crayon repeat step 4 using the 12-hour image as a guide. Use your pencil to draw arrows in the direction the clouds seem to be moving.

11. Quit the web browsing program and close your Internet connection.

12. Complete the questions on the How's the Weather? page.

HOW'S THE WEATHER? *(cont.)*

Follow the directions on the How's the Weather? Task sheet to complete the questions on this page.

Questions:

1. Describe the changes in the cloud patterns.

   _____

   _____

   _____

   _____

   _____

2. Was there a pattern in the way in which storms moved across the United States? If so, what was it?

   _____

   _____

   _____

   _____

   _____

   _____

   _____

3. Can you think of any reason that the storms might move in this direction?

   _____

   _____

   _____

   _____

   _____

CITIZENSHIP

Grade Level: 5–8

Content Area: Social Studies

Skills and Concepts: Using the Internet, multiculturalism, communication, consensus, task organization

Hardware:

- An IBM, Macintosh or compatible computer with a connection to the Internet
- a large screen projection device (See page 23.)

Software:

A web browsing program such as *Netscape* or *Mosaic*.

TCM Resource Book: *Cooperative Learning Activities for Social Studies* (TCM 655)

Other Materials:

- one copy per student of Requirements for Citizenship Activity Page (page 228)
- one copy per student of Citizenship Guide (page 229)
- one copy per student of Citizenship Award (page 230)

Summary:

The students will research the requirements for United States citizenship and create requirements for their group citizenship.

Before the Lesson:

Use the program to locate the FedWorld homepage at http://www.fedworld.gov. Use the search button to search for "citizenship requirements" This will take you to a document that contains text describing the requirements and process for becoming a United States citizen.

Procedure:

1. Divide the students into groups of four to six and lead them in a discussion of the idea of citizenship and what it means to be a citizen of the United States. Ask them if they know what is required to become a United States citizen.

2. Research the requirements for becoming a United States citizen. Using a large screen projection device, project the information found on FedWorld to discuss the requirements for citizenship. If you wish groups to find the information themselves, teach them to locate and print the information.

CITIZENSHIP *(cont.)*

3. Using Requirements for Citizenship Activity Page, have the groups write the requirements for being citizens of their group. Tell them to remember that each of them must be able to pass the requirements that they make up.

4. Have the group write their requirements in a Citizenship Guide.

5. Have each member pass the requirements of citizenship. Give out Citizenship Awards for those who pass.

Management:

One-Computer Classroom:

Use a large screen projection device to do this lesson as a whole class activity.

Pod or Lab:

Have students work in citizenship groups to complete the assignment.

Extension Activities:

- Use the FedWorld homepage as a starting point for research on the different offices of the cabinet. Have the students find out what each cabinet office does.

- Have the students explore FedWorld and evaluate its effectiveness in informing the public.

CITIZENSHIP *(cont.)*

REQUIREMENTS FOR CITIZENSHIP ACTIVITY PAGE

> You are going to plan requirements for citizenship within your group. Here are the three steps you need to take:
>
> First, discuss the requirements for citizenship within your group, and write the four requirements for citizenship on the Citizenship Guide page.
>
> Next, each person in your group must fulfill the requirements for citizenship.
>
> After your group has become citizens, join your class for a citizenship celebration.

❑ What are some of the things that you feel are important requirments to become citizens of your group?

_____

_____

❑ What will citizens have to know? (a pledge, a song, something about history or laws)

_____

_____

❑ What will citizens have to promise? (to protect and defend the Constitution, etc.)

_____

_____

❑ Will citizens have to take a test? If so, what will it cover?

_____

_____

❑ Will citizens have to prove anything? If so, what?

_____

❑ Notes:

_____

_____

_____

_____

CITIZENSHIP *(cont.)*

CITIZENSHIP GUIDE

1. You must know . . .

2. You must promise . . .

3. You must be tested on or for . . .

4. You must prove . . .

CITIZENSHIP *(cont.)*

Citizenship Award

This award signifies that

_____

has successfully completed the requirements for

_____

citizenship in the

_____

continent cooperative learning group.

Congratulations on a job well done!

Signed _____

Witnessed _____

Date _____

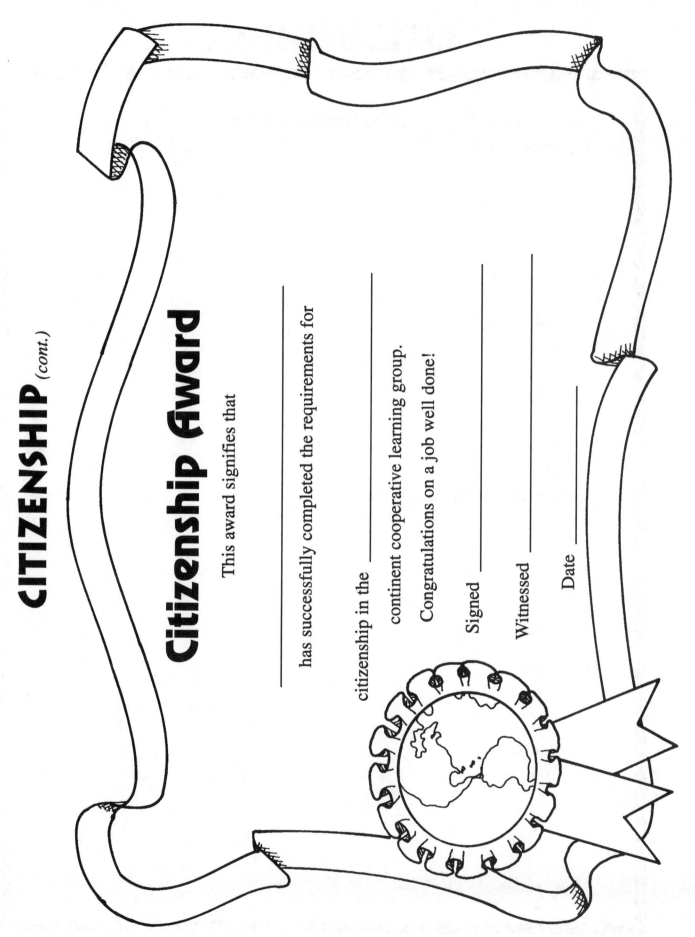

SHAKESPEARE

Grade Level: 8

Content Area: Literature

Skills and Concepts: Using the Internet WWW site, interpreting Shakespeare

Hardware:

- An IBM, Macintosh, or compatible computer with a connection to the Internet
- a large screen projection device optional (See page 23.)

Software:

A web browsing program such as *Netscape* or *Mosaic*

TCM Resource Book: *Shakespeare* (TCM 614)

Other Materials:

one page per student, Responses

Summary:

This is a lesson that would go with a unit on Shakespeare's *Romeo and Juliet*. In this lesson the students explore The Complete Works of Shakespeare homepage on the World Wide Web to determine the meanings of quotes.

Before the Lesson:

Explore The Complete Works of Shakespeare homepage http://the-tech.mit.edu/Shakespeare/works.html to become familiar with navigating through the page.

Procedure:

1. Explain to the students that they will be using an online version of *Romeo and Juliet* to help them find meanings for some important quotations in the story.

2. Hand out the worksheet (page 233) and read the quotes together. Have the students try to interpret the meaning out of context.

3. Click the link to *Romeo and Juliet* then explore the online book in search of the quotes.

Management:

One-Computer Classroom

If you are using a large screen projection device, you can show the entire class the Shakespeare homepage. Find each of the quotes together. Much of the text has hyperlink annotations, meaning that the words can be clicked to reveal a modern definition for some of the Shakespearean language. Have the students fill out their handouts for each of the quotes.

SHAKESPEARE *(cont.)*

Pod of Computers:

Have students work in pairs to interpret the quotes using the online text. Have the students fill in the handouts for each quote found.

Computer Lab:

Use the computer resources in the lab to allow a higher student ratio to computers and explore the online text.

Note: If your school is using a dial up connection it may be impossible or frankly too costly to use the pod or lab configurations for this lesson. Direct connect schools will have no problems as there is no charge for the time on line in most cases.

Extension Activities:

Have the students enter the quotation area of the Shakespeare page and find familiar quotes. Have them analyze why these quotes have stood the test of time and are still used today.

The Complete Works of William Shakespeare

This is a server of the complete works of William Shakespea provided by <u>The Tech</u>. New features are under development check the <u>What's New</u> page periodically.

The original electronic source for this server is the Complete Moby(tm) Shakespeare, <u>which is freely available online</u>. The may be differences between a copy of a play that you happen be familiar with and the one of this server. Don't worry, this very common phenomenon. You may want to read <u>a brief no on these differences</u>.

There are several pages available here:

- <u>About the glossary</u>
- <u>Search the texts</u>
- <u>A chronological listing</u> of plays
- A listing of the plays <u>by category</u>
- <u>Bartlett's familiar Shakespearean quotations</u>
- <u>Frequently asked questions</u> about this server

SHAKESPEARE *(cont.)*

RESPONSES

Explain the meanings of the following quotations from *Romeo and Juliet*.

1. "Down with the Capulets! Down with the Montagues!"

   _____

   _____

   _____

2. "Oh speak again, bright angel! For thou art
   As glorious to this night, being o'er my head
   As is a winged messenger of Heaven."

   _____

   _____

   _____

3. "Never was seen so black a day as this.
   Oh, woeful day, oh, woeful day!"

   _____

   _____

   _____

4. "Hold, there is forty ducats. Let me have a dram of poison."

   _____

   _____

   _____

5. "Take him and cut him out in little stars,
   And he will make the face of heaven so fine
   That all the world will be in love with night."

   _____

   _____

   _____

6. "Come, come with me, and we will make short work,
   For, by your leaves, you shall not stay alone
   Till Holy Church incorporate two in one."

   _____

   _____

   _____

POETRY ON THE NET

Grade Level: 5–8

Content Area: Literature

Skills and Concepts: Using the Internet WWW site, writing haiku poetry, publishing work on the Internet

Hardware:

- An IBM, Macintosh or compatible computer with a connection to the Internet
- a large screen projection device, optional (See page 23.)

Software:

- A web browsing program, such as *Netscape* or *Mosaic*.
- A word processing program

TCM Resource Book: *I Can Write a Poem* (TCM #326)

Other Materials:

One page per student, Haiku (pages 235 and 236)

Summary:

The students will write haiku poems that will be published on the Internet for people all over the world to see.

Before the Lesson:

Explore The Poetry Corner Homepage http://www.virtualnevada.com/orphanedthoughts.htm to become familiar with navigating through the page and submitting work.

Procedure:

1. If available, use a large screen projection device to show the class The Poetry Corner homepage. Move through the page looking for samples of student work that may be of interest to the class. Tell them that they will be writing poetry that will be submitted to this page so that other students all over the world can see it. Tell them that they can even get letters via e-mail from people who want to ask questions about their poems.

2. Teach the students the form of poetry you wish them to write. A handout for haiku is included for your use, but any form of poetry can be submitted. Have the students write their poems.

3. Revise, edit, and rewrite the poems using a word processing program. Be sure to include the name of the author and an e-mail address, if you have one. It is important that the final product be saved as a text file so that it can be easily submitted. Read the manual for your software to find out how this is done. Many times the file formats can be changed with the Save As command.

4. All the poems can be submitted at one time using one computer. Simply click the submit button at The Poetry Corner homepage and follow the directions.

5. Revisit the homepage in about a week and find your submissions.

Extension Activity:

Write to an author whose poem you enjoyed reading. Ask where he/she got his/her inspiration or what his/her process was for writing it.

POETRY ON THE NET *(cont.)*

HAIKU

1 3 4 5	
Japanese Haiku	5
1 2 3 4 5 6	7
Captures a moment in time	7
1 2 3 4	5
Snapshot memory.	5
Haiku has no rhyme	5
But has a special structure	7
To create within.	5
Each poem has three lines	5
With seventeen syllables	7
In five, seven, five.	5
When you write Haiku	5
Remember, freeze a moment,	7
Let it live in words.	5

Mark the syllables in the Haiku above. The first one is done for you. When you write Haiku, remember to "freeze" a moment. Here is an examle.

Wind, gently blowing

Up, around, and through the trees,

Plays tag with my kite.

Write a definition of Haiku. _____

_____

_____

_____

_____

_____

POETRY ON THE NET *(cont.)*

HAIKU

Now it's your turn to write Haiku!
Remember to count the syllables carefully.

Make a list of ten words to describe Spring and how you feel about Spring.

_____   _____   _____   _____   _____

_____   _____   _____   _____   _____

Use some of these words and ideas to finish this Haiku about Spring.

1 2   3   4   5
Opening blossoms _____ 5

_____ 7

_____ 5

Finish this Haiku about a puppy

_____ 5

_____ 7

1   2   3   4   5
Chews on my new shoe! _____ 5

Write a Haiku about your favorite sport.

_____ 5

_____ 7

_____ 5

Write a Haiku using one of your own ideas for a subject.

_____ 5

_____ 7

_____ 5

DRAWING THE LINE

Grade Level: 7–8

Content Area: Geography, Social Studies

Skills and Concepts: Using the Internet WWW site, physical and political geography, supporting a hypothesis

Hardware:

- An IBM, Macintosh or compatible computer with a connection to the Internet
- a large screen projection device, optional (See page 23.)

Software:

- A web browsing program such as *Netscape* or *Mosaic.*
- A word processing program

TCM Resource Book: *Colonial America* (TCM # 597)

Other Materials:

- one page per student, Drawing the Line (page 239)
- one page per student, Map of Thirteen Colonies (page 240)
- one green, red, blue, and brown crayon for each student

Purpose:

Using an online-interactive map of the United States, the students will see how physical geography shaped the formation of the political boundaries of the original 13 colonies.

Before the Lesson:

Spend some time exploring the interactive color relief map (http://www.zilker.net/~hal/aplus/). When you first arrive at the site, you are greeted by a color relief map of the United States with a grid superimposed. Click inside any of the squares to get a close-up view. Do the worksheet yourself to anticipate any problems that your class may have. If you have a large screen projection device, have it ready before this lesson. (See page 23.)

DRAWING THE LINE *(cont.)*

Procedure:

1. Ask the class if they know why the boundaries of the original 13 colonies are where they are. Take all responses, then ask if they think the physical geography had anything to do with the boundaries. Tell them that they will be using an online interactive map that was made by NASA using a satellite to see if geography might have had something to do with the borders.

2. Complete the activity sheets

Make your connection to the Web site and display the map on a large screen projection device. Start with the New England states by clicking the grid area that corresponds with it. You will zoom in on the area to reveal a detailed physical map. Have the students fill out the map and handout. Repeat this step, moving through each of the colonies.

3. Ask students to share the results of their work. Ask if they think that geography shaped some of the boundaries of the original colonies. Ask which ones seem to be most effected by geography and why they were effected.

MANAGEMENT:

One–Computer Classroom

Use a large screen projection device to do this lesson as a whole class activity. Have students fill in areas as you navigate through the maps.

Pod of Computers:

Have students work in groups of two or three to complete the assignment.

Note: In grading this assignment, you should not be concerned with the hypothesis the students make. The assignment should be graded on how well the students supported their hypothesis.

Extension Activities:

- Save the maps found as picture files for published reports or stories. In most web browsing programs, you do this by simply holding the mouse button down while pointing at the picture, then choose save from the menu.

- Repeat this activity for the state in which you live. Did geography shape the boundaries of your state?

DRAWING THE LINE *(cont.)*

DRAWING THE LINE

Name(s): _____ Date: _____

Did physical geography (what the land is like) help to shape the boundaries of the 13 original colonies? Use an interactive physical map to find out.

1. Look at the interactive map of the 13 original colonies. Then use the following color key to indicate each land form that might have effected the boundary.

    red = river

    blue = ocean or lake

    green = valley

    brown = mountains

2. In the following chart, explain how physical geography has effected the boundaries of the colonies. Remember to use cardinal directions to describe the border. (e.g., the western border of Pennsylvania).

State Name	Border Effected (use directions)	What geographical features do you believe affected the border?

DRAWING THE LINE *(cont.)*

MAP OF THE THIRTEEN COLONIES

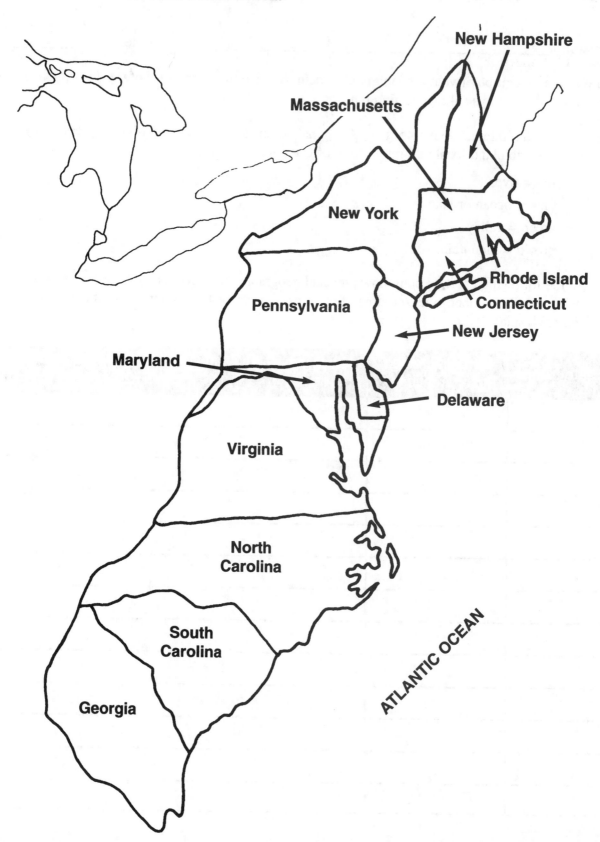

SPREADSHEETS

Grade Level: 6–8

Content Area: Math

Skills and Concepts: Gathering, organizing, and interpreting data; solving for unknowns; using formulas; using a spreadsheet; making generalizations

Hardware:

- An IBM or Macintosh compatible computer

- A printer

Software:

An Integrated Word Processing Program

Other Materials:

- What's Your Address? handout, one per student (page 243)

- Formulas, handout, one per student (page 244)

- What If ? handout, one per student (page 245)

Summary:

This activity is designed to run over two–four class periods. One–two days in groups or at desks, one–two days at the computer.

Before the Lesson:

Spend some time working with the spreadsheet program so that you become more comfortable with the tool. Most have very good built-in tutorials to help you learn to use the program.

Procedure:

1. Students may be grouped or work individually in stations for the activities, based upon the amount of computer resources available. (See Management section.) Tell the students that they will be developing a fictitious budget. They will be using the computer to help them keep track of their finances.

2. Teach the concepts presented in each handout prior to having the students complete them.

SPREADSHEETS *(cont.)*

Management:

One-Computer Classroom:

Have a template of the spreadsheet ready in which the students can input the formulas. Have the students rotate in a traditional fashion for this activity. (See page 113.)

Pod of Computers:

Use the rotational station method to facilitate the completion of this project. (See page 119.)

Computer Lab:

Make sure that the students have finished the preliminary activities prior to going to the lab.

Extension Activities:

- Have students make a blank spreadsheet with the same headings as the budget activities that follow. Make a list of six different amounts for each of the budget items and correspond them to the numbers on a die (e.g. 1 = $20.00, 2 = $30.00, 3 = $40.00, etc.). Roll the die to determine their costs for the budget items for each month. Talk about the probability of any of the amounts coming up. Discuss how the bottom line changes when new numbers are entered.

- Team with a science class in order to analyze the data for a given experiment. The scientist conducts the experiment and the mathematician analyzes the results.

- Take a survey of the class or school then organize and present the data in a school newspaper using a spreadsheet and word processor.

- Spreadsheets have a built-in graphing feature. Graph the results of a collection of data in order to visualize the meaning of the numbers.

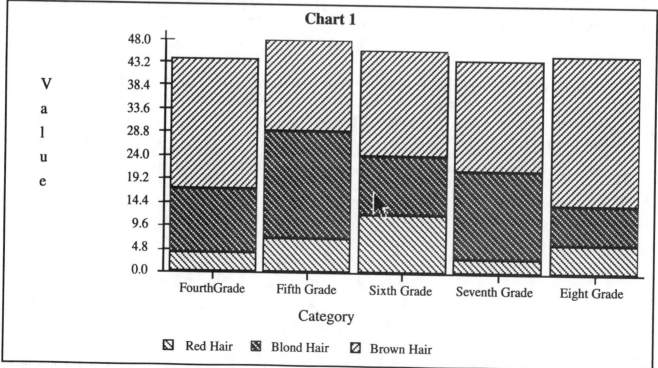

SPREADSHEETS *(cont.)*

WHAT'S YOUR ADDRESS?

Name: _____ Date: _____

When you finish school, it will be necessary for you to get a job to support yourself. You will have to think about all the necessities of life and how to pay for them. It is a good idea to make a budget so that you have enough money to pay for the necessities while leaving enough left over for saving and just having fun.

A **spreadsheet** is a great computer tool for making and keeping a budget. It is a table that helps you organize your data.

Below is a spreadsheet. Notice that it is divided into **columns** (running up and down) and **rows** (running side to side) The columns are lettered and the rows are numbered. Each box in the spread sheet is called a "cell." Each cell has an "address" which is a combination of the column letter and the row number in which the cell is located. For example: the address of the cell that contains the word "January" is A2.

My Budget

	A	B	C	D	E	F
1		Pay	Rent	Utilities	Food	Auto
2	January				$122.00	$65.64
3	February		$350.00	$88.97	$85.44	$95.01
4	March			$65.32	$93.48	$72.14
5	Total					

Part A: Follow the directions to fill in the empty cells of the spread sheet.

1. Write $350.00 in cell C2.

2. Write $375.00 in cell C4.

3. Write $1,000.00 in cells B2, B3, and B4.

4. Write $108.20 in cell D2.

5. Write the total of each column in row 5.

Part B: Using the spreadsheet, answer the following questions.

6. In what month did your rent go up?

7. What is the address of the cell that has the total paid for food during the three months?

8. What were the addresses of the cells you had to add to get the total in D5.

9. How much money did you spend in all?

SPREADSHEETS *(cont.)*

FORMULAS

Name: _____ Date: _____

A spreadsheet isn't just a table for organizing numbers. It is also a very sophisticated calculator that works with formulas. It can add, subtract, multiply, divide, average, and calculate percentages, as well as more complete advanced math functions.

In order to do these calculations, the computer has to know what you want to do. You have to give the spreadsheet a formula. A formula is a set of instructions for the computer to follow.

For example: If you wanted to add all your pay for the three months in the spreadsheet and have the total show in cell B5, you would enter this formula in B5:

$$= B2 + B3 + B4$$

Always start formulas with an equal sign. This lets the computer know that you are entering a formula and not a label like "January".

	A	B	C	D	E	F
1	Month	Pay	Rent	Utilities	Food	Auto
2	January	$1,000.00	$350.00	$108.20	$122.00	$65.64
3	February	$1,000.00	$350.00	$88.97	$ 85.44	$95.01
4	March	$1,000.00	$375.00	$65.32	$ 93.48	$72.14
5	Total	$3,000.00				

Answer the following questions.

1. What would the formula be for totaling column C?

2. What would the formula be for totaling column D?

3. What would the formula be for totaling column E?

4. What would the formula be for totaling column F?

5. Challenge: What would be the formula for finding out how much money you have left after paying all of your bills for the three months?

    = _____ - (_____ + _____ + _____ + _____)

SPREADSHEETS *(cont.)*

WHAT IF?

Name: _____ Date: _____

What makes a spreadsheet a powerful tool is that any time you change an amount in a cell, the formula automatically changes the calculation. This makes it easy to ask the "What if?" questions like:

What if my rent goes up?
What if my car breaks down?
What if I get a raise?

Now you are going to make a spreadsheet on the computer. Your teacher will tell you how to get a blank sheet, then follow the directions and answer the questions.

1. Use your mouse or arrow keys to locate and highlight the cell A2 and type in January.

2. Repeat this instruction for all the labels in the spreadsheet below. Include January, February, March, Total, Pay, Rent, Utilities, Food, and Auto.

3. Enter all the numbers in the spreadsheet below into the cells on your spreadsheet.

4. Locate cell B5 and type in the formula that will total column B. See the Formulas worksheet if you have a question.

5. Repeat these steps for columns C, D, E, and F.

	A	B	C	D	E	F
1	Month	Pay	Rent	Utilities	Food	Auto
2	January	$1,000.00	$350.00	$108.20	$122.00	$65.64
3	February	$1,000.00	$350.00	$88.97	$85.44	$95.01
4	March	$1,000.00	$375.00	$65.32	$93.48	$72.14
5	Total	$3,000.00				

1. What if your utilities go up in February to $111.99? Locate the cell and type in the new amount. What happens to the total line?

2. What if you go out to eat more in March, changing your food bill to $145.32?

3. What if your rent goes up to $415.00 in January and stays there?

4. If you enter the formula = B5 (C5 + D5 + E5 + F5) in cell F8, what information will this give you? After you answer the question try the formula.

THE DIGITAL DATABOOK

Grade Level: 6–8

Content Area: Language Arts, Organization

Skills and Concepts: address forms, setting up a database

Hardware:

- An IBM or Macintosh compatible computer
- Printer

Software:

Any integrated word processing (Works) program, such as *Microsoft Works* (Microsoft) or *Claris Works* (Claris) or any database such as *Fox Pro*.

Other Materials:

- The Parts worksheet (page 249 and 250)
- The Plan worksheet (page 251)
- Database Design Task Sheet (page 252)

Summary:

This is three days of lessons which teach students the basics of creating a database. This is designed as an optional companion lesson for the Form Letters lesson on page 187. When finished, students will have a database of addresses for companies whose products they enjoy. These addresses can be automatically inserted into a letter by using the mail merge command on most integrated word processing packages. For a description of database programs see pages 78–87.

Before the Lesson:

The teacher should become familiar with databases and their uses. Spend time working with your database program by taking the tutorial that is usually included in the program. Complete the lessons as the students would. Have the students bring lists of addresses of their favorite companies.

Procedure:

Day 1: The Parts

1. Tell the students that they will be creating a database of addresses of their favorite companies. Explain that databases are lists of information that can be sorted and used in several ways. (If you are planning to or have completed the Form Letters lesson on pages 187–189, tell the students that they will be using the database to automatically enter the addresses into their letters)

2. Go over the parts of a database: (For descriptions see pages 78–87)

   - database
   - fields
   - list view
   - records
   - data view
   - design view

THE DIGITAL DATABOOK *(cont.)*

3. Have students complete The Parts worksheet. If your students have access to computers in class, have some of the class use the tutorial included in most programs to train and reinforce the lesson instead of the worksheet.

Day 2: The Plan

1. Return and review the first day's worksheet of a database. Clarify any confusion about the vocabulary.

2. Tell the students that now that they know what the parts of a database are, the next step is to design a database that they will be using. It is important that before using the computer, you have an idea what you are going to be putting in the database.

3. Have the students brainstorm what fields that they might want in their database of company addresses. Some might include:

Name of the company	Description
Address	Type of product produced
City	Phone Number
State	e-mail address
Zip Code	URL (Internet Address)

4. Have the students design their database using The Plan worksheet. If your students have access to computers in class, have students who have not used the tutorial get experience with it.

Day 3: Using the Computer. (This lesson may need to be divided up into two lessons depending on the level and experience of your class.)

1. Use a large screen projection device or small groups around the computer to teach the students how to design a database using the program you have. Make sure to teach them how to switch into the different views: data, design, and list. Once the design is done, show the students how to enter and sort their records.

2. Return their corrected planning worksheet.

3. Have the students create their databases and enter the records that they have collected. The task sheet provided on page 252 will help with the sequence of the activity, but it is not specific as each database program is a little different.

Management:

One-Computer Classroom:

Use the Pass It On Method of teaching the program on page 132. You may want to set up the database together if time is limited. Then have students add their records to the database in rotation. The database can then be sorted to eliminate the duplicate records automatically.

The Pod:

Use the Rotational Station Method discussed on page 119. Other stations can include writing drafts of business letters that will be addressed by the database.

The Computer Lab:

Have each student create a database and enter the records. Be sure to have a disk for each student to save his/her database to.

THE DIGITAL DATABOOK *(cont.)*

Extension Activities:

- Have the students do a survey of student's name recognition of the companies. Then add a field for the amount of people who knew the company by name. A report that sorts these numbers from greatest to smallest or visa versa will give the student a list of best and least known companies.

- Keep track of the companies that write back to the students in field. This will be interesting for the students and valuable for the teacher. This will let you know who to tell the students not to write to the next year.

- Create a database of Pro or College sports teams. Enter a field for "Made the Playoffs." Use this to write those teams letters of encouragement. Many of the teams will send autographs and press packages back to the students. These addresses can be found in sports almanacs.

Management Tip:

Teachers can create a database design of important student information, like addresses, phone numbers, allergies, etc. before school starts for the year. Have each student rotate through the computer and enter his/her information during the first week. This becomes a tool that the teacher can add to at any time. Track notes that need to be turned in, book numbers, assignments completed, or anything that needs to be tracked. The sort function gives the teacher instant feedback on student's information or lack there-of.

THE DIGITAL DATABOOK *(cont.)*

THE PARTS

Name: _____ Date: _____

Databases are computerized lists of information that can be sorted in many different ways. Let's say that you had a database of all 5,000 of your friends' and family's names and addresses. You want to send party invitations to just your friends and not your family. A database can help by sorting out your friends from your family and print addresses for them. This is only one small example of the power of databases.

Parts

Databases have the two parts shown below:

Fields: These are the groups of information that you set up with headings

Last Name	Fist Name	Phone Number	Book Number	Field Trip
Bush	George	555-1234	E8	x
Clinton	Hillary	555-4856	E6	x
Marcos	Imilda	555-7346	E14	
Washington	George	555-1126	E21	x

Records: Each record is the information that you input on one person place or thing. It is the reason for having a database.

Views

The database can be viewed or looked at in three different ways:

Data view lets you input or view one record at a time.

THE DIGITAL DATABOOK *(cont.)*

THE PARTS *(cont.)*

	First name	Middle	Last name	Address1	City	State	Postal code	Area code	Phone1
	John	Q.	Doe	1234 Main Street	Anywhere	CA	95320	777	555-1234

Address Book (DB)

List view lets you see many records at once.

Design view lets you change or edit the fields or add more fields.

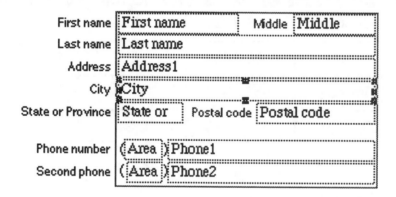

Answer the following questions about databases:

1. When I add the heading of "Address" to a database, what part am I adding?

2. What view will I need to be in to add a field to a database?

3. If I want to see all my records at once, what view will I need to be in?

4. What part would the name "John Smith" probably be in?

5. When you input one record at a time what view must you be in?

6. How many records are in the first picture shown in this exercise?

7. How many fields are in the first picture shown in this exercise?

8. Think of a way, other than an address book, that you might be able to use a database. Explain it below.

THE DIGITAL DATABOOK *(cont.)*

THE PLAN

Name: _____ Date: _____

Directions:

1. Insert the names of the fields that you will create for your database in the first table.

Field 1	Field 2	Field 3	Field 4

Field 5	Field 6	Field 7	Field 8

2. Using the Field names above, draw what you want your design view to look like. Make sure to draw rectangles large enough to fit the largest record in your list. Make sure that the record areas are in a logical position. A sample of a database design view is given for you.

First name	First name		Middle	Middle
Last name	Last name			
Address	Address1			
City	City			
State or Province	State or	Postal code	Postal code	
Phone number	(Area) Phone1			
Second phone	(Area) Phone2			

THE DIGITAL DATABOOK *(cont.)*

DATABASE DESIGN TASK SHEET

Use this sheet and your database plan to guide you through the task of creating a database. This is only an outline since each database program is different.

1. Start the database program.

2. Choose a new database.

3. Enter the field names.

4. Size the fields so that your biggest record will fit in the area provided for them.

5. Arrange the fields like you have them arranged in your plan.

6. Save the database with a name that you can remember. Where are you to save it? On a disk? On the hard drive?

7. Switch the program to data view.

8. Enter all your records in the fields. Note: The arrow keys or tab button will move you around the data view. The enter or return keys usually move the cursor to the next record. Save after each record.

9. When all the records are inputted, switch to list view and check out your list. Fix any errors.

10. Experiment with the sort function. Sort the name field alphabetically or the address field by number. Look at the other fields in your list and think about other ways to sort them.

11. Save the database once more.

12. Print the list and give it to your teacher.

13. Quit the program and clean up your area.

THE DIGITAL DATABOOK *(cont.)*

GRAPHING THE PLANT

Grade Level: 4–8

Content Area: Science, Math

Skills and Concepts: Graphing, analysis

Hardware:

- An IBM or Macintosh compatible computer
- Printer

Software:

A spreadsheet program such as *The Cruncher* (Davidson), *Microsoft Excel* (Microsoft), *Lotus 123* (Lotus), or as included in *Microsoft Works* (Microsoft) and *Claris Works* (Claris)

Other Materials:

- Plant Data Collection worksheet (page 255)
- plant seeds
- cups
- soil
- water
- fertilizer

Summary:

Students will test the effects of different fertilizer amounts on the growth of plant seeds. They will keep track of the data collected and graph the results using a spreadsheet. The students will then analyze the results using the graph.

Before the Lesson:

Have the students plant three different seeds in cups, one seed in each cup. Make sure that all cups, soil, and water amounts are the same (Constants). Only the fertilizer amounts are different (Variables). Give one plant no fertilizer, give another plant the recommended amount of fertilizer, give the third plant double the amount of fertilizer. Keep their plants separate from each others'. Tell the students to mark the bottom of each of the coresponding cups with 0 for no fertilizer, 1 for the recommended amount, and 2x for double the recommended amount. Keep the plants in equal sunlight and collect data once a week using the Plant Growth Data worksheet on page 255.

Become familiar with setting up a spreadsheet and graphing data. Teach the students how to set up their spreadsheets and insert a graph. Since this experiment is long term, a few students at a time can set up their graphing spreadsheets.

THE DIGITAL DATABOOK *(cont.)*

	A	B	C	D
1		Week 1	Week 2	Week 3
2	Plant 0			
3	Plant 1			
4	Plant 2			

Procedure:

1. For the duration of the experiment teach students to make a simple spreadsheet like the following, except extending the weeks out as long as you continue the experiment. The spreadsheet can be added to at any time you want.

2. Have the students input their growth data in the cells that correspond to the Plant and Week that it was taken.

3. Make a graph of rows 2, 3, and 4 and insert it below the data. In most programs, this can be done by highlighting the cells and choosing a chart or graph from one of the menus. Choose a multiple line graph and select "data appears in rows.'

4. Keep inputting the information for as long as you wish to continue the experiment. The graph will automatically update as you add or change data.

5. When the experiment is over, have the students print the graph and analyze the results. The graph can also be electronically "pasted" into a word processor so that students can type their analysis with the graph. This makes an impressive looking science report.

Management:

One-Computer Classroom:

This is a perfect activity for the one-computer classroom, as the spreadsheet can be completed any time for the duration of the experiment. Assign students to make their spreadsheets when they have free time or during a scheduled time. Have students who have completed their spreadsheets help others who need it. (See Traditonal Method)

The Pod:

This activity can be done any time during the duration of the experiment, so use this as a filler when you need a good station activity.

The Computer Lab:

This can easily be completed in one period of lab use.

Extensions:

- Have each student plant different types of seeds. Then compare the graphs to see if growth patterns are the same.

- Have students continue the experiment throughout the life cycle of the plant to track how fast each dies.

THE DIGITAL DATABOOK *(cont.)*

PLANT DATA COLLECTION

Name: _____ Date: _____

Fill in the information about the growth of your plants as completely as possible.

Date:	
	Height in cm
Plant 0	
Plant 1	
Plant 2	

Make notes about the appearance of each plant below:

Plant 0:

_____

Plant 1:

_____

Plant 2:

_____

Date:	
	Height in cm
Plant 0	
Plant 1	
Plant 2	

Make notes about the appearance of each plant below:

Plant 0:

_____

Plant 1:

_____

Plant 2:

_____

Date:	
	Height in cm
Plant 0	
Plant 1	
Plant 2	

Make notes about the appearance of each plant below:

Plant 0:

_____

Plant 1:

_____

Plant 2:

_____

THE DIGITAL DATABOOK *(cont.)*

SHOOTING PERCENTAGE

Grade Level: 5–8

Content Area: Math and Physical Education

Skills and Concepts: relationships between fractions, decimals and percentages

Hardware:

- An IBM or Macintosh compatible computer
- A printer

Software:

A spreadsheet program, such as *The Cruncher* (Davidson), *Microsoft Excel* (Microsoft), *Lotus 123* (Lotus), or as included in *Microsoft Works* (Microsoft) and *Claris Works* (Claris)

Other Materials:

- Shot Chart (page 258)
- Basketballs and hoops on the playground

Summary:

The students will gather data about the amount of shots made and missed. They will enter the information into a spreadsheet to convert to decimals and percentages.

Before the Lesson:

Become familiar with creating a spreadsheet, entering formulas, and formatting cells. Students should have an introductory knowledge of spreadsheets.

Procedure:

1. Tell the students that today they are going to be basketball stars. This means that they will be keeping their stats (statistics). Use the sports page to show them all the statistics that are taken on each player or group of players. Tell them that they are going to calculate their shooting percentages from different places on the court.

2. Pass out shot charts and explain that they will be taking different amounts of shots from different parts of the court. Go over the sheet and send the class out to take their shots and collect their data.

3. Discuss the formulas for finding a decimal: amount of shots made divided by amount of shots attempted.

4. Tell them that they will be making a spreadsheet that shows the decimal and percentage of shots that they made from each position. This can either be done by direct instruction on how to do the first set of shots or by simply allowing the students to discover how to set this up. This depends on their level of knowledge.

THE DIGITAL DATABOOK *(cont.)*

Below is one possible way of doing the spreadsheet.

	A	B	C	D	E	F
1		Shots Attempted	Shots Made	Decimal	Percentage	
2	Shot A					
3	Shot B					
4	Shot C					

Formula is =C2/B2

Make sure that the format is set at decimal and rounded.

Formula is =D2

Make sure that the format is set at percentage and rounded.

Management:

One-Computer Classroom:

Use a large screen projection device to demonstrate setting up the spreadsheet's first line. Have the students add their formulas and data to a single class spreadsheet starting below where the teacher demonstrated. The students can click on the cell in which the teacher put the formula to see his/her example. Rotate students through, giving them about 58 minutes to complete the formula and data entry.

The Pod:

Have half the students shoot while others are creating their spreadsheet. Then switch the groups.

The Computer Lab:

Do all the data collection prior to the lab time. Have the students discover how to set up the spreadsheet with only introductory knowledge and the formula for finding the percentage. Walk around and give hints to students who are stuck.

Extensions:

- Import all student's data to a single spreadsheet to calculate a class shooting average.

- Have the students analyze how this exercise relates to grading averages.

THE DIGITAL DATABOOK *(cont.)*

SHOT CHART

Name: _____ Date: _____

Directions: Look at the numbers on the picture of the basketball key. Go to those spots in order and follow the directions of the number below that is the same.

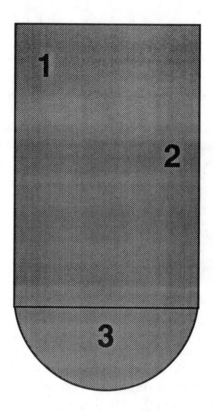

1. Take 13 shots from number one and record your results.

   Shots attempted = 13   Shots made = _____

2. Take 11 shots from number two and record your results.

   Shots attempted = 11   Shots made = _____

3. Take 7 shots from number three and record your results.

   Shots attempted = 7   Shots made = _____

What do you think was your highest percentage shot? Why do you think that?

What do you think was your lowest percentage shot? Why do you think that?

GLOSSARY OF TECH TERMS

adapter: Electronic piece that adapts to a device so the computer can control the device.

After Dark: A utility from Berkeley Systems called a screen saver.

AppleTalk: The AppleTalk network is how your Macintosh talks to your laser printer, other Macintoshes, or other machines. All these machines need to be hooked up in order to talk.

application: A computer software program you use.

bar code: The grouping of thin lines which when accessed by an electronic bar code reader reveal information.

baud (baud rate): The speed at which a modem can send or receive information.

bit: Short for binary digit. One bit is the smallest unit of information with which the computer can work.

bulletin board service (BBS): Service is usually set up by an online organization to provide or exchange information.

bundle: When you buy a particular product it often comes with another product(s) which is free.

button: The electronic item on a computer screen that is pushed in order for something to happen.

CD-ROM (Compact Disk Read-Only Memory): A disk which holds up to 600 megabytes of information.

CD-ROM player: The disk drive which allows the CD-ROM to be played.

clip art: The art work that is electronically cut and pasted onto documents.

CPU (Central Processing Unit): The "brains" of the computer. Often a tiny microprocessor chip which runs the entire system.

crash: When your computer stops working suddenly or the system breaks down. (A very bad deal!)

cursor: The little mark on the screen that sometimes blinks on and off. It will move when you move the mouse or press certain keys.

GLOSSARY OF TECH TERMS *(cont.)*

database: Collection of information stored in computerized form.

default: Anytime an automatic decision is made for you by the computer or software program.

desktop: The background on your screen when you are using a Macintosh or other Windows-like program.

desktop publishing: Process of creating printed documents that look professionally produced.

dialog box: A box or window on the screen that you can "dialog" with, communicate with, and make choices from.

digital: Information represented by numbers.

digital camera: Outputs images in digital form instead of regular photographic film.

disk: A thin, circular (or rectangular) object on which to store computer data.

disk drive: The part of the computer where the disk goes.

DOS (Disk Operating System): Many types of computers have systems called DOS. It usually refers to IBM PC or IBM-compatible computers.

download: To receive information (like a file) from another computer to yours through the modem. Or, you may take a copy of a document from a disk and download it onto your computer.

drag: Use the mouse to position the pointer over an object, press and hold the mouse button, and move the mouse.

e-mail: Short for electronic mail you can send or receive directly on your computer via modem or network.

ethernet: A local area network connecting computers together with cables so the computers can share the same information.

fiber optics: A communications system that uses dozens of hair-thin strands of glass that move information at the speed of light.

font: A style of type.

GLOSSARY OF TECH TERMS *(cont.)*

graphic: An electronic picture or design.

hacker: Computer enthusiast who is willing to "hack" away at understanding the computer for long periods of time.

hardware: The parts of the computer itself (modem, printer, hard drive, keyboard).

HyperCard/HyperStudio: Software applications which use multimedia and are interactive.

hypermedia: Programs in which any media (pictures or text) can be clicked to reveal something.

hypertext: Programs in which the text is an active button that can be clicked to reveal something.

IBM (International Business Machines): A very large computer company.

icon: Little pictures on the screen which represent files of other computer applications.

import: Bringing information from one document or computer screen into another document.

interactive: A program, game, or presentation where the user is able to interact and participate in what is going on.

interface: Connection between two items so they can work together.

Internet: Worldwide network of about half a million computer users belonging to research organizations, the military, institutions of learning, corporations, and so on.

K, KB (Kilobyte): A unit for measuring the size of things on hard disks or computer applications. It represents the memory of an item. One kilobyte is equal to 1,024 bytes.

keyboard: The piece of hardware that has the keys, like a typewriter.

GLOSSARY OF TECH TERMS *(cont.)*

LAN (Local Area Network): Connecting computers together in local proximity, like your school site.

laptop computer: A computer small enough to fit on your lap. They run on batteries and are portable.

laser printer: A printer which prints documents that look professionally printed.

laserdisc: (Also known as videodisc.) Similar to a music CD, but it also holds visual images as well. Information can be accessed by remote control or barcode.

laserdisc player: The machine which plays the laserdisc.

LCD Panel (Liquid Crystal Display): A liquid compound is wedged between two grids of electrodes to create an image. The LCD panel is a device which fits over the overhead projector and when connected to a computer will project whatever is on the computer screen onto a large viewing screen.

Macintosh: Type of Apple computer which was the first to use the windows and mouse formats.

Mb, MB (Megabyte): Short for a unit of measure, measuring the size of electronic items (like files and documents). One megabyte is equal to 1,048,567 bytes of memory.

memory: Temporary storage space in your computer as opposed to the permanent storage space on the hard disk. Think of the hard disk as a filing cabinet where everything is stored. Memory is your desk while you are temporarily working on the items inside of the filing cabinet.

menu: A displayed list of commands or options from which you can choose.

microprocessor: A single chip that contains the entire CPU (the brains of the computer).

modem: Device that allows computers to communicate with other computers via the telephone line.

monitor: Another word for the computer screen.

mouse: Small device that is connected to the keyboard which you move across the top of your desk to access the pointer or cursor on the screen.

GLOSSARY OF TECH TERMS *(cont.)*

mouse pad: A small pad on which you can roll your mouse. Designed to give you a better grip than a desktop.

MS-DOS (Microsoft Disk Operating System): This is the most commonly used system for IBM PC and IBM compatible computers.

multimedia: A computer presentation that involves still images, moving video, sound, animation, art, or a combination of all of these.

network: Communication or connection system that lets your computer talk with another computer, printer, hard disk, or other device.

OS (Operating System): The filing and utility system that a computer uses. There are three major operating systems—DOS, Windows, and Macintosh.

online: Communicating with other computers through your modem or network.

paint program: Software application that provides electronic versions of paintbrushes, paint cans, pencil, eraser, scissors, etc., in order to create illustrations.

PC (Personal Computer): Designed to be used by an individual person.

peripherals: Additions to your computer that add functionality, such as modems, scanners, and printers.

pixel: The dots of light on a computer monitor. Most monitors are 800 x 600 pixels.

platform: Refers to the operating environment your computer uses. The two main platforms are IBM and Macintosh.

port: A socket usually found on the back of a piece of hardware where a cable can be connected.

PowerBook: Apple's laptop computer.

Power Macintosh: An Apple Macintosh computer with Power PC capabilities (the 6100, 7100, and 8100 series).

printer: The device that takes the text and images sent from the computer and presents them on paper.

prompt: A symbol or question on the screen that "prompts" you to take action and tell the computer what to do next.

QuickTime®: Software product from Apple that is loaded onto your computer so you can run movies. This application compresses and then decompresses the movies. Movies require a great deal of space, so compression is important.

GLOSSARY OF TECH TERMS *(cont.)*

RAM (Random Access Memory): Electronic circuits in your computer which hold information. It is the temporary memory used while the computer is turned on. You will need to save any work you do onto a disk or a file on the hard drive; otherwise, your work will be lost when the computer is shut off. RAM is referred to as volatile because the contents disappear when the computer is turned off.

ROM (Read-Only Memory): Information stored on ROM remains intact. The information is usually programmed right onto the chip or disk and cannot be altered or added to. That is why it is called read-only.

scanner: Device that takes a picture of a document that exists outside of the computer and digitizes the image to put in the computer.

screen saver: If you leave your computer on for a long time, the image can burn onto the screen. A screen saver is a software application that blanks the screen and replaces the screen with an attractive little picture. By moving the mouse or touching a key, the screen saver shuts off and your original screen automatically comes back up.

SCSI (Pronounced SKUH-zee, an acronym for Small Computer System Interface): SCSI is a standard among hardware manufacturers for computer peripheral devices. The computer and CD-ROM drive exchange information through a SCSI cable connected to SCSI ports.

SCSI port: The SCSI port is the outlet at the back of the computer and the CD-ROM drive to which the SCSI cable is attached.

site license: A license to copy software to all the computers on your site.

software: The instructions for the computer which are stored on a disk. These disks must be loaded onto the hard drive of the computer so that the computer will know what to do. Some software applications are already loaded onto the computer.

sound card: An adapter that allows you to play sound on your computer.

spreadsheet program: Software program for financial or other number-related information processing. A spreadsheet is composed of rows and columns, with individual boxes (cells) inside of each to hold information.

SVGA (Super Video Graphics Adapter): Used to display sharp images with many colors on your computer.

GLOSSARY OF TECH TERMS *(cont.)*

telecommunications: Communications carried on by one computer to another through a telephone line and modem.

terminal: A screen and keyboard, along with any circuits necessary to connect it to a main computer.

toolbox: Many software applications, especially those with paint options, come with a toolbox which appears on the screen in the form of a palette.

upgrade: The choosing of a newer, more powerful package (hardware or software).

upload: Using a modem, you put one of your files onto a network (or online service) and load the file onto the service so other people have access to it.

URL (Uniform Resource Locator): The address of a given location or document on the Internet.

utility: A software program that is not used to create something (like an application) but rather is used to enhance your working environment. *After Dark* is a utility for your computer system.

video card (also known as an adapter or board): A piece of plastic or fiberglass on which electronic circuits are printed and memory and other chips are attached. This device determines the screen resolution (how many colors you see at one time) and how fast the screen images are displayed.

videodisc: See laserdisc.

virtual reality: A simulated environment through the use of a computer which appears to be real.

virus: A software program designed to destroy data on your computer or corrupt your system software. Some viruses are so destructive they can wipe out an entire disk. Viruses are created illegally and can travel from computer to computer through disks, networks, and modems. Using virus detection software is a safe way to protect your system.

window: Rectangular frame on the screen in which you see and work with a particular software application.

word processor: Software applications that allow you to type documents but with a variety of tools to make work time easier and more efficient.

WWW (World Wide Web): A global network of computers that uses hypermedia to jump from one computer to the next.

SUGGESTED SOFTWARE

The following is a list of suggested software organized by content area. Each title includes the publisher, type of hardware required, and a targeted grade level. Keep in mind that the perfect computer tool kit includes a writing and publishing program, a creativity and/or presentation program, tele-communications software, and several electronic learning programs based on the content that is taught. Many times schools have settled on a standard set of tools which they may have purchased on a site license basis. Always consult the person who is in charge of securing software before purchasing.

Arts & Creativity

Art Explorer	Aldus	3–8	IBM and Macintosh
Fine Artist	Microsoft	3 & up	IBM and Macintosh
Flying Colors	Davidson	3 & up	IBM and Macintosh
HyperCard Projects for Kids	Ventura	5 & up	Macintosh
HyperStudio	Roger Wagner	3 & up	IBM and Macintosh
Kid Cad	Davidson	2–8	IBM
Kid Pix 2	Broderbund	K–8	IBM and Macintosh
Kid Pix Studio	Broderbund	K–8	IBM and Macintosh
Microsoft Art Gallery CD	Microsoft	4 & up	IBM and Macintosh
The Multimedia Workshop	Davidson	5 & up	IBM and Macintosh
Print Shop Deluxe	Broderbund	All	IBM and Macintosh
Super Paint 3.5	Aldus	4–12	IBM and Macintosh

Desktop Publishing

Microsoft Publisher	Microsoft	4 & up	IBM and Macintosh
QuarkXpress	Quark	5 & up	Macintosh

SUGGESTED SOFTWARE (cont.)

General Learning

1995 Grolier's Multimedia Encyclopedia	Grolier	4 & up	IBM and Macintosh
Ace Detective	Mindplay	6 & up	Macintosh
Ace Publisher	Mindplay	6 & up	Macintosh
Ace Reporter	Mindplay	6 & up	Macintosh
Compton's Interactive Encyclopedia 1995, CD	Comptons	2 & up	IBM and Macintosh
Headline Harry and the Great Paper Race	Davidson	5 & up	IBM and Macintosh
Learn to Do Spreadsheets, CD	Allegro	4 & up	IBM
Learn to Do Word Processing	Allegro	4 & up	IBM
Microsoft Encarta '95, CD	Microsoft	4& up	IBM and Macintosh
Microsoft Musical Instruments, CD	Microsoft	4 & up	IBM and Macintosh
Sim Town, CD	Maxis	3–8	IBM and Macintosh
Time Traveler, CD	Orange Cherry	5 & up	IBM and Macintosh
World History: 20th Century, CD	Computer Vistas	4–12	IBM and Macintosh

Geography

3D Atlas, CD	Creative Wonders	5 & up	IBM and Macintosh
Crosscountry USA	Didatech	4–9	IBM and Macintosh
PC USA	Broderbund	4 & up	IBM
Picture Atlas of the World, CD	National Geographic	5 & up	IBM and Macintosh
US Atlas 5.0	Mindscape	3–12	IBM and Macintosh
US Geography	AEC	4–8	IBM and Macintosh
USA GeoGraph	MECC	1–7	IBM and Macintosh

Grammar

Billiards 'n' Homonyms	Heartsoft	3–8	Apple, IBM, and Macintosh
Essential Grammar	Gamco	4–10	Apple and IBM
Essential Punctuation	Gamco	4–10	Apple and IBM
Key Words: Elementary	Humanities	4–10	Apple, IBM, and Macintosh
Word Capture	Heartsoft	2–12	Apple, IBM, and Macintosh

SUGGESTED SOFTWARE *(cont.)*

Keyboarding

Mario Teaches Typing	Interplay	1–10	IBM and Macintosh
Mavis Beacon Teaches Typing 3.0	Mindscape	3–12	IBM and Macintosh

Language Arts

The Amazing Writing Machine	Broderbund	K–8	IBM and Macintosh
Parts of Speech	Gamco	4–10	IBM and Macintosh
Word City, CD	Magic Quest	3–9	Apple, IBM, and Macintosh
Word City, LaserDisc Companion	Magic Quest	3–9	Apple, IBM, and Macintosh
Word Cross	HI-TECH	All	Macintosh

Mathematics

Alge-Blaster 3	Davidson	7 & up	IBM and Macintosh
Alge-Blaster Plus!	Davidson	7 & up	IBM and Macintosh
Classroom Collection: Math 5-6, CD	Hartley	5–6	Macintosh
Classroom Collection: Math 7-8, CD	Hartley	7–8	Macintosh
Cruncher, CD	Davidson	5 & up	IBM and Macintosh
Fraction Action	Unicorn	3 & up	Apple, IBM, and Macintosh
Fraction Factory	Springboard	2–8	Apple and IBM
Fraction-Oids 1	Mindplay	4–8	Apple, IBM, and Macintosh
Fraction-Oids 2	Mindplay	4–8	Apple, IBM, and Macintosh
Geometric Golfer	MECC	5–12	Macintosh
Math 2, Solving Word Problems	Decision Development	5–8	Apple, IBM, and Macintosh
Math Ace	Magic Quest	3–12	IBM and Macintosh
Math Blaster Mystery	Davidson	5 & up	IBM and Macintosh
Math Blaster: Secret of the Lost City	Davidson	3–8	IBM and Macintosh
Math Dodger!	Arcadia	2–9	IBM and Macintosh
Math Workshop	Broderbund	K–8	IBM and Macintosh
Operation Neptune	Learning Company	5–9	IBM
Word Problem Game Show: Level C	Gamco	5–6	Apple and IBM
Word Problem Game Show: Level D	Gamco	7–8	Apple and IBM
Word Problem Square Off, Level 5–6	Gamco	5–6	Macintosh
Word Problem Square Off, Level 7–8	Gamco	7–8	Macintosh

SUGGESTED SOFTWARE (cont.)

Reading

20,000 Leagues Under the Sea, CD	Orange Cherry	4 & up	IBM and Macintosh
A Midsummer Night's Dream, CD	Bookworm	5 & up	Macintosh
Great Literature Plus	Bureau	4 & up	IBM
The History of American Literature	Clearvue	7–12	IBM and Macintosh
Little Women, CD	Bookworm	5 & up	Macintosh
Microsoft Bookshelf & Works, CD	Microsoft	4 & up	IBM and Macintosh
Myths & Legends	Queue	K–8	IBM and Macintosh
Paul Bunyan	Discis	6 & up	IBM and Macintosh
Pecos Bill, CD	Discis	6–12	IBM and Macintosh
Pow! Zap! Ker Plunk! Comic Book Maker!	Queue	K–8	IBM and Macintosh
Romeo & Juliet, CD	Bookworm	5 & up	Macintosh
Somebody Catch My Homework	Discis	6 & up	IBM and Macintosh
Tall Tales & American Folk Heroes	Queue	K–8	IBM and Macintosh
Tom Sawyer, CD	Bookworm	5 & up	Macintosh

Science

3-D Body Adventure	Knowledge Adventure	3 & up	IBM
A.D.A.M. Essentials, CD	Broderbund	7–12	IBM and Macintosh
Adventures in Astronomy	Entrex	5–11	Apple and IBM
Animals 2.0, CD	Mindscape	2–12	IBM and Macintosh
Beyond Planet Earth	Discovery	5 & up	IBM
Earth Treks	Magic Quest	4–12	IBM and Macintosh
Earthware Bundle	Heartsoft	5 & up	IBM and Macintosh
Eco-Adventures in the Oceans	Chariot	3 & up	IBM and Macintosh
Great Ocean Rescue, LD	Tom Snyder	3–6	IBM And Macintosh
In the Company of Whales	Discovery	2 & up	IBM And Macintosh
InnerBodyWorks	Tom Snyder	5 & up	IBM And Macintosh
Oceans Below, CD	Mindscape	3–12	IBM And Macintosh
Operation Frog	Scholastic	6 & up	IBM and Macintosh
Science III, Grades 5–6	AEC	5–6	Apple and IBM
Science IV, Grades 7–8	AEC	7–8	Apple and IBM
Story Starters: Science	Queue	K–8	Apple

SUGGESTED SOFTWARE *(cont.)*

Social Studies

Amazon Trail	MECC	4–10	IBM and Macintosh
Ancient Empires	Learning Company	5–9	IBM
Decisions, Decisions: Series	Tom Snyder	5–11	IBM and Macintosh
Exploration	Queue	6–12	IBM and Macintosh
Interactive Government Bundle	Heartsoft	7–12	IBM and Macintosh
Timeliner	Tom Snyder	4–12	IBM and Macintosh
The Twentieth Century	Clearvue	7–12	IBM and Macintosh
US History II, Grades 6–8	AEC	6–8	IBM
Writing Along the Oregon Trail	MECC	5–12	IBM and Macintosh

Spelling

Word Attack Plus	Davidson	4 & up	IBM and Macintosh

Teacher Utilities

Calendar Maker 4.1	CE Software	IBM and Macintosh
Exam in a Can: Series	IPS	IBM and Macintosh
Grade Busters Macintosh: Making the Grade	Jay Klein	IBM and Macintosh
Gradebook Plus	SVE	IBM and Macintosh
Grady Profile	Aurbach	Macintosh
QuickSeat/QuickCall	HI-TECH	Macintosh
Teacher's Tool Kit	HI-TECH	Macintosh
Worksheet Magic	Teacher Support	IBM and Macintosh

Vocabulary

English Vocabulary II	American Educational	4–6	IBM and Macintosh
Vocabulary Quest in the Land of the Unicorn	Unicorn	4–8	Apple and IBM

Word Processing/Writing

Children's Writing & Publishing Center	Learning Company	2–9	IBM and Macintosh
ClarisWorks in the Classroom	Claris	4 & up	Macintosh
Microsoft Word 6.0	Microsoft	3 & up	IBM and Macintosh
Writer's Workshop Bundle	Heartsoft	3 & up	IBM and Macintosh
Creative Writer	Microsoft	3 & up	IBM and Macintosh
Microsoft Works	Microsoft	3 & up	IBM and Macintosh

ONLINE SERVICES

◆ **National Geographic Kids Network**
Focus: Science, Social Studies, Geography
(800) 368-2728

◆ **America Online**
Offers The Electronic School House.
(800) 827-6364

◆ **AppleLink**
Official online service for educators who use Apple computers.
(508) 947-8181

◆ **Scholastic Network**
Only nationwide online service created specifically for educators.
(800) 246-2986

◆ **CompuServe**
One of the oldest existing telecommincation services. Variety of special interest forums.
(800) 848-8990

◆ **Classroom PRODIGY Service**
New network from same company designed especially for schools.
(800) PRODIGY ext. 629

◆ **GTE Educational Network Services**
Special Net service addresses various topics in special education.
(800) 927-3000

◆ **Internet**
You must belong to one of the services listed above or be a member of a local or state online network to access this huge international network. To locate such a network, call the Consortium for School Networking.
(202) 466-6296

◆ **eWorld**
Apple has created this online service which comes standard on all the Performa computers.
(800) 775-4556

TECHNOLOGY PUBLISHER INFORMATION

AIMS 9710 DeSoto Avenue Chatsworth, CA 91311 (800) 367-2467	**Claris Corporation** 5201 Patrick Henry Drive Santa Clara, CA 95052 (800) 544-8554
AIT: The Learning Source Box A Bloomington, IN 47402 (812) 339-2203	**Computer Curriculum Corporation (CCC)** 1287 Lawrence Station Sunnyvale, CA 94089 (800) 858-3672
Broderbund P.O. Box 6125 Novato, CA 94948-6125 (800) 521-6263	**Creative Wonders** 1450 Fashion Island Blvd. San Mateo, CA 94404 (800) 543-9778
Chariot Software Group 3659 Inda Street, Suite 100 San Diego, CA 92103 (619) 298-0202	**Davidson and Associates** 19840 Pioneer Avenue Torrance, CA 90503 (800) 545-7677

TECHNOLOGY PUBLISHER
INFORMATION *(cont.)*

Discis Knowledge Research, Inc.
90 Sheppard Avenue East, 7th Floor
Toronto, Ontario, Canada M2N #A1
(416) 250-6537

Grolier Electronic Publishing
Sherman Turnpike
Danbury, CT 06816
(800) 356-5590

EdMark
P.O. Box 3218
Redmond, WA 98073-3218
(800) 426-0856

Intellimation
130 Cremona Drive
Santa Barbara, CA 93116
(800) 346-8355

EduQuest/IBM
One Culver Road
Dayton, NJ 08810-9988
(800) 426-3327

Jay Klein Productions
1695 Summit Point Court
Colorado Springs, CO 80919
(719) 591-9815

Gamco
P.O. Box 1911M
Big Springs, TX 79721
(800) 896-1760

KidSoft
718 University Avenue, Suite 112
Los Gatos, CA 95030
(800) 345-6150

TECHNOLOGY PUBLISHER INFORMATION *(cont.)*

Laser Learning Technologies, Inc.
120 Lakeside Avenue, Suite 240
Seattle, WA 98122
(800) 722-3505

Micrograms
1404 N. Main Street
Rockford, IL 61103
(800) 338-4726

Lawrence Productions
1800 South 35th Street
Galesburg, MI 49053
(616) 665-7075

Microsoft Corporation
One Microsoft Way
Redmond, WA 98052
(800) 426-9400

The Learning Company
6493 Kaiser Drive
Fremont, CA 94555-9985
(800) 852-2255

Mindscape
88 Rowland Way
Novato, CA 94945
(800) 283-8499

MECC
6160 Summit Drive North
Minneapolis, MN 55430-4003
(800) 685-MECC

Misty City Software
11866 Slater Avenue NE, Suite 3
Kirkland, WA 98034
(206) 820-4298

TECHNOLOGY PUBLISHER INFORMATION *(cont.)*

National Geographic Educational Services
P.O. Box 98018
Washington, D.C. 20090-8018
(800) 368-2728

Queue, Inc.
338 Commerce Drive
Fairfield, CT 06432
(800) 232-2224

Optical Data Corporation
30 Technology Drive
Warren, NY 07059
(800) 248-8478

The Reading and Computing Place
14752 Beach Blvd., Suite 200
La Mirada, CA 90638
(800) 888-0553

Optimum Resource, Inc.
5 Hiltech Lane
Hilton Head, CA 92926
(800) 327-1473

Roger Wagner Publishing
P.O. Box 710582
Santee, CA 92072
(800) 421-6526

Orange Cherry/New Media Schoolhouse
P.O. Box 390
69 Westchester Avenue
Pound Ridge, NY 10576
(914) 764-4104

Sanctuary Woods
1825 S. Grant Street
San Mateo, CA 94402
(415) 286-6000

TECHNOLOGY PUBLISHER
INFORMATION *(cont.)*

Scholastic, Inc. 2931 East McCarty Street P.O. Box 7502 Jefferson City, MO 65102-9968 (800) 541-5513	**Thomson Learning Tools** 5101 Madison Road Cincinnati, OH 45227 (800) 354-9706
Society for Visual Education 6677 North Northwest Highway Chicago, IL 60631 (800) 829-1900	**Tom Snyder Productions** 80 Coolidge Hill Road Watertown, MA 02172 (800) 342-0236
Sunburst/Wings for Learning 101 Castleton Street Pleasantville, NY 10570 (800) 321-7511	**Troll Micro** 100 Corporate Drive Mahwah, NJ 07430 (900) 526-5289
Teacher Support Software 1035 N.W. 57th Street Gainesville, FL 32605-4486 (800) 228-2871	**Videodiscovery** 1700 Westlake Avenue North Seattle, WA 98109 (800) 548-3472

MAIL ORDER RESOURCES

Company Name: CD-ROM Warehouse
Address: P.O. Box 3013
1720 Oak Street
Lakewood, NJ 08701-9917

Phone: (800) 325-3166

Company Name: Creative Teacher
Address: 910 Ramona Avenue, Suite E
Grover Beach, CA 93433

Phone: (800) 336-1022

Company Name: Educational Resources
Address: 1550 Executive Drive
Elgin, IL 60123

Phone: (800) 624-2926

Company Name: Edutainment
Address: 932 Walnut Street
Louisville, CO 80027

Phone: (800) 338-3844

MAIL ORDER RESOURCES *(cont.)*

Company Name: Learning Services
Address: P.O. Box 10636
Eugene, OR 97440
Phone:
(800) 877-9378 West
(800) 877-3278 East

Company Name: MacWarehouse
Address: P.O. Box 3013
1720 Oak Street
Lakewood NJ 08701-9917
Phone:
(800) 255-6227

Company Name: Learning Zone
Address: 15815 S.E. 37th Street
Bellevue, WA 98006-1800
Phone:
(800) 381-9663

Company Name: Quality Computers
Address: 20200 Nine Mile Rd.
Saint Clare Shores, MI 48080
Phone:
(800) 777-3642

TECHNOLOGY-RELATED BOOKS

◆ Grant Writing

The Catalog of Federal Education Grants
(Time Saving Tips for Grant Hunting)
Capitol Publications, Inc.
Alexandria, VA
(800) 327-7203

Finding Funding
Corwin Press, Inc.
Thousand Oaks, CA
(805) 499-9734

◆ Internet

Navigating the Networks
Learned Information, Inc.
Medford, NJ
(609) 654-4888

Telecommunications and Education: Surfing and the Art of Change
NSBA
1680 Duke Street
Alexandria, VA 22314
(800) 706-6722

The Internet
Compaq Computer Corporation
Houston, TX
(800) 888-5858

Walking Through the World Wide Web (Macintosh and Windows)
Ventanta Press
Chapel Hill, NC
(919) 942-0220

An Incomplete Guide to the Internet and other Telecommunications Opportunities Especially for Teachers and Students K-12
NCSA Education Group
(217) 244-3049

Guide to Network Resource Tools
European Academic Research Networks Association
345 Kear St. Suite 200
Yorktown Heights, NY 10598
(914) 962-5864

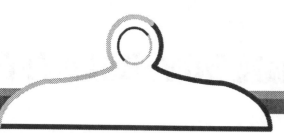

TECHNOLOGY FUNDING AND DONATIONS

Contrary to popular belief, the most common question asked concerning educational technology is not "How do I turn the thing on?" but the more serious question of "How do we pay for all of this?" With shrinking school budgets and the increasing demand for current innovation in the classroom, how can schools keep up? There are resources available for teachers and schools, and it is quite frequently just a matter of expressing a need, submitting an application, and formulating a technology plan. The following is a list of foundations, coalitions, technology educational funds, and the like which offer financial assistance to schools seeking technology.

1. **Foundation Center** has published a directory listing over 6,000 large foundations which donated over $9 billion dollars last year. This publication is called *The Foundation Directory*. It includes descriptions of grants, fundraising examples, and grant makers' priorities in addition to listings of these foundations. The cost is $195 for hardcover and $170 for softcover. There are other helpful publications available as well.

> Contact: The Foundation Center
> Dept. PR35
> 79 Fifth Avenue
> New York, NY 10003-3076
> (800) 424-9836

2. The **U.S. Department of Education** offers a listing of national educational technology groups and other resources through its Goals 2000 Resource Center. For more information call (800) USA-LEARN.

Also from the U.S. Department of Education is an annual listing of grants and fellowships offered by various offices of education. There are a variety of deadlines, levels of support, and eligibility requirements. The publication, *The Federal Register*, cost is $4.50.

> Contact: Superintendent of Documents
> U.S. Government Printing Office
> Washington, D.C. 20402

TECHNOLOGY FUNDING AND DONATIONS *(cont.)*

3. **Nike®** has a funding program called the "Just Do It" fund which supports disadvantaged youth. Grants range from $5,000 to $25,000. Grants are administered through the National Foundation for the Improvement of Education.

> Contact: NFIE
> Just Do It Teacher Grants
> 1201 16th Street NW
> Washington, D.C. 20036

4. **CompuMentor** is a nonprofit group which offers corporation-donated software and computer books at low cost to nonprofit groups and schools. DOS software is $25 and MAC is $6.

> Contact: CompuMentor
> 89 Stillman Street
> San Francisco, CA 94107

5. **Kraft General Foods** offers grants to K–12 programs focusing on educational reform, preparation for the future work force, at-risk students, and academic achievement. Priority is given to programs operating where company facilities are located.

> Contact: Director, Corporate Contribution
> Kraft General Foods
> Three Lakes Drive N3C
> Northfield, IL 60093

6. **Sony Electronics** supports programs encouraging the learning of technical and scientific skills required for tomorrow's work force.

> Contact: Corporate Communications
> Sony Electronics, Inc.
> One Sony Drive MD 3E2
> Park Ridge, NJ 07656

TECHNOLOGY FUNDING AND DONATIONS *(cont.)*

7. **Pew Charitable Trusts** provides grants in several areas including the restructuring of American education for higher performance, supporting the 21st century classroom, and strengthening the quality of teaching and learning in America's schools.

> Contact: The Pew Charitable Trusts
> One Commerce Square
> 2005 Market Street #1700
> Philadelphia, PA 19103

8. **The Software Publishers Association** and **Gifts in Kind America** are working together to collect donations of software for schools and nonprofit organizations nationwide. 1n 1993 over $16 million dollars worth of software was donated by groups such as Microsoft, Lotus, Egghead, Claris, Aldus, and WordPerfect.

> Contact: Gifts in Kind America
> 700 North Fairfax Street #300
> Alexandria, VA 22314

9. Last year the **Ford Foundation** contributed over $50 million to education and cultural projects. If your technology projects can coincide with the promotion of cultural diversity and the preservation of cultural traditions contact the Foundation for further information.

> Contact: Secretary
> Ford Foundation
> 320 East 43rd Street
> New York, NY 10017

10. The **Prudential Foundation** focuses mainly on educational projects that enrich the lives of disadvantaged and minority young children. Promotion of conflict-resolution projects is largely supported.

> Contact: The Prudential Foundation
> 751 Broad Street, 15th Floor
> Newark, NJ 07102

TECHNOLOGY FUNDING AND DONATIONS *(cont.)*

◆ **Adobe Systems**
Software company
Contact: Diane Compton, Human Resources Representative
1585 Charleston Rd., Mountain View, CA 94043
(415) 962-6643

◆ **Advanced Logic Research**
Personal computer manufacturer
Contact: Irene Rios, Corporate Contributions
9401 Geronimo, Irvine, CA 92718
(714) 581-6770

◆ **Aldus Corporation**
Software developer
Contact: Bonnie Alpert, Director of Corporate Contributions
411 First Ave. South, Suite 200, Seattle, WA 96104
(206) 441-8666

◆ **Apple Computer**
Hardware and software manufacturer
Contact: Fred Silverman, Director Community Affairs
20525 Mariana Ave. MS 385, Cupertino, CA 95014
(408) 974-2974

◆ **Software-Database Programs**
Contact: Tim Ornsby, Nonprofit Segment Manager
20101 Hamilton Ave., Tarzana, CA 90509-9977
(213) 329-8000

◆ **AST**
Personal computer manufacturer
Contact: Lorraine Peterson, Human Relations
16215 Alton Parkway, Irvine, CA 92713
(714) 727-4141

TECHNOLOGY FUNDING AND DONATIONS *(cont.)*

◆ **Amdahl**
Mainframe computers
Contact: Anthony Pazos, Senior Vice President, Human Resources & Corporate
Services
1250 East Arques Ave. MS 105, Sunnyvale, CA 94088
(408) 746-6000

◆ **AT&T Foundations & Charitable Contributions**
Telecommunications
Contact: Guidelines, AT&T Foundation
P.O. Box 1430, Wall, NJ 07719
(212) 605-6734

◆ **Borland**
Software developer
Contact: Product Donations
1800 Green Hills Rd., Scotts Valley, CA 95066
(408) 438-8400

◆ **Claris Corporation**
Software developer
Contact: Linda Higgins, Contributions Manager
5201 Patrick Henry Drive, Box 58168, Santa Clara, CA 95052
(408) 987-7000

◆ **Compaq Computer Corporation**
Personal computers
Contact: Lou Ann Champ, Corporate Contributions Administrator
P.O. Box 692000, Houston, TX 77269-2000
(713) 374-4625

◆ **Digital Equipment Corporation**
Voice Technology
Contact: Louis Karabetsos, Manager, Corporate Contributions
111 Powdermill Rd. MSO 1-814, Maynard, MA 01754
(508) 493-9210

TECHNOLOGY FUNDING AND DONATIONS *(cont.)*

◆ **Epson, America Inc.**
Printers, personal computers
Contact: Carolin Keith, Community Relations Manager
20770 Madrona Ave., Torrance, CA 90503
(213) 782-0770

◆ **Hewlett Packard Foundation & Corporate Contributions Program**
Computer printers
Contact: Roderick Carlson, Director, Corporate Grants
3000 Hanover St., P.O. Box 10301, Palo Alto, CA 94304
(415) 857-1501

◆ **IBM**
Computer hardware and software
Contact: James Parkel, Director, Corporate Support Programs
Old Orchard Rd., Armonk, NY 10504
(914) 765-1900

◆ **NEC America**
Computer technology
Contact: Susan Coleman, Public Relations Manager
401 Ellis St., P.O. Box 7241 M/V 4102, Mountain View, CA 94039
(415) 960-6000

◆ **Tektronix Foundation & Corporate Contributions**
Personal computers, printers, terminals
Contact Diana Smiley, Administrator
P.O. Box 500, Beaverton, OR 97077
503) 627-7085

◆ **Toshiba America Information Systems, Inc.**
Laptops, fax machines, photocopiers
Contact: Linda Bell
1 Bunker Hill, 601 W. 5th Street, 4th Floor, Los Angeles, CA 90071
(213) 623-4200

TECHNOLOGY FUNDING AND DONATIONS *(cont.)*

◆ Foundation Directories

Foundation Reporter
Corporate Giving Directory
(800) 877-8238

The Foundation Grants Index
(800) 424-9836

Directory of Major State Foundations
Logos Associates
P.O. Box 31
Woodsville, NH 03785-0031

◆ Finding Up-to-Date Federal Information

Education Funding Research Council
Federal Opportunities Books and Newsletters
(800) 876-0226

Capitol Publishers
Education and Foundation Grants Information
(800) 221-0425

NOTES

NOTES